ART AND EXISTENCE:
A Phenomenological Aesthetics

Also by Eugene F. Kaelin

An Existentialist Aesthetic

ART AND EXISTENCE
A Phenomenological Aesthetics

Eugene F. Kaelin

LEWISBURG
BUCKNELL UNIVERSITY PRESS

Library of Congress Catalogue Card Number: 74–101236

Associated University Presses, Inc.
Cranbury, New Jersey 08512

SBN: 8387 7582 9
Printed in the United States of America

The author wishes to thank the McGraw–Hill Book Company, New York, for permission to quote from The Meaning of Music *by Carroll C. Pratt; material used with permission of McGraw–Hill Book Company, © 1931.*

They also Serve who Only Stand and Wait.

To

The four women,
In the life of one man,
Who did.

CONTENTS

PREFACE

The philosopher practicing aesthetics as his major concern is often called upon to relate his professional activity and incidental discoveries to the needs of other disciplines. In this book I seek to trace the development of a distinctively existential-phenomenological account of aesthetic experiences. While phenomenology is not altogether unknown in the United States, either as a method of general philosophical or of specifically aesthetic inquiry, what is not too well known is the way in which the method may be used to produce the knowledge capable of bridging the chasm between the professional aesthetician, the art critic, and the practicing teacher of the various arts. The assumption is here made that creative communication is the aesthetician's field of inquiry, no matter what method he feels it necessary or appropriate to use, and that any account of creative communication must include some description of the various forms that making and appreciating works of art may take. If his descriptions prove adequate, they become of immediate interest to both student and teacher artist, as well as to the general public seeking an intellectual foundation for its love and appreciation of the products of art.

I have therefore here striven to fulfill the double demand placed upon the philosophical aesthetician's labors: to meet the rigorous requirements of my own profession, and to produce results that may be utilized by a reading public wider than the association of my colleagues.

The three chapters of Part I are devoted to a consideration of artistic creation considered as aesthetic communication. The first examines the dispute between emotivist and cognitivist on what, exactly, is communicated through art—feelings or knowledge; it concludes that the basic question is "How is something communicated through art when, in fact, it is?" Attempts to answer this question lead, however, to another dispute, that between idealistic and realistic aestheticians on the nature of expressive form. Croce is the idealist, and Alain and Valéry speak for the French realistic tradition. All three were perceptive critics of more than one art form, as well as philosophers and aestheticians, and the more one reads the critics, the less one is convinced that their philosophies bear any necessary relation to their perceptions, or that idealism or realism is a valid disjunction—either for the description of an act of human creation or, for that matter, of the ordinary objects of human experience.

If we can avoid the metaphysical disputes of our immediate forebears, the middle road is laid out by a return to the things themselves—to the artifacts created by human subjects and appreciated by an interested audience. In the second chapter, an attempt is made to discover in contemporary psychoanalytical theory and practice the basic conditions of communication through the arrangement of aesthetic materials.

Part I concludes with an existential-phenomenological account of human creativity. Chapter 3 summarizes the argument of my earlier book, *An Existentialist Aesthetic*, which contains a critical comparison of the aesthetic theories of Sartre and Merleau-Ponty. What is new in the present analysis is an original description of creative communication in existentialistic terms and the adumbration of a method for interpreting various contexts in which aesthetic expressiveness is found.

Having thus set up the larger human framework in which artist and audience may be said to communicate, I proceed to an examination of the particular effects of aesthetic expression deriving from the nature of the medium used by the artist. Prose fiction, the dance, painting, music, poetry, and films offer a rich and varied area for the application of the phenomenological *epoché*—that procedure by which a given aesthetic percipient attends to the unique qualitative appearance of the objects created for his enjoyment. Edmund Husserl (who invented the term, though hardly the practice) referred to the *epoché* as a "reduction" (of a natural or artificial object to the set of its appearances), or as moving from one attitude, the natural—in which an agent relates to objects of his environment either in action or by applying causal hypotheses in their explanation, to another, the phenomenological—in which one merely leaves oneself open to the play of the qualities of objects upon the attentive consciousness. What he maintained as a first principle of phenomenological methodology becomes for us the description of the one condition necessary for having an aesthetic experience at all. Once in the phenomenological attitude, we have "bracketed" the qualities into a single context of significance, which may then be analyzed and described.

Wherever possible, I have relied upon descriptions of individual works of art. Thus, Part II begins and ends with examples of practical criticism. Chapter 4 contains a summary of the generic characteristics of works of art, which becomes a postulate set for describing the method of aesthetic analysis to be used throughout the book. Each of the further specialized treatments, moreover, constitutes a further reading of the manner in which human transcendence fulfills itself through the manipulation of a particular art medium, beginning with that of the human body itself in dance. My message here is directed to teachers and students of the dance, since they are most highly motivated to understand how something containing one set of significance parameters in real life or in science may be transmuted into something else—a medium for aesthetic expression—as each movement is viewed only in a context with other movements, which in some manner fulfill or qualify the significance of the first. The same process is repeated for the other media mentioned above.

Part III contains my conclusion, an attempt to evaluate the work of Merleau-Ponty as central to European phenomenology. Its single chapter examines the reasons why Merleau-Ponty's earlier "philosophical anthropology" (explained in Chapters 3 and 5) was supplanted by "phenomenological ontology." Where earlier he had been content with describing how one reacts intuitively to an environment before the initial nonreflective attitudes come under the criticism of a reflective philosophy, in his later works he treated painting as a means of understanding the commitment of human beings to "Being" itself. In view of the preceding chapters on the aesthetics of Husserl, Heidegger, and Ingarden, we now find ourselves in a position to evaluate this shift in emphasis found in Merleau-Ponty's later reflections on art.

Substantively, the present book begins with a consideration of the claims made for the "purity" of the medium, then moves on to the arts as the language of creation, and to aesthetics as a general theory of linguistics (Croce, Collingwood, and Merleau-Ponty before Heidegger). Once this way has been lighted, the aesthetician comes to look upon art-works as sign-vehicles, whose significance is instituted and controlled by the organization of the sensory stimuli of which they are composed. Within the context of aesthetic expressiveness these stimuli are considered elements—insofar as they are the parts of which the context is constructed, or "counters"—insofar as our reading of them in the act of aesthetic contemplation reduces them to bare markers, the significance of which is understood as one is perceived in relation to the other.

If phenomenological theory in aesthetics has any currency on this side of the Atlantic, however, it has been severely prejudiced by phenomenologists' predilections for the more general, or eidetic, descriptions of aesthetic categories, applicable in essence to many works of art; accordingly, we have read too many accounts of "the work of art" (as if there were only one ideal type so described) and not enough descriptions of particular works of art. To combat this tendency, and to make the most basic type of object for aesthetic analysis appear in the first place, I have found it necessary to practice the basic phenomenological reduction, i.e., to bracket the context in which the communication of a novel significance takes place, and to describe what appears in particular cases. From there on it becomes possible for anyone who has had the experience of the work in question to become a qualified critic of criticism—which is perhaps only to say a "philosopher of art."

In multiplying my approaches to creative communication by considering aesthetic expressions in various arts media, I have hoped to fill in some of the missing perspectives that would allow a more adequate judgment on its nature. Thus, should someone tell me that the stick I see as bent is really straight after all, I should be in his debt for correcting my error. But even to do this, such a person would have to disclose some heretofore unrevealed perspective of aesthetic experience. For this reason I should be grateful to have this work interpreted as a struggle to see more clearly, and not as a pursuit of theory for the sake of theory itself. Phenomenology is only a method, and as such, is compatible with any acceptable theory that would pretend to explain the facts of human consciousness. In the realm of aesthetic experiences, however, the only proof of a pudding is to be found in the eating.

ACKNOWLEDGMENTS

For permission to quote from copyrighted material, I should like to thank the following publishers:

Art de France and Editions Hermann, Paris, France, for permission to cite passages from Merleau-Ponty's "L'oeil et l'esprit," vol. 1, pp. 197, 204, 206.

Arts in Society and the Regents of the University of Wisconsin for permission to reprint "The Arts and Communication," *Arts in Society* I,2 (1959):71-85.

Basil Blackwell, Publisher, Oxford, England, for permission to cite parts of the Macquarrie and Robinson translation of Martin Heidegger's *Being and Time*, 1962.

The Bobbs-Merrill Company, Inc., of Indianapolis, Indiana, for permission to quote from Eduard Hanslick, *The Beautiful in Music,* trans. by Gustav Cohen; copyright © 1967, by The Liberal Arts Press, Inc., reprinted by permission of The Bobbs-Merrill Company, Inc.

The University of Chicago Press, Chicago, Illinois, for permission to quote selected passages from *Emotion and Meaning in Music* by Leonard B. Meyer; copyright © 1956 by the University of Chicago Press.

Dennis Dobson, London, England, for permission to quote parts of Siegfried Kracauer's *Nature of Film,* 1960.

Editions Gallimard, Paris, France, for permission to quote from Maurice Merleau-Ponty's *Phénoménologie de la perception,* 1945, and *L'Oeil et l'esprit,* 1964; from Paul Valéry's *Charmes* (avec commentaire d'Alain), 1952; and from Alain's [Emile Chartier's] *Vingt leçons sur les beaux-arts,* 1931; and for permission to use my own translations of parts of Alain's *Eléments de philosophie,* 1941, and *Vingt leçons sur les beaux-arts.*

The Hafner Publishing Company, New York, for permission to quote from the Bernard translation of Kant's *Critique of Judgment,* 1951.

Harcourt, Brace & World, Inc., for permission to cite passages from Virginia Woolf's *To the Lighthouse,* printed in the Harbrace Modern Classic Series, 1927.

Harper and Row, Publishers, Inc., for permission to quote passages from William S. Newman's *Understanding Music,* 1952; and for permission to make my own translations of selected passages from Martin Heidegger's *Unterwegs zur Sprache,* 1959, as well as for permission to use the not-yet-published translations of passages from Heidegger's *Vorträge und Aufsätze,* particularly "Building Dwelling Thinking," and ". . . Poetically Man Dwells," by Albert Hofstadter.

The Harvard University Press, Cambridge, Mass., for permission to quote from Susanne K. Langer's *Philosophy in a New Key,* 1942.

Humanitas for permission to reprint "Art and Existence," 4 (1968):181-210.

The Johns Hopkins Press, Baltimore, Maryland, for permission to quote from *The Artist as Creator* by Milton C. Nahm; copyright © The Johns Hopkins Press, 1956.

The Journal of Aesthetics and Art Criticism, Cleveland, Ohio, for permission to quote parts of "The Form and Function of Music," by Carroll C. Pratt, 1954.

Vittorio Klostermann, Frankfurt am Main, West Germany, for permission to cite my own translations of Heidegger's *Holzwege,* 1950, *Was ist Metaphysik?,* 1960, and *Erläuterungen zu Hölderlins Dichtung,* 1951.

The National Association for Physical Education of College Women, for permission to reprint a revised version of "Being in the Body," National Educational Association Publications, Washington, D.C.: *NAPECW Reports,* 1964, pp. 84-103.

Günther Neske Verlag, Pfullingen, West Germany, for permission to use materials from Heidegger's *Unterwegs zur Sprache,* 1959, and *Vorträge und Aufsätze,* 1954, with concurrent permission of Harper and Row Publishers, New York.

The Max Niemeyer Verlag, Tübingen, West Germany, for permission to use my own translations of passages from Heidegger's *Was Heisst Denken?,* 1961, and *Einführung in die Metaphysik,* 1953, and from Roman Ingarden's *Untersuchungen zur Ontologie der Kunst,* 1962.

Martinus Nijhoff, The Hague, Netherlands, for permission to use my own translation of a passage from Edmund Husserl's *Cartesianische Meditationen,* 1963.

The Northwestern University Press, for permission to cite my own translations of Merleau-Ponty's "L'oeil et l'esprit," full translation of the text (by Carleton Dallery) being available in *The Primacy of Perception*, in the 1964 edition of J. M. Edie; and to incorporate portions of *Signs*, 1964, by Merleau-Ponty, in the conclusion of this book.

The Oxford University Press, for permission to quote from *The Theory of Film* by Siegfried Kracauer, 1965.

Prentice-Hall, Inc., Englewood Cliffs, New Jersey, for permission to cite portions of *Art and Existentialism* by Arturo B. Fallico, copyright © 1962; material used by permission of Prentice-Hall, Inc., Englewood Cliffs, New Jersey.

Princeton University Press, Princeton, New Jersey, for permission to use my own translations of Paul Valéry's *Charmes*, 1952.

The Prothmann Associates, Baldwin, New York, for their permission to reproduce all photographic materials, figures 1-10, from the Stoedtner-Prothmann Collection.

The G. P. Putnam's Sons, New York, for permission to quote from John Dewey's *Art as Experience*; reprinted by permission of G. P. Putnam's Sons from *Art as Experience* by John Dewey. Copyright © 1934 by John Dewey; renewed 1962 by Roberta Dewey.

Quadrangle Books, Chicago, Illinois, for permission to reprint "The Visibility of Things Seen," from *An Invitation to Phenomenology*, ed. by J. M. Edie, 1965, 30-58.

Routledge & Kegan Paul, Ltd., London, England, for permission to use my own translation of a passage from Merleau-Ponty's *Phenomenology of Perception*; full translation by Colin Smith available in the Routledge and Kegan Paul edition of 1962.

School Review and the University of Chicago Press for permission to reprint "Method and Methodology in Literary Criticism," 72 (1964):289-308, copyright © 1964 by the University of Chicago Press.

Charles Scribner's Sons, New York, for permission to quote passages from Susanne K. Langer's *Feeling and Form,* 1953.

The estate of Dame Edith Sitwell, David Higham Associates, Ltd., controllers, for permission to cite her correspondence with the editors of the London *Observer,* as reported by *Time Magazine* on November 12, 1951, p. 31, with concurrent permission of the Vanguard Press, Inc., of New York.

The Wisconsin Film Society Press, Madison, Wisconsin, for permission to reprint two film reviews from *Classics of the Film,* ed. by Arthur Lennig, 1965, pp. 106-9 and 132-37.

I should also like to thank the following individuals:

Mrs. Lili Kracauer, for permission to quote from her late husband's *From Caligari to Hitler,* The Princeton University Press, 1947.

Mr. Arthur Lennig, for permission to reprint my reviews of *Variety* and *Nicht Mehr Fliehen* from his *Classics of the Film,* The Wisconsin Film Society Press, 1965.

Professor Leonard B. Meyer, for his permission to cite portions of his *Emotion and Meaning in Music,* University of Chicago Press, 1956.

Professor Sieghardt M. Riegel, Department of German, University of Wisconsin, Madison, for his suggestions and criticism of my translations of Heidegger's thoughts on the relations between poetry and philosophy.

ART AND EXISTENCE:
A Phenomenological Aesthetics

PART I

Artistic Creation as Aesthetic Communication

1

THE ARTS AND COMMUNICATION

I

One of the definable roles of the aesthetician in our time is to narrow the gap between artists and their society of appreciators. At present, when this gap seems to be at its maximum, a careful analysis of the process of communication is a shocking necessity. Too often we are prone to explain situations that are only remotely analogous by using identical models. That this has been the case between speech and artistic expression is obvious to only too few contemporary aestheticians. Benedetto Croce's case is most significant. In his aesthetics, which he called a general theory of linguistics, a person who speaks is said to be forming a system of vocal gestures that convey all there is to be conveyed of his sensuous intuitions, or impressions. Indeed, the speaker's expression and his intuition are identical.[1]

When this model is applied to the arts, however, there results an unhappy divorce between the inner activity of the mind, which organizes impressions, and the outer manipulation of materials, which puts before an appreciative audience a mere artifact, or symbol of this inner activity. Thus an art-work is said to be an expression of the mind, not something primarily executed, through techniques, in the materials of the artist's craft. What one perceives in looking at the physical execution of the art-work is, therefore, a symbol of a symbol.

Croce's problem is much more complicated than such a simplified presentation appears to admit. Reflective artists do concede a distinction between their craftsmanship or technique, which may be successfully taught because it is formulable in idea and communicable in essence, and their inspiration, which is unique and therefore indefinable and incommunicable outside the individual work of art. To this distinction Croce's theory gives at least a specious explanation, but not without commitment to some very dubious metaphysics. Any theory that can explain, without the metaphysical trappings of idealism, both the communication of the artist with his audience and the distinction between technique and inspiration, deserves closer attention. In the second part of this chapter I shall consider the outlines of such a theory.

My present attention is limited to a discussion of the inadequacy of the idealist's model for explaining communication. If the intuition of the artist is the art-work, then, supposedly, the making of a solid object is only an afterthought, an inessential and often unsuccessful attempt to communicate to some audience the artist's vision (intuition, idea). The fallacy of such a view is readily apparent. The critic has before him only the afterthought, which for any number of reasons may be as different from the original generating thought as paint on canvas, a physical object, differs from an idea, defined by Croce as spiritual activity. Can the critic, under such an assumption, ever talk about the work of art? Whoever coined the phrase "intentional fallacy" has shown that reputable critics, at least, cannot. A critic must judge the physical object before him. And so must the artist, presumably when he signs his work. Can we assume that critic and artist see the same object if what they are looking at is an idea? In an effort to answer this question, let us examine more closely the model of communication–significant discourse–used by Croce and his followers to explain the art process.

When a person hears a word, he infers a meaning associated with that word for all persons capable of using the same language. If there is some doubt concerning the meaning of a particular vocable, both partners in the act can check their communication by referring to a standard dictionary of the language spoken. What could be a simpler, and more inexact, model for artistic creation?

The first suggestion that comes to mind is that the model breaks down for lack of a dictionary to verify the "terms" of artistic communication. This is true, and always has been; the realization of this truth, therefore, goes nowhere to explain the gap between contemporary artists and their audience. Moreover, if no one has yet constructed a list of emotions, or ideas and images that correspond with line character, color harmony and contrast, space tensions, and the like, the reason seems to be that such a task cannot be performed; the lexicographer of aesthetic meanings would be attempting the impossible. A dictionary can be composed for those words or symbols, and those alone, which already possess a fixed meaning in a given language. The artist, on the contrary, is dedicated to finding, or expressing, new meanings. Realizing that it is a fallacy to judge his own artistic merit on his feelings or intentions, he must assume the task of discovering a new idea by manipulating the materials of his medium. Experimentation is as necessary to the artist as it is to the scientist; for both, a dictionary can only follow discovery.

If the artist's gestures have meaning, they are of the same kind as the first words of children, who also discover the meanings of their words after having learned to use them. The model for this kind of communication has already been suggested by G. H. Mead in his *Mind, Self and Society*. For Mead, the meaning of any gesture is a reaction to it, and when two individuals react to the same gesture in identical ways there has been communication.[2] Instead of Idea-Gesture-Idea, we have the model of Gesture-Reaction$_1$, Reaction$_2$.

The advantage of this model is that, in terms of artistic communication, there is no necessary distinction between the artist's "idea" and the work which allegedly serves as symbol of that idea. The artifact would be the art-work; it would be a sign rather than a symbol. Where the meaning of a symbol is fixed by convention, that of a sign emerges from a social process of interacting organisms. Thus, the "meaning" of any given art-work is never exhausted by any one viewing of it; a classic becomes such by generations of appreciative responses to the artist's complex gesture. Analysis and informed discussion have never killed a work of art.

It is my purpose to show in the second part of this chapter that such a model has already been used by at least two recent aestheticians, and that, if carried out to its logical conclusions, it would tend to bring the artist back into contact with his audience without the unreasonable demand that he change his habits, however difficult to understand or censurable they might at present seem to be. Contemporary art has meaning, if only we understand that we, as audience, must collaborate with the artist for that meaning to emerge. The social process commonly called "artistic communication" is amenable to empirical investigation. Both creator and appreciator are implicated, being united by an aesthetically describable work of art, judgments on which are capable of reasoned verification.

II

Croce's basic insight, that art is in some sense a language, has been considerably obscured by recent British and American aestheticians because of an inability to agree on the nature of the function served by that language. Some, like I. A. Richards, subscribe to an emotive theory, while others, like Morris Weitz at one time in his career, espouse a cognitive theory, whereby the arts are said to give us knowledge of a specifiable sort. Richards was concerned primarily with the language of literature, and Weitz with a general philosophy of the arts. We may sketch their antithetical views in an effort to show that the rhetoric of the one and the logic of the other demand a third discipline to complete the modern aesthetic trivium. There remains to be supplied the grammar of artistic forms, already clearly described by two French aestheticians, Alain and Valéry.

For Richards, the language of poetry is emotive because, considered with reference to a set of verifying conditions, the statements of poetry would all be false. A poetic statement is therefore a pseudo-statement, whose acceptability is defined "entirely by its effect in releasing or organizing our impulses or attitudes (due regard being had for the better or worse organizations of these *inter se*)."[3] For Weitz, on the other hand, literary statements in general, although making no original claim to truth, are nonetheless capable of implying other statements that do make verifiable truth-claims. Thus, in analyzing the "meaning" of Richard Wright's *Native Son,* Weitz shows how the surface meaning of the story can be understood to "imply" a general truth; the life of a Black as depicted in the novel illustrates the idea that when freedom of the individual is externally restricted it becomes nothing more than the ability to destroy, first others and then oneself.[4] Weitz has borrowed D. H. Parker's distinction between surface and depth meanings, and presented them in the dress of modern logic. Sidney Zink achieved the same result in terms of the more classical logic in his "The Cognitive Element in Art."[5]

Both Richards and Weitz are operating within the realm of empirical aesthetics, but neither of their descriptions seems to do justice to the aesthetic problems. Neither Richards, the sensitive reader of poetry and intelligent theoretician, nor Weitz, the sensitive theoretician and intelligent reader of poetry, has found an adequate explanation for the human sensitivity and intelligence implicated in the complete art process. The inadequacy of both their positions is apparent from the inability to generalize the principle of the aesthetic language as each considers it. Forgetting for the most part about the regard owing the organization of attitudes and impulses *inter se,* Richards could talk meaningfully only about poetry, or at most about the literary arts. Weitz has at least tried the generalization,[6] but his description of the truth-claims of painting and music, based upon the analogy of those implicit in the Christian's gesture of prayer, has failed to convince, most probably because the analogy with the prayerful attitude was only partially developed. After all, Richards might very well say that the prayerful attitude is one whose embodiment in ritual makes religion a true artistic activity. One activity, two points of view. Need we pay our money and take our choice?

Not necessarily. It is obvious that art can and does embody the emotional states of the artist, likewise that an audience may be emotionally moved by the contemplation of such an embodiment, and it is just as obvious that at least some forms of art contain depth meanings, or, if you like, second-order assertions. But nothing is to be gained by belaboring the obvious. A solution to this dilemma can be had only by reconsidering the notion of meaning as it is applied to art-forms—all of them, to each considered on its own terms.

The first step in this positive portion of my analysis is, therefore, to elucidate the notion of a "pure" art form, or, as the discussion is known in contemporary analysis, of the value of the medium in aesthetic communications. History will come to our aid: in France the twenties were roaring with still another literary debate, *viz.*, whether the office of poetry was to express a mood, idea, or anything else, or whether poetry was a musical form, to be judged as an aesthetic act merely in reference to such a form. If poetry were meant to express anything, in the sense of referring to an idea or emotion of the poet, then the creation of the artist would be not unlike the creation of God, who first entertained ideas, or exemplars, of the things to be created. This is the cognitivist position, which easily lends itself to an idealistic interpretation, such as Croce's.

But if the creation is purely mental, then the outward manipulation of the materials that constitute the physical work of art is merely secondary, technique as opposed to inspiration, and the ideal work of art would be of sights unseen and sounds unheard. Fortunately or unfortunately, museum habitués are more interested in the sights that are seen and concert-goers in the sounds that are heard—even if these sights and sounds are becoming more and more difficult to "understand."

Those creations which can be appreciated are of the body, a gesture of the body itself: a movement of the arms or legs in a dance; of the vocal chords in song; of the hand holding brush, tube of paint, pencil, or burin; of the fingers plucking a string, stroking a key of clavier, piano, or typewriter. And all meanings are embodied in some physical context. The idea, the feeling, cannot exist outside the context of a reaction to the physical object. This is what Charles Morris meant when he said that an aesthetic sign refers, if refer it must, only to itself.[7] When poetry is judged with reference to the potentialities of its particular medium, it is judged in its "purity." Only a study of the possibilities of the medium in question will enable us to judge the mechanics of the aesthetic language operating through that medium.

The French aestheticians who have been most articulate on this subject are Paul Valéry (1871-1945) and Emile Chartier (pseud., Alain, 1868-1951). From their point of view, a poem, the physical object created by the poetic artist, is composed of words, neither of emotions nor of ideas; and the value of the poem is to be found in the words, not in the emotion or the idea that the words may contain. But prose too is composed of words, and is not for that reason poetry. The consolation of Molière's *bourgeois gentilhomme,* who spoke prose naturally and poetry with difficulty, was not that his words were a kind of poetry, albeit inferior in aesthetic quality, but that he had been speaking in an art form almost since birth. Valéry suggested that a valid distinction between poetry and prose could be drawn by considering each in its purity, i.e., by eliminating from poetry all that is prose (or any other type of expression, such as painting, music, etc.) and accepting the residue as "pure poetry." When this process of eliminating the accidental characteristics of the genre was accomplished (as Clive Bell eliminated the representative function even of his favorite, Giotto, to arrive at the "significant form" of pure painting), there remains only the form of the poetic words. Pure poetry was thus described as a form, a system of vocal gestures whose value lies in their temporal sequence, in those relations one to the other which define their "weight" (*pesanteur*), number, and sonority.

Marcel Proust has one of his characters praise the following line of Racine as the epitome of poetic expression, signifying, as it does, nothing at all: La fille de Minos et de Pasiphaé.[8] One thing is clear; conventional meanings associated with words oftentimes hinder true poetic expression, and no idea is poetry if not expressed in some words. "The daughter of Minos and Pasiphae," for example, serves heavily to organize the drama of *Phèdre*; her parentage is foreboding of the evil in her future. But the drama is a complex medium, served here by poetic expression. What of the poetry?

In translating only the referential idea of the line,

which is irrelevant to the artistic, technical value of the poetry as such, we do not violate the prose-poetry distinction. Pure poetry can be neither translated nor paraphrased; any attempt to do either destroys its "purity." The value of the quoted line comes from its weight: the initial "i" is lengthened by the "ll," and the purity of the vowel sound is maintained first of all by the mute quality of the "e" in "fille," repeated in the "de," and secondly by its repetition in the first syllable of "Minos." The stress of the second syllable of this word announces the pause of the caesura, the sixth syllable of the classical French alexandrine. Following the caesura, there is a break in the original continuity, a brief staccato between the "et" and the "de" (the accented "e" being separated from the unaccented by the two consonants), which ultimately flows on into a blending of the labial consonants (p, ph) with the assonance of the vowels (a, a), this final legato being reinforced by the stress of the terminating accented syllable.

Technical jargon? Not at all; the technique of the poet is the source of the value in his art. All that the technical critic can do is to describe what is perceived in the object. Poets like Valéry are self-conscious craftsmen, truly aware of the possibilities of their medium, and hence doubly valuable to aestheticians. Henry James, another self-conscious artisan, wrote with similar illumination on the craft of fiction.[9] Craftsmanship endows materials with aesthetic form.

An alternative way of talking about the arts is exemplified in the ordinary language of Louis Armstrong, who in response to the question, "What is jazz?" is supposed to have said: "Man, if I haf ta tell ya, yull neva know." And it is not to be supposed here that Satchmo himself did not know. A propos of his poetry, Valéry said something similar:

> My verse has the meaning that one lends to it. The one I give it is valid only for me, and cannot be opposed to anyone else's. It is an error contrary to the nature of poetry, and one which would be fatal to it, to pretend that for every poem there is a true meaning, unique and conforming or identical to some thought of the author.[10]

The poem, one in form, is multiple in "meaning." Alain was to use this insight to construct a complete aesthetic theory. If the arts can truly be said to compose a language, then one ought to be able to describe that language, both generically and specifically. In the latter case, art objects, i.e., the formed material of the different genres, constitute expressive vehicles. Since Alain's *Système des Beaux-Arts* is almost wholly occupied with the specific arts (and a primary source is more valuable than a commentary), we shall consider artistic expression only in its generic sense. To describe how art is a language, we must describe *how* art objects express *what* they do.

First, the "what." If it can be taken as axiomatic that the creative act of the artist is a bodily act, that reference to an externalized idea (or emotion) of the artist can never be adequate, since an art object is obviously neither a feeling nor an idea, but an art-fact—i.e., an object constructed or reconstructed by the attitudes of the artist—then artistic expression is of nothing if not of itself. The idea of the art-work is not external to the work; it is the work. The idea is given shape as the matter of the work is formed by the artist. To use a metaphor taken from the early semiotic work of Charles Morris, syntax, and not semantics, gives its rule to art. Syntactically, one brush stroke leads to another; one tone calls for development and final resolution; one word seeks its complement. The relations of aesthetic signs are all internal, and must be considered concretely, i.e., in context. This is the truth of artistic semiotic, and an adequate explanation of the art-work's unity. Depth meanings or emotional fulfillment there may be, but whether or not, they are, in themselves, irrelevant to a description of the purely artistic value. Reading for depth meanings, or for sense titillation however sublimated, is low-grade appreciation, if such readings lead the attention away from the form of the object itself. The person who looks on one of Caravaggio's still-life representations and sees grapes has been misled from the object of contemplation. Likewise, the reader of Wright's *Native Son* aware of a truth-claim. A novel, when it is a good one, claims only one thing: the attention of an appreciative audience, and this to itself.

The error of the semantic view is apparent when we consider the "how" of artistic expression. Since art is considered to be a language by both emotivist and cognitivist, its signs are mistaken for conventional symbols having a meaning external to them. By means of such symbols the artist is alleged to communicate his ideas or feelings. In his social-psychological study of language, G. H. Mead called such an attitude "the error of the philologist." One could not look to the mind of the speaker for the idea to be expressed, because in the first instance of communication there was no mind prior to the symbol. Language, for Mead, was the social phenomenon that conditioned the appearance of mind, and its study therefore was more properly genetic. Alain perceived this same error of philology in aesthetics, as well as the advantages of the genetic method:

> The first meaning of a sign, make note of it, is the effect that it produces on others. The child is acquainted first of all with the human text by purely mechanical memory, and then he deciphers the meaning on the face of his fellow-man. A sign is explained by the other. And the other, in his turn, receives his own sign reflected by a human face: each learns then, from the other; and this is a beautiful friendship.[11]

Meaning and society, like craftsmanship and form, are inseparable concepts. The meaning of an art-work grows out of social interaction: in the clearest exemplification of the idea, the gestures of one dancer harmonize with those of another. The dance is a conversation of gestures signifying nothing, for all the sound and fury. This conversation is understood when an audience reacts in kind, here kinaesthetically.

As for Richards, reactions of an audience may be purely emotional. This is one way to appreciate art-works; and it may be the conception of an idea that is only implicit in the work, as in Weitz's appreciation. But whatever they are, they may both be said to constitute a third dimension of artistic semiotic, one which may very well be entitled "pragmatic," to continue our metaphor in Morris's terminology (semantics, syntactics, pragmatics).[12] For an understanding of this third dimension, Charles S. Peirce's semiotic theory is perhaps clearer; the meaning of the art-sign is rightfully its interpretant, the reaction of some subject to the gesture of the artist. Real masterworks are those to which perhaps only their creators responded in the first instance, but whose individuality as expressive works of art has grown through time. Their basic formal unity is viewed and reviewed, and the interpretations given to it constitute the multiplicity of meaning aesthetic relativists insist upon in describing art objects.

Such is the account given by Alain to the meaning of works of art. An adequate semiotic interpretation of art-works will not stress the semantic dimension, as Weitz seems to have done, nor the pragmatic, as Richards most certainly has done. If Alain is guilty of having stressed the syntactic dimension, the reason is that it seems to be at least a necessary condition for the existence of the other two. Any surplus of meaning—significance or signification—must be attachable to a well-formed formula bearing its own syntactical meaning.

To summarize Alain's position, we may say that he divided languages, as did Auguste Comte, into two kinds: those signifying "absolutely" and those signifying "relatively." The absolute language is composed of gestures which, semantically considered, are primitive signs referring only to themselves and whose meaning therefore accrues in a social process of interpretation. Art-works are said to be such signs; and if this contention is acceptable, it can be seen that meaning in art is a social phenomenon taking place between the artist and his society by means of the created work. From the nature of the sign described it is apparent that the artist learns as much from his work as does his audience. The artist is his first appreciator, and, in a word of Alain, is the first one surprised to discover "his" idea.

The signs of the relative language, on the other hand, are arbitrary symbols. The scientific and algebraic languages exemplify the ideal of communication made possible by such signs. Any ordinary language will afford another example. But in judging the works of prose artists, the semantical meanings of the words used may be considered in the same light as representation in painting. In other words, the relative language may become an element of the absolute; since words will always have a representational content, the form of a novel or short story will always be a concrete whole, or significant context. What is said, having no absolute aesthetic value in itself, will become aesthetic as it is given expression or concretion within the author's total gesture, or style.

It is apparent now where the ambiguity in the conception of the literary media lies. According to Alain and Valéry, words are the materials of both prose and poetry: words as sonorous entities in the case of poetry, and as embodying a semantic reference in the case of prose. But in neither case do the referents of the words constitute the aesthetic "meaning" of the work of art. In both cases our aesthetic reaction is to the purely formal character of the work considered only with reference to itself, i.e., to its own internal structure. If we consider these structures carefully, we shall see that words function differently in the two kinds of contexts.

The question of the meaning of art-works has heretofore been settled by reference to a property of the medium with which poets and novelists (or essayists and philosophers) must work. How easy to understand then why more careful aestheticians[13] have maintained that knowledge can result from only some kinds of art-works, and why the less careful have had difficulty in showing that knowledge may be garnered from all art media. There has been, in terms of classical logic, a mistaking of an accidental for an essential property of the genus of art-facts. The essential property of this genus is the forming activity of the artist; but let this not mean Crocean intuition. Croce, no less than Hegel, needs turning right side up. Creation is the act of the human body, a gesture that has meaning through the interpretive response of an appreciative audience.

In conclusion, it might be said that recent French aesthetics gives a fruitful suggestion for adjudicating the issue between the conflicting claims of the emotive and cognitive theorists. Whatever one thinks of the distinction drawn by the Frenchmen between prose and poetry, it is clear that the accidental property of the prose medium cannot be generalized successfully to apply to all other media. There may even be some question as to whether such generalization is possible for any one given property. Our thesis is simply that the work of Alain and Valéry offers a new avenue of approach toward the analysis of art objects considered as expressive vehicles. The theory is one having a great deal of consistency with the practice of contemporary artists, who tend more and more to abstract from subject matter in their attempt to exploit the expressiveness of their respective media.

In modernist art, we are presented with the creative act itself, as it is made possible by given materials. This is what Alain saw so clearly:

> The human body, by its structure, offers us two forms of the natural language: the gesture and the voice. One sees immediately that the dance corresponds to the first, and music to the second. However, if one wishes to understand in what sense art is language, one must consider language as its sources. And it is clear that the first and most powerful language is action. To act is to signify.[14]

What the artist thinks is never so important as what he does.

Linguistics may reach fruition as aesthetic theory if aestheticians continue their research into the arts as actually practiced by the artists of their own time. Since "modern" art is our art, it should become the object of interest to our aestheticians. The modern artist's interest in form calls for reinforcement by aesthetic analysis of form, whether abstract or concrete; and, if such reinforcement is given, aestheticians may be able to fulfill their function of bringing together artists and their audience. In order to achieve this level of communication, emotivists and cognitivists must be supplemented by formalists. In painting this has already been done in the criticism of Bell and Fry; recently, in literature, the not-so-new school of New Criticism has taken a step in the right direction; and music affords almost a model of abstract formal analysis. If we keep in mind the obvious fact that some forms are concrete and others abstract, we need not fear the "formalist" label.

Implications of the formalist theory are great at present, for both artist and society. In general, if our attitudes before works of art become more aesthetic in the sense defined above, we should no longer hear from members of society: "What's the message? That doesn't resemble anything! I don't like it." From here there is only a short step to "Let's censor it." Nor should we hear from the artist: "I work for myself; the people are too insensitive to judge." The artist and his audience discover the artistic idea in the same way, by observing what has been done. Aestheticians have only to enter into the conversation. They have only to relearn their language as a child does—from day to day. In the absence of this learning process, we can only wait for the evaluation of the future.

It is not unfitting to presume that, in the ages to follow, anthropologists will look upon the art of our time and see, in Ortega y Gasset's phrase, a will to style. "Theirs," they will say, "was a 'dehumanized art'; we can see in it only a complex gesture, a form that seems to express nothing, i.e., everything, or whatever you like. And if you insist that we tell you *what* it is, you will never know."

Perhaps, in light of the above, the best avenue of future research for aestheticians is to consult the work of practicing psychoanalysts; they, too, are presented with a context of expression—its meaning obscure yet somehow contained in and decipherable from the bodily activity of a patient that must stand warrant for his "mental" intention. To pursue the point, we are invited to look and see to what degree, if any, an artist's behavior is similar to the subconscious expression of emotional or cognitive states by neurotic or psychotic individuals.

If the comparison seems shocking, we need only take the poet at his word, that great wit to madness is near allied. Going beyond the established bound of convention, creative artists, like madmen, push our communicative medium beyond the realm of the obvious. And where the medium is the message, the ongoing embodiment of a human act, it may be of some comfort to critics to understand that in our consideration theirs is a psychoanalytic procedure. As every successful analyst already knows, his "patient" stands in need of a cooperative, understanding gesture for communication to take place.

NOTES

1. Benedetto Croce, *Aesthetic,* D. Ainslie trans. (London: Macmillan, 1922), pp. 8–9.

2. See G. H. Mead, *Mind, Self and Society* (Chicago: The University of Chicago Press, 1934), Part II, "Mind," *passim.*

3. From selections of his *Science and Poetry,* 2d ed., revised (London: Kegan Paul, Trench, Trubner and Co., Ltd., 1935). Reprinted in E. Vivas and M. Krieger, *The Problems of Aesthetics* (New York and Toronto: Rinehart and Co., 1953), p. 585.

4. Morris Weitz, *Philosophy of the Arts* (Cambridge, Mass.: Harvard University Press, 1950), pp. 137ff.

5. In *Ethics* 64 (April 1954):186–204.

6. Weitz, *Philosophy of Arts,* 134–52.

7. See his "Esthetics and the Theory of Signs," *Journal of Unified Science* 8 (June 1938):131–50.

8. Jean Racine, *Phèdre,* I, 1.

9. In *The Art of Fiction and Other Essays* (New York: Oxford University Press, 1948).

10. "Préface à un commentaire," *La Nouvelle Revue Française* 34 (Feb. 1930):216–21. Reprinted in *Charmes* (Paris: Gallimard, 1929).

11. *Eléments de philosophie,* 20th ed. (Paris: Gallimard, 1953). First published as *81 chapîtres sur l'esprit et les passions* (Paris: Block, 1917). Translation mine.

12. Charles Morris, *Foundations of a Theory of Signs* (Chicago: University of Chicago Press, 1938). Vol. 1, no. 2 in *International Encyclopedia of Unified Science.*

Although this early monograph has been superseded by much of Morris's later work, the fitness of the metaphor I have used to explain the various dimensions of meaning in the art-work seems patent. It was suggested to me by C. Arthur Berndtson in a lecture on aesthetics at the University of Missouri. In recent times, it has been used by J. L. Jarrett in *The Quest for Beauty* (Englewood Cliffs, N.J.: Prentice-Hall, Inc., 1957), pp. 207ff., for similar purposes.

13. Sidney Zink, "The Cognitive Element in Art," *Ethics* 64 (1954): 186–204.

14. Alain [pseud. Emile Chartier], *Système des beaux arts,* 28th ed. (Paris: Gallimard, 1953), p. 60. Translation mine.

2

ART, AESTHETICS, AND PSYCHOANALYSIS

I

The purpose of this chapter is to isolate one direction aesthetic theory has taken in our own time and to indicate what phenomena in art and in psychoanalysis may be taken as support for the new theoretical insight. If the results are more suggestive than definitive, the reason may be found in this limitation of scope.

One of the consequences of Croce's[1] aesthetic doctrine can be neatly summarized into a paradox, that art expresses the inexpressible. But the use of paradox may be deemed by some to defeat the aesthetician's theoretical purpose; his language may do no more than shock us into thinking that theoreticians of art, if not artists themselves, ought to be able to express more clearly what is clearly expressible. To point out that the aesthetician's locution harbors a contradiction in terms, however, may do nothing more than expose our own insensitivity to the expressiveness of language. For the paradox remains profoundly true if given the proper interpretation; so true, in fact, as to state in as succinct a manner as possible the very axiom of aesthetic inquiry, that works of art express what is possible to be expressed only in terms of a given medium.

Two immediate objections to our interpretation of this "axiom" must be met. The first is that no test of the statement can be made when one starts out to investigate just what is expressed in a given artistic context. If I am reading a poem and ask the question "What does it mean?", the tools of verbal analysis can yield only a paraphrase, and not the poem; what is expressed in poetic structures cannot be reduced to a simple verbal equivalent. A fortiori, then, a picture, statue, or building. A poem does not mean; it *is,* as the poet might have said. In the same vein, a picture as a work of art does not picture; it is. How can we ever be sure, then, that art-works express anything? This objection is based upon a logical point of inquiry, and must be evaluated in the same terms.

In answer, let us consider a point of logic itself. Certain logicians insist upon the distinction between the meaning of a sentence, called a "proposition," and its physical occurrence, the sentence itself as written or stated. And the reason for this insistence is that the same proposition may be expressed by two different sentences either in different languages or in the same language. But there are others who insist upon talking only about sentences or statements, defining the logician's business as dealing with the structure of formulae and their transformations; any addition of the problem of meaning to this task could, in their eyes, only confuse the strictly logical issue. Which approach is valid for the artistic language?

It is clear that statements are statements because they mean, and that in order to mean they must be well constructed according to clearly defined rules of semantics. Thus, behind the meaning of any logical statement there will be found a vocabulary (supplied by a dictionary), rules of grammar (supplied by usage), and, as a test, a requirement of translatability (supplied by an understanding). When we apply these criteria to the language of art, as Susanne Langer has shown[2], we find that nothing corresponds to the first two. There is no dictionary meaning assignable to the elements of an artistic construct, and no rules the application of which will assure a "meaningful" statement. If this is true for the first two criteria, why should one continue to look for authentication in the third? Thus, without taking sides in the logical dispute noted above, we may merely answer the objection by saying that the rules of verbal expression apply only to verbal expressions, and not to art-works. But in so answering have we given satisfaction to those who pointed out the original difficulty? Hardly. A test there must be. But where to find it, if not in a "counter-statement?" The answer to this query is so obvious that it is rarely recognized. The only possible test for the meaning of an art-work is the experience of it, and a qualified viewer of the work is the man who has had the experience. It is for this reason that artists and critics, in answer to the question "What does it mean?" usually retort with a dry "Look again, read again; the work means itself." And in so doing, they merely state what their experience tells them is axiomatic for any inquiry into the facts of aesthetic experience. Art is to be enjoyed; its meaning is its enjoyment.

The second objection is to question the nature of this "axiom." To refer again to the logical model, an axiom is composed in part of indefinable notions, constitutes as a whole an undemonstrable proposition, and is itself used to demonstrate the truth of other propositions, which constitute the theorems of the system defined by the set of axioms selected. All attempts to prove the axioms are bootless; by trying, one could only reason in a circle. Once again it is clear that the analogy with logical procedure is of limited utility. Aesthetic inquiry can never be of the nature of a formal linguistic system; in purporting to give a reasoned explanation of facts, it must be empirical and yield no "proofs." In what sense, then, is our axiom an axiom?

In answer, consider an artist's usual statement, "My work speaks for itself; no comment is necessary." By answering in this way the artist merely states our axiom in another form. But what is being claimed? What, indeed, but the self-sufficiency of the pictorial? Anyone possessing normal visual receptors is capable of "understanding" the painting without a set of verbal footnotes, including perhaps the title. A portrait is meaningful even when the person being painted remains unknown. The experience is, and by rights ought to be, entirely visual. As a painter, speaking about paintings, the man is claiming what seems to him self-evidently true: a painting is a visual experience, and is not to be judged as if it were a verbal expression. This is, of course, no proof of the axiom, but an interpretation of it, and serves merely to state the ground for judging the success of a painting. To judge a painting as if it were a logical disquisition seems decidedly unfair both to the painter in question and to logicians in general. To each his own form of expression.

We may concede the artist his claim, and admit that the language of painting is the "language of vision." The only task remaining would be to examine the psychological theory and practice that may tend to yield independent support for the artist's contention. Is there any psychological phenomenon that can be taken as evidence for nonverbal communication? If there is, and if its mechanism may be made clear, psychologists will have been found to be extremely helpful in sharpening aesthetic theory, which, we are told, tends to be rather dull.

II

In an effort to determine the contribution, if any, made by psychoanalytic practice to aesthetic theory, the distinction drawn by Herbert Read[3] between the process, governed by psychology, and the product of art, which is the domain of aesthetics proper, may be denied on the grounds that any "inspiration" having its source in the subconscious mind of the author is more properly considered a part of the art object than a mere source of motivation for the artist's activity. The inspired idea is one that comes to fruition in expression.

But theories of inspiration are various and complex. Plato, espousing a theory of external inspiration, linked the activities of artists, prophets, lovers, and madmen, and subsumed them under the rubric of the irrational; each of these classes of individuals is composed of men "beside themselves." The theory of external inspiration, having a specious application to art considered imitative, is obviously inadequate to describe the movements in contemporary art, becoming more and more subjective.

Contemporary artists appeal, in the main[4], to a theory of internal inspiration, making reference to the subconscious processes of the creative mind. Ehrenzweig[5], writing as a psychoanalytical aesthetician, explains this preference of contemporary artists by referring to a pan-genital crisis provoked by the erect posture of the human species which hid from view the female genitalia. The artist is thus said to invent forms disguising the subconscious wishes of his libido, which, following the upright walking habit of the human species, could no longer be freely expressed in social contacts. Such disguise is necessitated by the action of the super-ego, or censor.

Similar assumptions have been made by two recent movements in painting. Max Ernst adopted the dadaist slogan, *épater le bourgeois*, to shock a predominantly middle-class audience into a realization of its basic sexuality, giving a not-so-hidden portrayal of the libido in such works as *La Phallustrade* and *L'effet d'attouchement*. The surrealists, creating an impression of a super-real world by amalgamating images of veridical perceptions with dream fantasy, likewise reduced the action of the censor to lay bare man's underlying sexual motivation. The weaknesses of both these movements as attempts to marry psychoanalysis and aesthetics are their obvious unfairness to psychoanalytical theory; the gestures and actions most meaningful to the analyst are the *unconsciously* expressed desires, and not those consciously exploited for an aesthetic effect. Interesting as these schools may be, they lack the essential connection we seek between psychoanalytic and aesthetic theory.

It has always been the bane of aesthetics to have suffered from a plethora of theories and a dearth of facts. Aestheticians have for the most part proceeded rationalistically from a more or less fruitful intuition to the deduction of what must be the case in the experience of particular works of art. The more successful approach would seem to be the empirical method of inducing the generalizations of aesthetic theory from a clearly defined set of aesthetic facts. For these, clearly, we are confronted with the work of artists and critics. Gyorgy Kepes[6] is the artist who defines his work as the development of a "language of vision." And this contention is supported by art educators, who maintain that the meaning of a work in the visual arts cannot be reduced to a literal linguistic statement.

But it would be a mistake to limit this concept of a nonverbal language to painting alone. Poets likewise maintain that their work cannot be limited to a literal statement, or paraphrase; the manner of phrasing is as important as what is phrased to the message of the poem. In a recent trial seeking to determine the status of a poem by a member of the "Beat Generation," novelist and critic Mark Shorer claimed to understand the import of the poem, *Howl*, by Allen Ginsberg, but refused to translate a line of it into prose, claiming that if this could be done, the poem would not be a poem. Even poetry is communication that may be properly described as nonverbal, since the effect of poetry is only in part a function of the referral property of words.

To generalize, it may be stated that nonverbal communication is the primary aesthetic fact. To the aestheticians, then, goes the job of explaining how this fact takes place. Various explanations have been given.

On the continent, Alain[7] and Valéry[8], as stated above, likened an art-work to a primitive sign that signifies "absolutely" rather than "relatively." The primitive signs of art differ from the conventional ones of ordinary languages in that they have no fixed or assigned meanings, and no fixed rules to govern any combinations into which they may enter; their meaning is established by individual reaction or interpretation of the context in which they occur. More recently André Malraux[9] tried to show the similarity in the ways poetry and paintings communicate, finding the "form" or "style" the significant element, as opposed to recognizable images or assigned meanings. He is obviously working in the tradition of Alain and Valéry. Maurice Merleau-Ponty[10], an existentialist aesthetician, agrees in essence with Malraux, although he denies that the purpose of an art-work is merely to exhibit the "style" of the author. For him, art is an indirect language, an expression, in which the individual elements have perhaps no assignable meaning, but gain a meaning by entering into the particular relations they do within context. And a representative "content" may very well be considered as one of the elements of the total form of the art-work. The proper way to read a poem or view a picture, then, is to unite what is said directly and what is said indirectly; one must read the words of the poem to understand what is said, and "read" the spaces between the words to interpret the indirect meaning of the poem.

In contemporary American and British literary criticism this phenomenon is given the name of "oblique reference," or "obliquity," and Susanne Langer[11] explains the same phenomenon by making a similar distinction in kinds of symbols: ordinary languages are discursive media, and art-works are nondiscursive, or presentational symbols. The meaning of a symbol of the latter sort is presented within the structure of the symbol and is "understood" when the art-work is perceived. Ballard[12] describes the mechanism of this meaning relation as the elaboration of analogies; and Ruesch and Kees[13] use a similar concept to differentiate discursive thought (digital computation) from the nondiscursive (analogic computation).

But the question remains, "By what process or mechanism do nonverbal expressions become communicative?" Here, I take it, is the contribution of the psychoanalyst to aesthetic theory. After all, nonverbal communication takes place each time a verbally blocked patient is led to recovery by a psychotherapist, whether through free drawing, through successful Rorschach or TAT projective testing. Moreover, if one examines closely the nature of the objects used in both Rorschach and the TAT tests, one will be able to see the grounds for the uniqueness of artistic expression.

Consider, first, the use of free drawing. Margaret Naumburg[14] describes a cure wrought exclusively by this means. At the beginning of therapy the patient was ignorant of the "meaning" of her works; she was led to it by the analyst. And the society that evolved between the patient and the therapist—this first act of communication—was a necessary condition for the appearance of that meaning. Next, the Rorschach technique. A series of ambiguous images are presented for interpretation, as in modern "abstract" art. The images are what they are; their meaning is "read into" them. Finally, the TAT technique: unambiguous images are interpreted. Recognizable content remains constant; its meaning shifts from subject to subject, as may the meaning of a more traditional painting. In short, the meaning of the images used in projective techniques varies from one patient to another, even when the form perceived is relatively constant. Meaning accrues to an art-work in similar fashion, if Alain and Valéry are correct. And for it to accrue, there must be this intimate society between the artist and his audience.

In answer to still another question, "What is the ultimate worth of aesthetic expressions?" it could be answered that social community is the ultimate value subserved by even the most antisocial of artists, and that an artist may succeed, where a propagandist fails, in molding public opinion.

III

To summarize, the propensity of aestheticians to proceed on theoretical grounds alone has led to a profusion of conflicting theories and produced little agreement on what constitutes the facts of their discipline. Nor have the theoreticians of art succeeded in isolating the mechanism by which the essential fact, nonverbal communication, takes place.

It seems appropriate therefore to suggest that aesthetics be conceived as the descriptive study of the area in which nonverbal communication does take place by means of the perception of an art-work. Then a study of successful psychoanalytical cures achieved by the use of similar objects of perception in therapy should yield further information concerning the manner in which such communication comes about.

Finally, if this account is fruitful, aestheticians may be led to abandon the model of significant speech to explain artistic communication. The meaning of the art-work cannot be claimed to be understood first in the artist's mind, and then translated by means of technical aptitude into some physical medium. The artist does not mean; his work does. Like the verbally blocked patient, or autistic personality, he may very well not know what he wants to say, except in the very vague sense of having an impulse (which is verbally blocked) to say something.

His creation is a means of discovering what is meant. In other words, the physical act of creation usually precedes the artist's understanding of his art-work's significance.

Communication will then have taken place nonverbally when artist and audience respond to the work in similar ways. Society grows from this interplay, along with the mutual understanding of the art object. Since the meaning of the work cannot be described, but only shown, the task, for critics, is restricted to an analysis of the object presented for appreciation. They must work in the hope that this society may develop. Such is the practical consequence of Croce's assertion that art expresses what cannot otherwise be expressed.

To go beyond the data of this chapter, it might be speculated that religious communities have grown up around the production of art-works, as is attested by the religious significance of the prehistoric cave paintings. In this process, the so-called mystery of communication has become endowed with the quality of the sacred.

In recent times the claims of classical psychoanalysis have been challenged by the growing school of existentialist philosophers and psychologists. Since a small group of existentialists have been successful artists and critics as well as exponents of the newer psychological trend, it behoves us to look at their testimony on the function of art in the working out of human existence. We move, then, from art considered as any form of nonverbal expression in which a creative personality achieves ego fulfillment to an explanation of the ways in which human existence establishes itself as both creative and personal by introducing novel significance into our common world.

The difference is a nuance. Retained throughout the change in point of view is the Crocean notion that art gives knowledge of the radically individual.

If our quest is to succeed, we must end with a description of a method for interpreting the significance of a particular work of art.

NOTES

1. Benedetto Croce, *Aesthetic,* Trans. by D. Ainslie (London: Macmillan, 1922).

2. Susanne K. Langer, *Philosophy in a New Key,* paperback reprint (New York: Penguin Books, 1948).

3. Herbert Read, "Psychoanalysis and the Problem of Esthetic Value," *International Journal of Psychoanalysis* 32 (1951): 73–82.

4. See Brewster Ghiselin, ed., *The Creative Process* (New York: Mentor Books, 1955).

5. Anton Ehrenzweig, "Unconscious Form-creation in Art," *British Journal of Medical Psychology* 21 (1948): 185–214; 22 (1949): 88–109.

6. *The Language of Vision* (Chicago: Paul Theobald, 1944).

7. Alain (Emile Chartier), *Système des beaux arts,* 28th ed. (Paris: Gallimard, 1953).

8. Paul Valéry, *Introduction à la poétique* (Paris: Gallimard, 1938).

9. *Les Voix du silence,* in *La Gallérie de la Pléiade* (Paris: Nouvelle Revue Française, 1951).

10. Maurice Merleau-Ponty, "Le language indirect et les voix du silence," *Les Temps Modernes* 7 (1952): 2113–44; 8 (1952): 70–94.

11. Langer, *Philosophy in a New Key,* and *Feeling and Form* (New York: Scribner's Sons, 1953).

12. E. G. Ballard, *Art and Analysis* (The Hague: Nyhoff, 1957).

13. Jurgen Ruesch and Weldon Kees, *Non-verbal Communication* (Berkeley and Los Angeles: University of California Press, 1956).

14. Margaret Naumburg, *Psychoneurotic Art: Its Function in Psychotherapy* (New York: Grune and Stratton, Inc., 1953).

3

ART AND EXISTENCE

The drive of existentialism, as a philosophical interpretation of the significance of human experience, has for the most part been felt only in peripheral disciplines: in theology, as supplying the ground for a description of "the ultimate concern" of human behavior,[1] and in psychiatry, as affording an alternative account of human motivation to that offered in Freudian determinism.[2] Some attempts have been made to extend the mode of thought to the problems of education,[3] and at least one philosopher has striven to show the interrelations between the existentialist treatment of human behavior and aesthetic accounts of art creation, criticism, and appreciation.[4]

As a doctrine insisting upon the efficacy of the creative human impulse, existential philosophy has done nothing more than to follow the direction of Husserl to return to the things themselves for an understanding of their significance, and to admit that if man's conduct is to a certain extent determined by the conditions under which he lives, it is nonetheless true likewise that some men not only can but do create a new environment for themselves, thereby changing the conditions under which they live. Indeed, without accounting for this aspect of human creativity, anthropological and sociological theory would seem to be out of contact with the facts they are intended to explain.

The cultural determinism of anthropologists and sociologists is, of course, a regulative principle of scientific reasoning, and not a result established by such thinking; it allows the researcher to proceed as if his rule were universally true, and is useful for the interpretation of statistical results. People can be classified into groups, and groups noted to behave in uniform ways; as long as there exists a control group whose individuals behave in ways significantly different from those of the experimental group, it is possible to employ the joint method of agreement and difference to establish empirically that a member of a culture, group, or other classificatory schema is caused to behave in the way he does.

The empirical question is changed, however, when it is observed that human individuals may react to their class or classification in such a way that this reaction itself becomes a new factor in the experimental situation, creating a motivation for change not explicable by any sociological "typology." Such reactions to classification may range from meek acceptance to outright revolt; American society has been, and will continue to be, the scene of myriad examples of both. To consider the example of Negroes alone, the Uncle Toms and the Black Power activists are cases in point. What explains this difference in motivation? What explains the situation in which certain members of a socio-economic grouping accept the classification of others, whereas others of the same group maintain their right to auto-determination, accepting no tags and refusing to behave as others are convinced they ought? Explanations have been many and various: from freedom of the will to sheer perversity; from spontaneity of action to the dialectical relationship between self and the other, or, perhaps most fancifully, between being and nothingness.

Whatever the explanation in scientific or in metaphysical terms, the fact seems obvious enough. Human behavior is sometimes essential, as deriving from universal properties attributable to some general laws of nature—physical, physiological, biological, psychological, cultural, as the case may be, and sometimes existential, as deriving from a personal reaction of distinct individuals as they live through the human condition according to the laws of the various kinds of universes mentioned above. That one set of determinants be labeled "facticity" and the other "transcendence" is of little consequence here. If there were no situation determining the behavior of each individual, the latter would have no objects presented to his choice, nor any means with which to attain them; and if the individual were not capable of transcending or modifying his situation by a personal reaction to his own appraisal of the environment, there would be no accounting for humanly significant social change or cultural evolution.

So far the behavioral sciences have been successful in describing certain aspects of man's facticity, but when the equally apparent facts of human behavior attributable to man's transcendance have been written off as "abnormal" or "deviant" or "chance," one may be led to suspect that the scientist in question has confused his regulative principle with matters of fact. This is the case every time the expert appeals to the newness of his discipline, or to the practical ignorance of "all" the causes necessary for a complete explanation of human behavior.

Whether or not our predictive science is relatively new and imprecise and our knowledge only fragmentary, the appearance of creative art on the social scene is a fact, and, viewed from the perspective of the multitudes of uncreative mankind, represents a prime example of deviant behavior. And some cultures, compounding the felony, continue to erect institutions and to spend a goodly proportion of their wealth on at least the preservation of both successful and unsuccessful art products. All societies do, to some extent, and this is some sort of explanation.

But how rationalize the love or tolerance of deviance without claiming that such love is itself normal and therefore to be expected? It would be too easy to claim that we normal scientists observe the normality of social approval even though what is approved is a deviation from the norm. After all, a true scientist is as rare a bird as a true artist—creation comes hard in both areas of human endeavor—and none would cite social approval as the criterion of his worth, either as he or his society views it. Society approves of both science and art for their results; of science, for its codification of warranted belief and predictions of things to come, and of art, for its discovery and preservation of a uniquely human significance.

If scientific or positivistic accounts of artistic behavior have been found wanting, the reason would seem to be their inability to handle the unique and the individual in purely essential terms and not in the alleged fact that the proper essential terms are not yet available to us. If a piece of metal refuses to behave like gold under experimental conditions, we are rightly led to expect that it is not gold even if it glitters; the man mistaking iron-pyrite for gold is aptly called a fool, but if a man refuses to behave as we were led to suspect, we are quite apt to crown his efforts by calling him an artist. And this comes as a surprise to no one who realizes that an artist is only a man, who, from the moment he was able to perceive, found himself already in possession of one of the necessary tools for evaluating his environment. Of course, if we could know what a man is, we could make the same sort of predictions about his behavior that we do about the behavior of anything else. But our ignorance of his nature is not merely *de facto*; since man is the creature without a nature, i.e., an experimental animal always capable of individually modifying the conditions of any experiment of which he is the subject, our ignorance of his behavior prior to his actions or reactions is a matter of necessity and *de jure*. It is not absurd to observe that even he may not know how he will react, whether or not he knows how he is expected to act. Like the experimenting scientist himself, he may discover the significance of his action only after the fact. But this is to say nothing more, perhaps, than what has already been written: by their fruits you shall know them. Man is the creator, and nowhere so plainly as in art.

Treatises on aesthetics linking human freedom with the creation of expressive art are not wanting. Milton Nahm's *The Artist as Creator*[5] is a nonexistential treatment of the subject; and Arturo B. Fallico's *Art and Existentialism* is one of the best examples of existential jargon yet applied to our commonplace experiences of both freedom and aesthetic activity.[6] Of these two works, Nahm's is the more useful, even for my existentialistic purposes.

Noting that aesthetic speculation on human creativity has suffered from poorly conceived metaphysics, Nahm indicates that pretended explanations of man, the creator, by appealing to supposed knowledge of the creation of God, the demiurgic maker, are useless, in that they appeal to the unknown to explain the unknown, even though such attempts at explanation did create an interest in human genius. He then proceeds to show that human genius later became treated in terms of the imagination, which operates under the conditions of inspiration as a kind of "unconditioned originality." Subsequently, in Croce, aesthetic intuition becomes the initial act of expression and the ultimate prerational basis of all scientific concepts.[7]

Although it is admitted that this second stage of development has led men to search for evidence in the facts of aesthetic experiences, especially with the nature and functioning of works of fine art, Croce's intuitionism is noted as suffering a double defect: it reduces aesthetic knowledge to matters of fact (rather than "judgments of value"), and conceives of the mind of the artist as creating without his body's manipulating sensuous materials. In this sense, human creation is a real event, but wholly "spiritual." But, surely, to locate the work of art in the artist's head, if not his spirit, is to miss one of the prevailing facts of inspiration: that the existence of materials conditions the formation of images, and that the force of the human imagination is expended in the rearrangement of materials at the service of a specific human value and significance. Thus, it would be equally false to claim that man does not create at all on grounds that he merely rearranges what is already at his disposal; he creates precisely by manipulating materials in accordance with specific human values, such as the perception of human feelings in a clear and tense presentation, which before the act of expression were vague and diffused throughout the creative organism. Nahm concludes: "We have asserted . . . that to produce the new in this way, within the limitations imposed by material, signs, feelings and under the conditions of limiting conceptions and values, is to specify the meaning of freedom in art."[8]

In Nahm's view, a work created under the conditions of freedom is both intelligible and original, classifiable and individual,[9] but neither at the expense of the other. A work may be perfect with respect to a type and yet original with respect to the significance communicated through the type, or aesthetic genus. Indeed, the ultimate value of art is claimed to be a communication between human freedoms:

> In terms of these values [perfection and originality], we have argued that it is precisely the function of fine art to *create the creator,* in Kant's words, to awaken the man of taste 'to a feeling of his own originality' and to stir him 'to examine his art in freedom.'[10]

Thus he claims, "The test of the freedom of the fine artist is his success or failure in leading the man of taste to create new values by specifying generic facts and by individualizing the content of aesthetic classes."[11]

Nahm's attempts to refute Croce with Kant are interesting, especially since Croce rightly considered himself a Kantian of sorts. Both Kant and Croce argued that aesthetic judgment is possible without a concept or rule; both considered the artist to be truly creative without being able to explain how or why such creation takes place; and both denied that one could create anything according to a prevised plan, since genius gives its own rule to art. Nor should it be forgotten that, for Kant, the manifold of impressions given to human consciousness comes already formed by the intuitions of space and time, considered as forms of sensibility, equally in play whether the subject is merely observing a fact of nature or making an object he discovers to be beautiful. Kant's idealism is transcendental, but idealism nonetheless.

Freedom, for Kant, is experienced in art as the play of our cognitive faculties. An object is intuited for which no concept is adequate, and the play continues, not as an invitation to reverie, but as an experience valued for its own sake—the felt pleasure in the harmony of the imagination (supplying a manifold of impressions) and the understanding (supplying an indeterminate concept such as unity in beauty, or totality and power in the mathematically and dynamically sublime). The creator is said to work not by rules from the past, but through his own genius, which gives its rule (freedom) to his product. Whence, the true *originality* of art, which may become *exemplary* only because the mark of its success is the presence of the indeterminate concept that becomes the standard or rule for the judgment of others. And this means only that all judgments of the work must be referred to the unity, totality, or power of the work in question.

The "aesthetical idea" purveyed in an artistic creation is incapable of representation in concepts although, according to Kant, it may occasion much thought. In thinking these thoughts while beholding the manifold, the viewer of works of fine art is moved to an appreciation of his own freedom—not to employ Kant's "supersensible substrate of humanity." Art is no mirror to nature; it presents a distinctly human significance and elaborates a community of persons—a society, if you will—capable of experiencing that significance.

Thus it remains profoundly true that in making works of fine art men do transcend themselves, i.e., become other than what they were;[12] for in so doing they are creating an environment that refuses to be ignored, a new order of facticity through which and by which men communicate their individuality. In existentialistic terms this is what is meant by art's creating the creator. But as stated in these existentialistic terms, the claim seems much clearer.

II

Where Nahm offers his own definition of a work of art as a concrete significant form,[13] in an attempt to avoid aesthetic idealism as it was elaborated by Croce, he succeeds; but where he continues to appeal to aesthetic categories, such as the tragic, the comic, the sublime, and so on, for an understanding of the perfection of a type, he fails to adopt what is most living in the thought of Croce—the consideration that aesthetic knowledge is not strictly classifiable, being individual and bearing its own significance. Arturo Fallico, on the other hand, perhaps because he is an artist or because he has read Croce more thoroughly than the existentialists, has retained the insight of the great Italian without being able wholly to compensate for his idealistic shortcomings. In *Art and Existentialism,* we read at least three times that an artist is pregnant with his idea, he knows not how; that he can neither will nor not will to create on demand; that it is all or nothing, a spiritual fact or nonexistent.

Croce, of course, was himself impregnated by Kant who stated simply:

> . . . the author of a product for which he is indebted to his genius does not know himself how he has come by his ideas; and he has not the power to devise the like at pleasure or in accordance with a plan, and to communicate it to others in precepts that will enable them to produce similar products.[14]

And Croce delivered himself of the idea in words of his native Italian, which have allowed us to comprehend both the idea and its paternity. It states only that an aesthetic idea is a discovery of the human mind; in Kant, at least, this discovery is not incompatible with the manipulation of sensuous counters that are the expression of the idea.

Yet we read in Fallico:

> The aesthetic enactment is like pregnancy: there cannot be a 'little' of it; it is there or it is not. And as in pregnancy, the act of conceiving is distinguishable from that of delivery into the open world. It is possible to conceive, but to have difficulty in the delivery. Our analogy breaks down only at one point: in art, the 'baby' is fully delivered to and for oneself (which is the only necessary form of its delivery), even before it is delivered in the construction of the public directive record of it.[15]

And we understand that he has accepted Croce's distinction between the creative, inner, and spiritual act and its public externalization. It is as if there were no alternative model for the explanation of aesthetic communication to that afforded by speech: idea-expression-idea.[16]

The testimony of many so-called "modern" artists is eloquent on the role of physical manipulation in the control of "inspiration," so that a newer model, one that considers the finished work itself the artist's expression, becomes an imperious demand. In short, it stipulates that an artist has communicated with me when both he and I have "internalized" the work in the same way by responding to it in similar fashion. We recognize once again the model for aesthetic communication stemming from the social psychology of Mead as contained in his *Mind, Self and Society*.[17] It is neither idealistic nor materialistic, and has the added advantage of gibing with ordinary experience.

In Fallico's favor it should be noted that his purpose is not a strictly aesthetic endeavor: he is not trying to give a phenomenological description of art-works in general, nor even of a particular work, though he mentions many. His explanatory purpose is served, he believes, if we can examine in general the ontological structures of human beings on the one hand, and the structures of aesthetic experience as the creation, criticism, or appreciation of art-works on the other;[18] if the one throws a light on the other, then some sort of explanation is available.

Or is it? Certainly not, if both sides of the explanatory circle are initially unknown. How does one solve an equation with two unknowns, each dependent upon the other? One may start, as Fallico does, by asking the question, "How is the very being of the existing individual constituted so that art is possible?" And one could answer the question by transcendental deduction, as Kant pursued a similar answer to a similar question: We have knowledge. How is it possible? Kant's appeal to the forms of intuition, categories, and reasoning principles as the structures that allow knowledge is plausible only if we assume that knowledge is what he claims it to be. And his answer sketches only one possible solution. For this ploy to work, we must be assured that knowledge is what we claim it to be, and give a phenomenological description of the process by which we acquire it. This is what Husserl thought he had added to Kantian philosophy, and he expressly denied that transcendental deduction was a satisfactory substitute for phenomenological reduction, even though latter-day Husserlians, such as Sartre, have maintained their substitutivity.

The problem becomes still more complicated when Fallico reverses the procedure, and asks, "What can art mean in the light of the fact that human existence is as it is?" Here, of course, even if we possess a valid phenomenological description of human existence we should still face the problem of justifying the transcendental deduction from it, i.e., that, given one description of the human condition, art *must* mean this, that, or the other. And, on the face of it, this would seem to be more difficult than the former. For, if we did know (by acquaintance and phenomenological description) that human existence is what Fallico describes it to be, how could we establish that the meaning of art is necessarily what he takes it to be? Either we have an explanatory circle of the vicious and non-Heideggerian type, or we have a valid phenomenological account of the one or the other portion of it, which obviates the necessity of appealing to anything beyond. And it is for this reason that such sentences as

> The possibility of being-self-in-its-world-together-with-other-selves which constitutes the aesthetic word is, in phi-

losophy, somehow proposed as the possibility which is becoming actualized as life-in-the-world.[19]

are empty of content. We know that the artist is free, within limits, to bring his creation into existence; he comes to know this willy-nilly by making a successful work of art. But observing him, we can see how this is done; and if we have the command of the language and the true desire to avoid jargon of any kind, existentialist or other, we can give some kind of description. To do so is to give a phenomenological account of the manner in which individuals have worked out the problems of a personal choice of existence—a project to which we may now turn.

III

If Nahm's error was his retreat from the Crocean insight, as to the radical individuality of the work of art, into an ultimate retrenchment in a neo-Aristotelian system of type-classifications, Fallico is led astray by his acceptance of Croce without at the same time succeeding in producing the phenomenological descriptions that would lend further credence to the illustrious Italian's claims. Indeed, Fallico's existentialism gives only a quasi-metaphysical interpretation of artistic creation. It is not enough, however, to show parallelism between two kinds of structures; to give a phenomenological account of human freedom in creation we must describe the processes by which human ontology is exemplified in the act of making successful works of art. Its essence must still be read from the phenomenon itself.

In this respect, Nahm's account is relatively more faithful to the aims of phenomenology than Fallico's. His descriptions may be deficient in that they are not borne out by further observation, but they are an attempt to do justice to what actually happens when an artist does in fact create. In Fallico's lucubrations, on the other hand, both creation and the nature of the human personality must be assumed to be known, in order for his parallelism between the structures of creativity and the patterns of human behavior to be understood. There is room, then, for still another account of artistic creation.

The best existentialist treatments of aesthetic experience are still those of Sartre and Merleau-Ponty.[20] As by now is well known, Sartre gives two explanations of human freedom. In his earlier, Husserlian-inspired treatises, man is said to be free insofar as he is capable of imagining the existence of an object not present to his senses. We can perceive the structures of our real environment, conceive of a lack therein, and purpose to restructure the same environment in such a way that the lack is fulfilled. Images are intentional or conscious events in which consciousness relates itself to an absent object. The object exists only as intended. In an act of aesthetic perception, the physical art object is only an analogue; its perception merely motivates the consciousness to intend its imaginal correlate. And to a certain extent, these claims are borne out by a consideration of works of art. A portrait, a landscape, any realistic scene does enable consciousness to attend to a referential meaning attributed to the art-work considered as an iconic sign.[21]

The difficulty begins when we analyze this account. First of all, his excursions into the ontology of being and nothingness (added only after the completion of his *l'Imaginaire*[22]) have not added to our *aesthetic* knowledge, since in *L'Etre et le néant*[23] his subject was ontology, and not aesthetic experience. Fallico has failed to note this distinction. Secondly, when we apply Sartre's phenomenological descriptions of the imagining consciousness to our experiences of works of art, we find that they are limited to only one kind of aesthetic object, a representational work. The moment the work tends to deviate from the realistic—as it may, to complete abstraction or nonobjectivity—we are hard put to describe the intentional correlate of the physical analogue in any terms other than what we perceive in the actual work.

In his essay on the origins of a work of art, Heidegger asks the pertinent question:

> But where and how then does this universal essence exist so that the work of art may correspond with it? With which essence of which thing, then, should a Grecian temple correspond? Who could assert the impossible, that in the edifice the idea in general of the temple is represented?[24]

A nonobjective work of art represents nothing, yet is experienceable as a unique and individual significance, not as an essence, or idea of anything at all. But to make this clear one must show how significance accrues to or appears within a single perception of the work in question.

In order to turn this trick, Merleau-Ponty makes appeal to the phenomenological structures of perception itself. The value of what one sees is on the surface of a work of art; it is felt within the structures of the human corporeal schema, or body proper, as it intends an object in an organized sensuous field. The object and its field are related as figure and ground held in a single tense and vibrating positioning—there, before the intending subject. The significance of the gestalt as it forms or evanesces before the subject's vision is the tension felt in its perception; and as such, it constitutes a modification of the perceiver's bodily schema or basic spatiality, which is defined by a range of the controlled responses of the living organism.

The underlying gestaltism of Merleau-Ponty's thought, linking the intuition of a form with the significance of its organization, goes a long way to answer some of the lingering questions of aesthetics—especially questions as to the relative values of materials, form, and expression. The materials are all sensuous; the form is the felt tension of materials fusing into closure and significance. Yet still another question remains unanswered: how does the experience of representational works achieve its ultimate significance when it contains, by definition, elements that are not seen, but only referred to?

Where Sartre's doctrine is "thick," Merleau-Ponty's is "thin." To emphasize the imaginal values of representational works of art at the expense of the perceptual values of their sensuous surfaces, as Sartre does, is to ignore an important fact of aesthetic creation: that the meaning of a representational painting, literary work, and the like, is controlled by the manner of presenting an idea or image on the surface of the work.[25] That, too, is a relation of tension, or unification of two correlative functional terms into a single comprehensive experience. Call it "the total expressiveness" of a representational work.

This too must become "internalized" within the field of organismic responses if we are to have the experience of the work.

Merleau-Ponty's latest attempt to overcome the thinness of his original doctrine and to explain this secondary phenomenon of internalization was, however, a failure. His statement, in "l'Oeil et l'esprit,"

> That's why the dilemma of the figurative versus the nonfigurative in painting is badly put: it is true at one and the same time and without contradiction to state that no grape has ever been what it is in the most figurative painting, and that no painting, even an abstract one, can elude Being: Caravaggio's grape is the grape itself.[26]

contains a paradox solvable only in terms of an ontology of vision. In short, aesthetic perception of representational works follows the same pattern by which a human subject assimilates any visual object, in a readaptive response to visual stimulation felt by the tension of the intentional arc of the body proper (humanly controlled spatiality):

> One senses perhaps . . . everything communicated by this little word, to see. Vision is not a certain modification of thought or presence to the self; it is rather the means given to me for being absent from myself, of being present, from within, to that fission in Being only at the end of which I close in again upon myself.[27]

Hence, seeing is grasping at a distance, an intentional movement outward toward the seen object and return to a renewed and revivified homeostatic condition of enriched bodily presence.

It *may* be true that our perception of visual objects is felt as space tensions; it *is* true that paintings are constructed of space tensions. Both experiences present a phenomenon of nature, the subjective and objective aspects of experience in fusion. But why call this "Being" when the word "phenomenon" already encloses all there is to the experience? It successfully conveys the idea that visual experiences, and *a fortiori* experiences of paintings, are neither univocally "subjective" nor "objective," but a tensely felt relationship between our visual (corporeal) apparatus and the objects of our environment.[28] And if this is true, there is more to seeing than what meets the eye.

Merleau-Ponty, like Fallico, has abandoned the phenomenology of aesthetic perception for speculative ontology, and has failed to provide an adequate description of the manner in which our experience of depth (representational) paintings "thickens" into the comprehension of the allegedly real presence of their referential objects. To call a real visual object a space tension, felt within the intentional arc of a single living bodily schema, is to reduce the value of a represented object within the structures of a painting's depth to a single function of presenting space. This happens in paintings, of course; both Giotto and Cézanne were masters of the art. But such theoretical reduction of depth to surface values makes it impossible for us to understand any further thickening of the surface, such as occurs when objects are viewed in relation, presenting a further symbolic meaning—e.g., a circular form presents space; but it sometimes becomes a halo, indicating the sanctity of the person whose head it surrounds. Merleau-Ponty's account gives no support for any kind of iconological or symbolic reference.

The reasons should be obvious; some paintings contain surface alone. And for these Merleau-Ponty's phenomenology of painting is adequate. But other paintings contain images and perhaps even an idea, and for these he can give no adequate explanation. I propose, in what follows, to get out of this impasse by constructing a phenomenological view of creation in art embodying the theories of both Sartre and Merleau-Ponty. I shall avoid referring to the dialectic of "Being" and "Nothingness" of the one, and to the commerce between "brute being" and "wild-flowering mind" of the other. Three notions should suffice: imagination, perception, and context of significance. Then, following my analysis, I shall draw my conclusions concerning the nature of the creative and appreciative personalities.

IV

Existential-phenomenological accounts of aesthetic communication have failed so far because no one has kept the whole of the problem in sight. Sartre stressed the imagination, thereby putting the creator's activity at a premium; Merleau-Ponty stressed perception, thereby emphasizing the viewer's contribution. And before either of these had written a word on the subject, Roman Ingarden had applied the method of Husserl to describe the nature of aesthetic objects,[29] which, if I am right, constitute the means by which the communication takes place within the overall social process.

It would seem obvious that, if we are to achieve our aims of describing the manner in which aesthetic objects of all types and genders mediate between the experiences of human subjects, some attention must be given all three of these factors. And if we actually succeed in the task, we shall have gone a long way toward explaining the value of aesthetic expression to both individuals and to society. Imagination, perception, and the institutions of society are all amenable to phenomenological investigation, and should not be exceedingly difficult to describe. We need only perform the reduction and read the significance that spreads itself before us in context.

1. *Imagination.* Imagining is a conscious event in which we become aware of an intentional object. But it does not happen in a vacuum. I can imagine objects or events only because I have perceived objects and events of a like kind. Sartre admits the point by referring to a "savoir imageant," or latent conceptual knowledge that informs each imaginal projection. But for the store of such latent concepts, I must have had a still more primary relation to the world—call it perception if you will—by which I have gained the significance contained therein as "sedimented" meanings. In this way, Merleau-Ponty's thesis of the "primacy of perception" seems to be borne out, not only for knowledge in general, but for artistic creation as well. Or has it? Let us look again.

Consider an act of painterly creation. It is engaged. The artist is occupied with constructing a sensuous surface with such counters as lines, colors, and volumes. These must appear; and in their appearance, they constitute a field of ongoing expression. Either as a past event held only in memory (if the creation is purely imaginary) or as a present expanse of visual field (if the creation is physical and controlled through the manipulation of materials), the institution of a set of qualitative relationships forms a part of human facticity, or the determinate situation against which the agent must work if his action is to be effective. His freedom is to act, to accept, or to change what has already been instituted. This can be done only through the imagination, by which the painter projects further qualitative relationships not yet a part of the established situation. Here the causal influence is from the future, not the past; and from the creator's viewpoint, the work is an end toward which he continues to work. When the second stroke is made on canvas or wood and a new perception replaces the first, a new present results; it is there to be perceived, or is grasped in a new act of intending the painter's world.

This reference to the painter's world is no mystical reference to a privileged habitation of artistic genius. Heidegger's analysis of "the worlding of the world"[30] is empirically sound; madmen, poets, and children often lose themselves in worlds of their own creation; but then so do sane adult men and women when they are concerned with a system of referential relations defined by their own personal interests or involvements. The painter's world is only more obvious in that he leaves a visual pattern for the understanding of his involvements. It is for this reason, of course, that psychoanalysts may choose to use drawing or painting as a communicative tool, especially, as we have seen, where the patient is for some reason verbally blocked.[31] In the case of the creative painter, moreover, the expression is purer, since his world, as seen in his work of art, is entirely visual. His work begins with the past (perception), is interpreted in the light of the future (imagination), and culminates in a new and meaningful present. And when that moment has been achieved, he may respond to his work in the same way that any sensitive viewer responds to the same work.

Such a view of artistic creation cannot put the premium on either the imagination or perception. Both are involved, even if the work is nonobjective.

When the context of significance becomes more complicated, when lines, colors, and volumes represent objects, and represented objects present ideas, the situation has not changed essentially. The painting may be motivated by an idea, and achieved through the relations of represented objects; or the idea may be discovered by an adventitious relation between objects. In either case, if the painter is to communicate, all this depth structuring of his universe must be presented to our vision for the significance to be perceived.

An idea may be the initial motivating factor. And if so, it may be a sedimented meaning of a past or present culture, or an entirely new conception. The new conception can arise only from an evaluation of present or past knowledge; older, received meanings may be made to gain new significance for being put into a novel setting. All we need to make the explanation is an understanding of facticity and transcendence—of the known, determinate situation and the human subject's capability of getting beyond it. Nothing is necessary beyond the memory of the past, the imagination of the future, and the perception of the present.

If Heidegger is right, this is the essence of human existence—the possibility of being simultaneously or equiprimordially (*gleichursprünglich*) ahead of itself, already in a world, alongside entities. In choosing the imagination as the principal means of man's creative concern, Sartre chose existentiality, which he called "transcendence," as the means of man's freedom of expression. But his analyses of Baudelaire, Jean Genet, and

Tintoretto show to what extent the other two determinants of human freedom are required. Call them the "past" and "a new present" if you like, or, if you prefer, call them "facticity" and "fallenness."

It may be objected here that my account, like Fallico's, has begun to lapse into ontological "explanation." To an extent this is true, but there is a difference. I am not simultaneously examining art to establish ontological conclusions, and human existence to establish aesthetic conclusions. I am, however, examining the manner in which a painter must act in terms of the materials at his disposal and the strength of his own imagination to rearrange them, in order to discover how human existence is revealed in art. And I think I may have succeeded in showing that, although it is true that a painter creates his own universe in terms of the future existence of his artifact, he cannot do so without taking into account the common world of other human subjects whose materials he actually manipulates. He may project any aim or value he wishes, but to communicate with others he must use common materials and embody them in a meaningful present experience. Hence, the artist's freedom is not absolute. To be maximally effective in society, he must adjust to the plastic qualities of his materials, put them into a significant context, and finally perceive the significance as he has embodied it. Without the first of these characteristics his "work" remains a dream (or Crocean expression); without the second, his work has no meaning; and without the third, he does not himself participate in the aesthetic communication.

2. *The context of significance*. What I refer to by this name has variously been called "the work of art," "the aesthetic object," or "the object of criticism." In more

ordinary terms, it is what we appreciate when we attend to the artist's creation. Ordinary language philosophers are right in their objection to the use of the definite article as a way of distinguishing a physical perception—the painting that hangs on a wall—from the intentional object that was first projected by the creator and then comprehended by an appreciator who adopted the correct attitude for intending, or attending to, the same object. Although their point is made linguistically, and has metaphysical consequences, a whole philosophy of art criticism is at stake.

Consider the linguistic point first. The reference of the definite article to a unique entity is obviously well-taken. The "the" in "the aesthetic object" does serve to point out a unique referent; but it is used in conjunction with the epithet "aesthetic," which presumably refers to an object of some kind other than the merely physical. Thus any description of an aesthetic object is considered accurate if it is couched in terms other than those commonly used to refer to the materials of the physical correlate. No doubt this has often been intended, as by Croce and Fallico, who distinguish between "the expression" and its "externalization" and between "the enactment" and "reenactment" of the first creative word.

Idealists, such as Croce and Fallico, have not learned the methodological lessons of phenomenology, which is precisely to abstain from any metaphysical statements whatsoever. The difference between the "natural attitude" and the "phenomenological" is precisely one's decision to put into brackets any belief concerning the reality of the objects intended. If natural objects are explicable by reference to a series of causal determinants conditioning their appearance, the phenomenologist merely refuses to follow the naturalist's route, and suspends his belief in causality. He puts brackets around the object as it is intended, and describes what he finds enclosed therein.

Quite obviously, bracketing the world is a procedure, not a substantive commitment, and to call the object "real" or "unreal" violates the method. It simply makes no difference whether the object is purely imaginary or is there as a part of the real world to be perceived. What is examined phenomenologically is the appearance of a new significance, whether it is achieved through the manipulation of psychical or physical materials. I have already shown that a phenomenological description of the imagination entails some aspects of a perceived situation, and that the same sort of description for communication by means of artistic creation entails an ultimate return to a perceived situation. Metaphysically, then, there is no ground for determining the uniqueness of purely aesthetic objects. Idealists must strain their explanations in order to cover the act of "externalization," and "realists" must at least complete their monism with some account of the manner in which aesthetic objects become reflected in the mental activity of perceiving minds.

But aesthetic objects are unique. If it is not metaphysical, the difference between a "physical" and an "aesthetic" object may be only linguistic, as Paul Ziff has maintained.[32] In other words, the difference may be attributed solely to the way in which the various objects are described, either in physical or phenomenological terms. Such a distinction is useful, but fails to solve the question at issue, which is not *the nature* of aesthetic *objects,* but the difference in kind between physical and phenomenological *descriptions.* It is taken for granted that the ordinary language user can distinguish descriptions of the same work as physical and as phenomenological. No one, after all, could mistake a quantitative account of light or sound waves for a qualitative description of space tensions or musical intervals, and no one in his right mind could mistake the printed pages of a poem for the cluster of images they represent. True enough, physics is not psychology, and the structure of a sign vehicle need have no isomorphic parallel to the structure of a poem. If the ordinary language user can understand this much, he can likewise understand that there is something peculiar about the aesthetic perception of art objects.

The same conclusion may be drawn from a consideration of the "good reasons" school of aesthetic judgment. Admitting that some judgments of aesthetic worth are good and some bad, depending upon the reasons given for the judgment of approval or disapproval, some analytical philosophers have refused to stipulate any criteria for making aesthetic judgments, since each judgment must be verified by reference to the circumstances or context in which the judgment has arisen. In doing so, they have emphasized the point that there is no single rule or quality by reference to which judgments are made. This too is a denial of the uniqueness of an aesthetic kind —"the good," as this expression is applied to works of art. Kant and Croce had both warned against this sort of aesthetic generalization. But to deny the uniqueness of an aesthetic rule, valid for many objects (Kant), or the existence of aesthetic kinds and concepts (Croce), is not to deny the uniqueness of an aesthetic object; indeed it is to maintain the individuality of the contexts in which such objects make their appearance. And invariably when the analytical philosopher deigns to give a good reason for his aesthetic choice, it is in terms of the working of an individual work of art. For the most part, however, he is content to indicate the manner in which aesthetic judgments are to be made—by others, and presumably, in particular, by art critics.

It shall be taken as established, then, that there is no unique "work of art" in the sense that a special kind of metaphysical object is intended by the use of that expression; nor is there a single rule that may be applied to many works of art in the determination of their individual worth. And, if the truth be said, we become aware of works of art in the various sets of circumstances or contexts in which they appear. Judgments of value, finally, are warranted by appealing to features of the various works as they appear. But this means only that the value or significance of a work of art is always felt in context.

In broadest scope this context is defined by the relation between a subject and the object perceived. This relation may be called variously "imagining," "perceiving," "minding," or "feeling." Which of the terms is apposite depends upon the character of the object intended. As Ingarden has shown, aesthetic objects may be composed of a series of strata, each significant in itself and adding significance to the total "polyphonic harmony," which is the gestalt appearance of their functioning within context. For convenience's sake, I shall arrange the strata in accordance with their "thickness," as explained above.[33] We may begin with the surface.

The expressiveness of certain aesthetic objects is exhausted on the surface: absolute music, architecture, nonobjective painting, the dance, and the like. Aesthetic surfaces are composites of sensory elements or "counters." These surface counters are established by discriminations between sounds and silences; lines or colors and their backgrounds; positive or negative spaces of masses; and movements of the human body. Merleau-Ponty's phenomenological account of our perception of these counters indicates the extent to which the human corporeal schema is affected in their perception. Their expressiveness or significance is felt as a tension in the intentional relation between the perceiving organism and the object coming to closure. The "emotion," if such it must be called, is nothing more than the manner in which the object moves us as we attend to its closing.

The phenomenon of closure performs a double function in this description. It indicates the manner in which psychological elements—visual, aural, and/or kinaesthetic—are grouped into significant unities. It thus corresponds to Kant's "indeterminate concept" by which the understanding is said to unify the sensible images of intuition, and indicates the first "value" of aesthetic perception, the clearness that Nietzsche called "the Appolonian" dimension of art. The experience of the phenomenon, in our readaptive response to the actual closing of sensuous counters, yields not only a perception of the clearness, but a feeling of the tension in the act of closing. This second function of closure describes the expressive quality of the form in question, or the Nietzschean "Dionysian" component of aesthetic perception. In the most basic sense of the term, we have "judged" the work when we have felt its tension; i.e., we have had the experience when we have felt the tension of its funding counters.

The appearance of depth counters, however, alters the context. Where the only test of a valid perception of the surface work is the actual presence of visual clarity and intensity, certain organizations of sensuous surfaces represent objects not present to our perceptive organs. Lines, volumes, and spaces may fund to suggest objects of a familiar, natural kind. Thus a drawing of the human figure is easily recognized as being either masculine or feminine, especially if the figure is a nude. And in our perception of this kind of drawing, the nude is present only to the imagination. Degrees of naturalism in the representation may thrust our attention back to the surface qualities, as in Caravaggio's grapes in Merleau-Ponty's account; or pictorial "statements" may be made by special manners of handling the surface. Thus Renoir's impressionistic treatment of the nude feminine bust suggests softness, tenderness, and innocence, while Kirchner can take the same subject and render it as blatantly harsh, animalistic, and crassly provocative. In the one form of expression the object demurely retreats behind the picture plane, the soft pinks of flesh made more radiant by the surrounding muted greens, while Kirchner's prostitute thrusts her pointed breasts, the surrounding blacks emphasizing their livid purple pointedness, this side of the picture plane as if to violate the privacy of our lived space. Put a halo around the first, and we should accept the sanctity of the representation, while the same touch on the second would strain our credulity or awaken our ironic sensibilities.

The object that appears, the further images it may evoke, or the ideas it may present when viewed in relation to others, introduces further play of the imagination and understanding. Such aesthetic objects call out "depth" structures, and necessitate a criterion of relevance for the interpretation of the depth meanings of the experience. Ultimately, of course, the relevance is supplied and controlled by the relatedness of counters: surface to depth, depth to depth, and overall depth to overall surface, which is the total expressiveness itself. The sole rule to follow in the determination of total expressiveness of an aesthetic context is that no counter—surface or depth—has an absolute significance; or conversely, that each counter has only that significance which its relatedness to other counters makes apparent.

If this account of the expressive context of works of art is accurate, the correct role of the imagination is to supply the cognition of represented objects; and beyond this function, once the objects are cognized, the understanding itself may be involved in the interpretation of the relation between them. That our perception remains primary in aesthetic experiences is not owing to the fact that represented objects are presented to our vision by similar or identical space tensions in the natural and phenomenological attitudes, but that any interpretation of the depth must be brought back to the expressing surface as the ultimate control of the image or the idea expressed.

3. *Perception.* Aesthetic communication is completed with the perceptual closing of related counters fusing into significance for a number of viewers. But what this significance in each case happens to be is controlled by the nature of the counters and their relations. No statement about aesthetic experiences in general may prejudice the freedom of the artist to construct his object as he sees fit, nor the manner in which a sensitive viewer is free to interpret it. The structures of the perceptual field suffice to limit both systems of freedom, and guarantee the possibility of communication by means of the art-work.

Since communication takes place with the internalization of a single meaning or significance, it suffices, in order to explain aesthetic communication, to trace the manner in which both creator and appreciator intend the same object.

First, the creator. Even if the work began by the sheerest act of the imagination (the combining of counters seen only in "the mind's eye"), there is only one test of the creator's claim to have created the physical analogue that corresponds to it. And as the enemies of intentionalist criticism point out, if the artist has been successful in the manipulation of his medium, there can be no difference between the physical artifact and its imaginary intention. To discover the artist's intention in such cases, we need only consult the perceptual object he has constructed; and if he has, by hypothesis, failed to achieve his intention in physical materials, there would be no point in examining the physical object for the intention. To rewrite a word of Croce, the only aesthetical idea about which we can speak is the one that has been overtly expressed in the physical materials of the common world. Granted, then, that creation may begin with imaginary "inspiration," the test of its success is the perception of the object made.

A communicated idea cannot remain the private property of its originator. And since some aesthetic ideas are created by the very act of manipulating a sensuous medium in a technique of discovery, some original ideas are never properly speaking wholly imaginary. In this latter manner of creation, morever, there is no problem of externalization at all, no derogation of physical manipulation to techniques; the creator internalizes his idea in the same way as his viewers—by perceiving the context in which the significance has arisen. The problem arises only when we assume that "the aesthetic object" is something purely internal; it is precisely that of understanding how such objects become externalized in the world of perceptual events, and of correctly evaluating the function of craftsmanship in art.

The viewer, on the other hand, may be thought of as having an unlimited freedom of interpretation to associate images and ideas with the perceived surface. But certainly this is not the case either. "The aesthetic object" is not something contemplated in an act of reverie, only motivated by the perception of the moodal qualities of a given surface. To consider an image or an idea as "the significance" of the context of its appearance, is to violate the relativity of meaning to context. In some works of art images appear and ideas are presented. They then become counters having their significance by virtue of a relation to other counters—in particular the surface whose organization constitutes a style, manner, or technique, which in turn possesses a significance modifying that of the depth. One may honestly be in doubt about the depth significance of the work in question. If so, an interpretive hypothesis is in order, and the hypothesis can be checked only by referral to the original context.

The task of a philosophical aesthetics can only be the elaboration of a set of categories whose application to a unique context of significance "explains" the appearance of that significance. Surface, depth, and total expressiveness may do for starters, but further investigation on the various kinds of sensuous surfaces must be performed in order to discover the limits of aesthetic expression in a given art medium. The history of the development of modern art in many art media indicates that this search is still going on. Perhaps some day even our teachers of classical music may be led to a comprehension of the significance in electronic music. Experimentalists in the theater, poetry, the dance, and painting seem already to have won their battle. Each successful discovery has added to our understanding of the structures of aesthetic objects.

V

The preceding phenomenological account of artistic creation, describing the creative and appreciative acts as they converge upon a single context of significance, gives credence to the opinion of R. G. Collingwood that an artist creates in order to get his feelings clear.[34]

An aesthetician working in the idealistic tradition of Croce,[35] Collingwood distinguished between "psychic expression" and "artistic expression." In the former, the subject merely undergoes a reaction to environmental stimulation, expressed in muscular, circulatory, and glandular changes within the organism. Such feelings constitute the state of every organism excitable by its environment. Aesthetic expression is the means for introducing clarity into these basic psychic conditions, by selecting certain of the brute, and for the most part, unconscious "feelings" for expression in art. When such feelings are expressed artistically, they are brought to full consciousness, under conditions of control. The controlled bodily reactions constitute a basic human "language," which enables the artist to convert his sense impressions into ideas of the imagination by expressing them in a public context.

Collingwood's theory has a clear-cut advantage over its Crocean counterpart. The Englishman is not committed to a theory of creation in which the mental elaboration of an image must precede the manipulation of physical or phenomenological counters. Creation is still considered a discovery. The discovery is made when a successful image has been constructed, and is registered as a bodily reaction become fully conscious. Like Croce, Collingwood considers the artist to be a subject in search of identity, who achieves this aim when his feelings have been clarified. But unlike Croce, Collingwood offers a criterion for the clarification of feelings, by associating bodily reactions with the structures of the imaginal construct. Lastly, he offers a criterion for differentiating good from bad art: good art clarifies feeling, and thus intensifies consciousness, whereas bad art works toward the corruption of consciousness, in that it falsifies, denies, or otherwise conceals the basic springs of human feeling.

In other words, Collingwood came as close as anybody to describing how the arts function as a language of feeling. What he lacked was a description of the context of significance that would yield a methodological procedure for ensuring communication between consciousnesses, a clear distinction between perceptions and images, and a view of artistic technique that would allow for the teachability of aesthetic expressions.[36] It seems clear, if I can get my feelings clear by manipulating the sensuous materials of a physical medium, that my "image" is of the sensuous materials so arranged; that if I can recognize the clarity of my feeling expressed in the image, I can explain, and therefore teach, at least this manner of recognition; and that both of these conditions are results of my correctly perceiving the context of aesthetic expressiveness I have constructed.[37]

The central positive doctrine established in Collingwood's thesis is that the expressing subject does not know what his feeling is; he is said to express it in order to discover it. The ultimate value of aesthetic expressions would then be the discovery of my own personality: of those feelings (some of which are forced upon me by my environment) which correlate most clearly with my true self. The self, then, must be such as to be developed by expression.

Art educators and certain psychoanalysts have always made this assumption, the former to justify the inclusion of the creative arts in the educational curriculum and the latter to introduce communication between themselves and their patients, who are (and may remain) unknown to both participants in the therapeutic sessions. Essentialist thought has never been able to achieve these aims. Although the Delphic oracle was ominous in more ways than one, instructing Socrates, who sought the conditions of the good life, to know himself, the founder of ethics had no way of assimilating the message. Even Polonius offered similar advice to his departing son, "To thine own self be true." What is the process by which self-knowledge is achieved? Educators continue to look for the essential determinants of adolescent behavior; psychoanalysts, of the Freudian school at least, to look for the true self in the frustration of past drives emanating from the *id.* Socrates sought an essence that could not be defined, being individual, and Polonius merely advised Laertes of the existentialist's dilemma: how to be true to oneself, when oneself is an ongoing process of development into the future.

Heidegger and Sartre have done the most toward supplying the missing information and the lacking hermeneutical tools of analysis. Sartre understood the projective character of human selfhood, but he ran aground on a metaphysical reef. How can one understand what the initial (and final) project of human transcendence is, when the choice of project is said to have been taken outside of time and space?[38] Within the one time and space of the real world, however, one may determine the essence of a given personality, if only one rejects the notion of essence as *quidditas* or nature, and observes how a person behaves under known stimulation. Heidegger has never committed Sartre's error. For him an essence is not what a thing is, but a manner in which something comes into being and remains as it is. Existence does not precede essence,[39] but the essence of a human being does lie in his existence:[40] in how he lives, feels, and expresses himself. And the ultimate empirical test of the authenticity of the choice of one self as opposed to another is whether the individual resolutely faces the consequences of having made a prior decision. The essence of the human being, then, is found in the repetition of a manner of existence, in the continued acceptance of a personally projected goal as the determining motive for one's action.

Art illuminates this process in a number of ways. The initial creation clarifies a given choice. It can only grow out of a primary relation between the creator and his situation; he is always in the world. When he judges his work to be good, he repeats the value of his initial choice. He may become so enamored of his initial choice that he never deviates from a given style. Thus we can speak of a work of art as a David, Ingres, Mondrian, Rembrandt, and so on. Only Picasso seems to be bent upon a continual destruction and reconstruction of his style; perhaps only he understands, in a preontological way, that he must continually remake himself.

If he or any other artist were mistaken, the object of choice is still there—to be perceived by any sensitive observer. We call the more sensitive of the observers "critics," and hearken to their words as to the testimony of the object. What is witnessed in that testimony is the freedom of the human personality.

Society has already entered thc picture when the object has been made. Certain sub-institutions of the society will concern themselves with its preservation and appreciation: the museum and the school. And the reason for all of this is the simple basic fact that art itself is an institution, perhaps the most free, permitting the expression of any human impulse. The individual pole of that institution is provided by the imagination as it projects a goal into the future; the social pole, by the communality of the materials and the uses to which the art object is put. We need only repeat that the artist's freedom is relative, not absolute; it is always engaged, and projects a common future. The individual may use it to find out who and what he is; the society may use it to discover what it is—by a recognition of the values (freedom, clarity, and intensity of feeling) it presents; we may use it to commune with the best in our fellow man.

If the truth be known, therefore, the art institution reveals the being of man, and achieves its highest expression in allowing the most intimate kind of our being-with-others. It is not enough to call art the expression of a human personality, as if the personality preexisted its expression in art; rather, it is the expression of a relative human freedom in which the creator and his audience discover what he and they are. In this sense, the ultimate value of art lies in its revelation of the truth—in a clearer picture of humanity in the making.[41] The creator is still being created.

If our argument is to be made complete, we must continue our investigation of the existential-phenomenological account of artistic communication by giving a succinct statement of the method, not as it applies to the artist's personality, but as it may be used to provide an objective description of a unique artistic significance. Moreover, since the conditions of creation and appreciation differ from medium to medium, special attention must be placed on the differences of artistic media.

In order to give added point to the demonstration, we shall in the next two chapters consider the method as it may be applied in an educational context; and the remainder of this volume will be dedicated to a study of the ways in which media other than prose fiction (Chapter 4) and the dance (Chapter 5) are amenable to a similar analysis. The concluding chapter will contain an explanation of the historical context in which this method was developed.

NOTES

1. See Paul Tillich, *Systematic Theology* (Chicago: The University of Chicago Press, 1951), vol. 1.
2. See Rollo May *et al.*, ed., *Existence: A New Dimension in Psychiatry and Psychology* (New York: Basic Books, Inc., 1958).
3. See Van Cleve Morris, *Existentialism in Education* (New York: Harper and Row, 1966).
4. See Arturo B. Fallico, *Art and Existentialism* (Englewood Cliffs, N.J.: Prentice-Hall, 1962).

5. Subtitled "An Essay of Human Freedom" (Baltimore: The Johns Hopkins Press, 1956).

6. In spite of Professor Fallico's statement:

I have tried to avoid technical jargon, keeping in mind the average intelligent reader. One difficulty, inherent in a work of this sort, could not be eliminated. This is what might be called 'the difficulty of saying the obvious.' (p. viii)

7. Pp. 328–29.

8. *Ibid.*, p. 329.

9. *Ibid.*

10. *Ibid.*, italics mine.

11. *Ibid.*, pp. 329–30.

12. See Edmund B. Feldman, "Man Transcends Himself through Art," *Arts in Society* II, 1 (1962):90–98.

13. Pp. 217–40.

14. Immanuel Kant, *Critique of Judgment*, Bernard trans. (New York: Hafner Publishing Co., 1951), p. 151.

15. Pp. 148–49.

16. See Chapter 1, "The Arts and Communication," above.

17. Chicago: The University of Chicago Press, 1934.

18. *Ibid.*, p. 52.

19. *Ibid.*, p. 167.

20. See my *An Existentialist Aesthetic* (Madison: The University of Wisconsin Press, 1962).

21. See Charles W. Morris, "Esthetics and the Theory of Signs," *The Journal of Unified Science* 8 (1939):131–50, and its criticism in Kingsley Price, "Is a Work of Art a Symbol?", *Journal of Philosophy* 50 (1953):485–503.

22. Eighteenth edition, Paris: Gallimard, 1948. Original, 1939.

23. Paris: Gallimard, 1943. Translated as *Being and Nothingness* by Hazel Barnes (New York: Philosophical Library, 1956).

24. See my "Notes Toward an Understanding of Heidegger's Aesthetics," in Lee and Mandelbaum, eds., *Phenomenology and Existentialism* (Baltimore: The Johns Hopkins Press, 1967), pp. 59–92.

25. See Chapter 6, below, "The Visibility of Things Seen."

26. "L'Oeil et l'esprit," *Les Temps Modernes* 17 (1961):225. My translation.

27. *Ibid.*, p. 222. My translation.

28. See Chapter 6, "The Visibility of Things Seen."

29. See his *Das literarische Kunstwerk* (Halle: Max Niemeyer Verlag, 1931).

30. See his *Sein und Zeit* (Tübingen: Niemeyer Verlag, 1957), pp.

63–88, and *Vom Wesen des Grundes* (Frankfurt a.M.: Klosterman, 1955).

31. See Margaret Naumburg, *Psychoneurotic Art: Its Function in Psychotherapy* (New York: Grune and Stratton, 1953).

32. In "Art and the 'Object of Art,'" in Wm. Elton, ed., *Essays in Aesthetics and Language* (Oxford: Blackwell, 1954), pp. 170–86.

33. See pp. 71–72.

34. See his *The Principles of Art,* paperback reprint (New York: Oxford University Press, 1958), *passim.*

35. See John Hospers, "The Croce-Collingwood Theory of Art," *Philosophy* 31 (1956):291–308.

36. See my "Aesthetics and the Teaching of Art," *Studies in Art Education,* 5 (1964):42–56.

37. See my "The Existential Ground for Aesthetic Education," *Studies in Art Education* (1966), pp. 3–12.

38. *Being and Nothingness,* pp. 463–67, and, especially, "The Time of the World," pp. 204–16.

39. Sartre, *L'Existentialisme est un humanisme* (Paris: Nagel, 1946), pp. 17–19.

40. Heidegger, *Sein und Zeit,* p. 42. Compare his criticism of Sartre's use of the term "essence," in *Über den Humanismus* (Frankfurt a.M.: Kostermann, 1946), pp. 14–19.

41. For Heidegger's interpretation of this process, see my "Notes Toward an Understanding of Heidegger's Aesthetics," and "The Existential Ground for Aesthetic Education."

PART II

The Role of the Medium

4

METHOD AND METHODOLOGY IN LITERARY CRITICISM*

I

The program for instruction in any field of intellectual endeavor depends upon methods, and any discourse upon methods to be employed in the solution of an intellectual problem is rightfully termed "methodology." In the following, aesthetics will be interpreted as the methodology of criticism, which in turn is to be considered a method of art analysis. Instruction in literary criticism, therefore, must contain two elements: the laying down of a workable method of analysis (aesthetics), and *travaux pratiques* in the use of the method laid down (criticism). The distinction roughly parallels the usual educational distinction between theory and practice, which remains sound if the differenda do not lose contact in their separation. Accordingly, my thesis demands two sections: the first, dedicated to what I take to be a methodologically sound aesthetic theory; and the second, to an illustration of the theory in practice.

If, on the one hand, the method sought is to be something other than general cultural history, and, on the other, is to yield specifically aesthetic results by treating its objects as something other than moral sermons or pseudo-scientific and quasi-philosophical treatises, it becomes imperative to conceive of some generally workable idea of aesthetic expression considered as a whole, and then to proceed to an analysis of the particular case of literature. I shall arrange the results into a small set of postulates.

Postulate 1. *Aesthetic expressions are context bound.* There is no "meaning" for any gesture taken out of context, and no context can meaningfully take in the whole of the universe (everything that can be truthfully said). The universe of discourse defining the limits of significance for criticism is, therefore, what is usually referred to as the "work of art," or as the "object of criticism." In practice, this postulate limits critical sense to statements about a single work of a single author, and tends to concentrate attention, rather than disperse it over the widest range possible. Thus, it would be considered critical nonsense to refer to a work of art as "romantic" or "classical," since to classify the given work with others resembling it in one way or another leads the attention away from the specific romantic or classical quality of the given piece and places it on the class of objects of which the work is a member.

The temptation to classify, moreover, leads humanists to travesty scientific minds, when, in character, they should be engaged not with facts, either particular or general, but with the experiencing of the quality, or value, of a given object. In a similar vein, Blaise Pascal distinguished between *l'esprit géométrique* and *l'esprit de finesse,* roughly between analysis and synthesis, which he thought proper for scientists and humanists respectively. Following the rules of aesthetic positivism, Taine and his disciples of our own day have illustrated the need for a peculiarly humanistic method,[1] which cannot be attained without the maximum concentration on the specific values of a particular work. It is my hope that this method can be supplied by aesthetic theory.

Postulate 2. *The context of an aesthetic expression, and hence of its significance, is constructed uniquely and exhaustively by the network of relations set up by "the counters" of the given medium.*

I refer here to the medial symbols, markers, or elements with which the artist must think in solving his qualitative problems,[2] and which, taken in relation, form the sensuous surface of the work. In music, the medium is composed of sounds and silences; anything that can be meaningfully said about music as an aesthetic expression must be traceable to sounds and silences. Painting, the visual medium, has for its context of significance anything that may be seen: lines and forms, colors and space. Architecture uses mass and force, and the like. Although ultrapurists, those aestheticians who restrict artistic significance to the medial values alone, needlessly restrict the aesthetic context in that their music never has a program, their painting a subject, or their architecture a function, the truth of the matter is that some music does have a program; some paintings, and very good ones at that, are figurative; and any piece of architecture having no function is no building at all. The problem to be conceived here is a "thickening of the surface."

When the sounds of nature are "pictured" in the sounds and silences of music, when the lines and forms of painting suggest recognizable forms of nature, when the masses and forces of structural concrete or steel permit and intensify the life within, the context of analysis must broaden to allow for the inclusion of this intellectual "depth." Representation of objects, suggestion of images, and conception of ideas—all depth qualities—may add considerably to, and enrich the context of relatedness that is the artist's expression. In fact, if much of the musical medium and all of nonobjective painting are but limited surface expression, it is not impossible to conceive of an expression without a sensuous surface.[3]

Since the marks on paper used to express mathematical truths are irrelevant to the value of the latter, mathematics in its ultra-purity could be considered a surfaceless aesthetic expression. The analytical trick in the case of a mathematical theorem as an art object would be to explain how the relatedness of abstract ideas could be experienced as a quality. This is a gift few mathematicians possess, and still fewer have been able to give coherent accounts of their process of thought: Einstein claimed to work with "visual phenomena and motor responses"; Poincaré wrote that his "aesthetic sense" enabled him to choose the most fruitful patterns of relatedness, especially when he had been frustrated for some time in finding the felicitous solutions to his problem, which usually came when his mind was "idling."[4]

Since its medium is defined by spoken and written words and their attendant meanings, literature in its purity is a surface and depth art. Its surface is composed of the words as sounded or read, and its depth is the organized meaning given expression in the words. The word "texture" is useful for the organization of the surface counters; and "structure" serves well for the depth.

Postulate 3. *The aesthetic expressiveness of a work of*

art is the experience of the relatedness of the surface counters and their representations out of which the total context is constructed.

As indicated above, the work of art may be a surface expression only, hence nonobjective; or it may be a depth expression in which an object, image, or idea is presented by means of the surface. Although literature, using words, is always a depth art, the relative values of the surface and depth may vary greatly: from a very tense and musical surface that is poetry,

> In Xanadu did Kubla Khan
> A stately pleasure-dome decree

to the looser, more prosaic timbre of a symbolic narrative,

> Call me Ishmael. Some years ago—never mind how long precisely—having little or no money in my purse, and nothing particular to interest me on shore, I thought I would sail about a little and see the watery part of the world.

Both of the examples cited above have rhythm, a surface quality perceived whenever the words are read, aloud or in perceptive silence; and each rhythm is adapted to the necessities of the total work. In Coleridge's poetry, the musical values of the words dominate over the sense; whereas the rhythm of Melville's prose sets one looking for an idea that is to follow.

In each case the surface serves the purpose of the total expressiveness of the piece; if ever one became unaware of the surface values, he could lay no claim to having experienced the work. The complete analysis of a literary work, of course, entails our ability to relate surface and depth, texture and structure, into a single experience. Being felt, or experienced, this expressiveness is not discursive; it is had or it is missed, but it cannot be rendered into words whose function it is to purvey information. Experience the difference between:

> Man and plants are both natural events, subject to growth.

and

> The force that through the green fuse drives the flower
> Drives my green age . . .

and you will have experienced the difference between the use of words primarily to convey information (their discursive use) and the use of words to construct an aesthetic context (their nondiscursive use).

So much for the general aesthetic postulates. The task now becomes that of considering the manner in which words are used nondiscursively in the particular aesthetic contexts we call "literary."

The basic counters of the literary medium are the words; and, as noted above, the articulation of the words has a double effect. Perceptually, the words are sounds or marks on paper, and both of these features of words as articulated may go to constitute the texture of a literary work. But along with their perceptual values, be they aural or visual, one will find a second level of articulation: that of meaning. Any meanings represented constitute the depth of the work; and theoretically, at least, there are no limits to the levels of meaning one can find as valid constituents of the aesthetic object.

The meaning may be denotative or connotative. The

word "mother" denotes the class of women having borne a child, and connotes precisely "woman having borne a child," if the meaning of words is limited to their conventional intention. Objectively considered, the connotations of a word are all the ideas or characteristics (and only those) necessary to define the class of objects denoted. These objective connotations (sometimes referred to as "comprehension" of the term) are theoretical limits, strictly possible only in the realm of mathematics and logic, whose entities are uniquely definable. To make up for this restriction, the literary artist has a whole range of subjective connotations with which to play. Witness the doggerel poem:

M is for the million things she gave me . . .

each line of which exploits one of the subjective connotations associated with the word "Mother." Recall, too, Dame Edith Sitwell's dismay at one reader's inability to understand "Emily-colored hands," which according to the author was a misquotation. She later explained,

> I did not write "Emily-colored hands," a hideous phrase. I wrote "Emily colored *primulas*," which to anyone who has progressed in poetry reading beyond the *White Cliffs of Dover* calls to mind the pink cheeks of young country girls.[5]

Whatever the limitations imposed upon the meanings of poetry by the use of a private language by obscurantist poets, the context in which the personally meaningful metaphors are used will further qualify, and thus limit, the meanings of literary expressions.

Every symbol, in fact, has its meaning, not externally,

but internally to the context of expression. A device for relating one level of significance in that context to another, the literary symbol serves to reinforce the internal structure of a work. Faulkner's unbeatable three-legged horse, attended by the Negro boy possessing the gift of tongues, serves to relate the allegorical content of *The Fable,* the Christian myth, with the first-level events in the life of the unknown soldier. The soldier himself is a symbol for Christ, and to prove it obligingly disappears from his coffin after a three-day vigil by the mercenaries who were charged with the recovery of his body. The body was to be used for the purpose of commemorating the death of the soldier in the service of humanity, and the ceremonial was to be observed by all nations.

Symbolism is thus a literary technique for enriching the depth structures of a work; the greater the levels of significance, the greater the intensity of expression. Mechanically, symbolism is a relatively simple device: words are organized to represent objects; and the objects are related to represent ideas. On the higher levels of literary interpretation, usually called "symbolic," one set of ideas may be so organized as to represent another, and so on. This is not to say that the aesthetic significance of the work is exhausted by an analysis of the various levels of meanings and their interrelations. The whole network of structural relations must be experienced in relation to the surface presenting the novel's depth. This experience is the total aesthetic expressiveness of the literary work.

In the example to follow I shall attempt to show how one event in the novel may be interpreted as a symbol for the very novel of which it is a single event. Although this process violates the logical theory of types (proscribing for any set of symbols a reference to itself), the art of literature is not limited to the techniques of logical expression, and may indeed gain for willfully breaking them.

It is useful for purposes of critical analysis to envisage the depth structures of novels and short stories as a function of character and plot, both of which are virtual "creations"[6] emerging from the articulation of connotative and denotative meanings. Moreover, they are not independent: character depends upon the events that influence the lives of the fictional characters, and in a philosophical viewpoint allowing for a degree of personal freedom, the decisions and actions of the various characters may influence the course of events. In still other novels, the events and the characters may be all but undistinguishable, as in *Molloy* by Beckett.

The formal structures of character and plot[7] likewise allow the expression of serious philosophical ideas: morality and metaphysics, respectively. And these latter may be used as structural principles for integrating the structure of the story. Thus we find "naturalistic" stories in which the events determine the life of the characters, the whole being presented in reportorial style (e.g., Dreiser's *Sister Carrie*), and "humanistic" stories in which the characters qualify the nature of events (e.g., Cather's *My Antonía*). An impressionistic style serves well to present a story based upon the metaphysics of subjective idealism, as in parts of Sartre's *Nausea*; and the symbolic mode of presentation fits well with the transcendental idealism of Melville's several novels, perhaps most clearly in *Moby Dick*.

This confluence of literary analysis and philosophical speculation has a second basis, the explanation of which will yield a further hermeneutical tool. Since the literary object is a closed context, enclosing within itself all the significance it bears, it is comparable in structure to the metaphysical concepts of "universe," "world," "cosmos," and the like. The author has constructed a unique universe, just as the metaphysician is trying to disclose the principle or principles upon which the structures of the "real" universe depend. Universe for universe, however, this basis of comparison affords no philosopher's stone to transmute bad into good literature.

The interpretive tool it does allow is the resultant necessity, when in doubt, to make a hypothesis for the description of a novel's structure. In some cases this may not be necessary, depending upon the didactic purposes of the authors concerned (cf. Huxley's *Point-Counterpoint,* in which the musical device is used to unify varied voices on a general hedonic theme); on the other hand, the individual interpreter may never succeed in discovering the unifying principle of even the most successfully unified work.

The source of an interpretive hypothesis may be anything: cultural history, the works of the same or other authors, philosophy, psychology, or what have you; but the rules of the game demand that the hypothesis be tried against the experienced events of the given universe—the facts of nature for the scientist or philosopher, and the facts of the narrative for the literary critic. And if one suggested hypothesis does not work, then the critic is authorized to discard it, sometimes in spite of what the author has claimed, and—in the case of truly visionary authors—almost always in spite of the prevailing climate of opinion.

But the successful unification of the structure is not "the meaning," the aesthetic significance of the piece.

Criticism only begins when the depth has been understood. The critic must yet relate, almost always in a second or third reading, what he has understood to the texture of the vehicle used by the author in presenting his universe of meaning. To use a trite example, the bite of wit and the ironic play of paradox can never be understood or felt without an understanding of the textural qualifications of the written or spoken message:

"Do you love me, honey?"
"I adore you, sweetheart."
"How do you love me?"
"In the pig's blue eye."

The last ironical response is enough to change anyone's honey into the bitterest of wormwood—depending upon the circumstances that surround the conversation, and that, by filling in the context, qualify its meaning.

All the critic can do is to put a perceptive and imaginative individual into a receptive mood; he cannot verbalize the total expressiveness of the aesthetic object, which must be felt according to the patterning of human feeling determined by the textural-structural relations of the aesthetic context. If my description of aesthetic contexts is a workable methodological account of the method of criticism, that is the limit of the possibility of education within the literary medium. To move from

"Yes, of course, if it's fine tomorrow," said Mrs. Ramsay. "But you'll have to be up with the lark," she added.

to

It was done; it was finished. Yes, she thought, laying

down her brush in extreme fatigue, I have had my vision.

is to perform a complicated score. The art of teaching literature has for its end the realization of the values inherent in the total context.

II

To the Lighthouse opens in the middle of a conversation between a mother and son, and, while the father and the same son, accompanied by his favorite daughter and two other persons, land at a lighthouse off the Isles of Skye, the novel closes with an exclamation by an artist that her portrait is done. Thus, for the beginning and the end—of the novel, of a portrait, and of a planned trip, all of which, so related, become the same event in different perspective. But for a novel by Henry James of that title, this one might have been called *The Portrait of a Lady*.

The lady involved is Mrs. Ramsay, the mother of eight children and wife of an oafish metaphysician who had published his first book before the age of twenty-five and nothing thereafter. At the beginning of the novel, she sits before a window knitting and incidentally posing for a picture with her youngest son, James. The boy has asked whether he might make a trip to the off-shore lighthouse just before the first written words of the novel. (The question, implied, is part of the novel's context.) The painter is one Lily Briscoe, whose work is being watched by the sympathetic critic, William Bankes. Through the window we are introduced into Mrs. Ramsay's world.

Everything there is not honey and light; but as Mrs.

Ramsay looks out and Lily Briscoe looks in, the reader enjoys a double vision: the one perspective shows us the inner world of Mrs. Ramsay, whose actions are motivated by love and sympathy, and who, like the long, third stroke of the spinning beam of the lighthouse, becomes a principle by virtue of which other things are seen. What is seen through her constitutes a second set of objects presented to the reader's attention. The most important of these, of course, are James and his father.

Mrs. Ramsay knows by feeling, becoming one in intimacy with the objects she becomes conscious of. The not-so-dim analogue of carnal knowledge that is sexual union passes through Lily Briscoe's mind in her attempts to capture Mrs. Ramsay's personality:

> What art was there, known to love or cunning, by which one pressed through into those secret chambers? What device for becoming, like waters poured into one jar, inextricably the same, one with the object one adored? Could the body achieve, or the mind, subtly mingling in the intricate passages of the brain? or the heart? Could loving, as people called it, make her and Mrs. Ramsay one? For it was not knowledge but unity she desired, not inscriptions on tablets, nothing that could be written in any language known to men, but intimacy itself, which is knowledge, she had thought, leaning her head on Mrs. Ramsay's knee.

If Lily could put that personality into the symbols of her own medium, what would it become? The answer, "a triangular purple shape," an abstract rendering of Mrs. Ramsay reading to James; so muses the critic, Bankes. Using his sympathy for an aesthetic object, he explains,

> Mother and child then—objects of universal veneration, and in this case the mother was famous for her beauty—might be reduced . . . to a purple shadow without irreverence.

But Lily, wiser in the ways of intuition, corrects his naïveté:

> But the picture was not of them, she said. Or, not in his sense. There were other senses too in which one might reverence them. By a shadow here and a light there, for instance.

As the reader grasps the second level significance (the flashing light of the lighthouse, if my hypothesis is correct), the author continues,

> Her tribute took that form if, as she vaguely supposed, a picture must be a tribute. A mother and child might be reduced to shadow without irreverence. A light here required a shadow there.

In that other universe, the one represented by the everyday, academic lives of the Ramsays, the mother and child are merely shadows to the failing light of the father. Here on vacation the values are reversed, and the light is thrown off by the mother and son; the father does not fit into the picture.

Receiving all of Mrs. Ramsay's affectionate sympathy and always demanding more, he is incapable of reciprocating, bogged down like David Hume in the mud of his own logic. His knowledge, about "subjects and objects and the nature of reality," is all conceptual; being general, and separated from its objects by the distance of the signs he must use to think with, it is a good two degrees removed from the reality he would like to describe. But to his wife his mind was of the very first order:

> For if thought is like the keyboard of a piano, divided into so many notes, or like the alphabet is ranged in twenty-six letters all in order, then his splendid mind had no sort of difficulty in running over those letters one by one, firmly and accurately, until it had reached, say, the letter Q. He reached Q. Very few people in the whole of England ever reach Q . . . But after Q? What comes next? After Q there are a number of letters the last of which is scarcely visible to mortal eyes, but glimmers red in the distance. Z is only reached once by one man in a generation. Still, if he could reach R it would be something. Here at least was Q.

It comes as no surprise that Mr. Ramsay will dig in before he reaches Z, and continue smugly talking nonsense about "Locke, Hume, Berkeley, and the causes of the French Revolution"; or that his young son, who loves his mother, detests his father.

The first part of the book presents the events of one afternoon and evening: Mrs. Ramsay's sitting, James's deception, Mr. Ramsay's blundering into Lily Briscoe and William Bankes while reading poetry, the engagement of Minta Doyle and Paul Rayley, the symbolic reading of *The Fisherman and his Wife,* the chaotic dinner party of the family and their friends—academicians, lovers, painter, poet and critic, all presided over by Mrs. Ramsay, who alone makes a single event of this curious gathering of unrelated passions. In keeping with Mrs. Ramsay's distrust of the discursive intellect, this one moment in time somewhat resembles the picture pasted pastiche her son James was making at her feet, cutting the images from an illustrated catalogue and putting them together to be seen all at once in a single act of vision. This is *how* we see through The Window, Part I of the book.

In spite of her feelings for her son, however, Mrs. Ramsay is forced to acknowledge that the weather the next day would not permit a trip to the lighthouse. The pastiche of the events surrounding the Ramsays and viewed from The Window endures one half of a day; it takes up some 186 pages of writing.

For the purposes of the story, then, the time of the clock is relatively unimportant, or more properly said, is reduced to its strictest relevance in the lives of the individuals in the story. In explicating this hypothesis we shall discover the central phenomenon related in the novel.

The third part is an extended narrative of correlative events: James's piloting his father and sister to the lighthouse, ten years after the first project, and Lily Briscoe's final vision in the presence of Mr. Carmichael. Only artists (the painter and the poet) are permitted the ultimate realization. But, as Mrs. Ramsay muses in Part I, artists should marry critics and thus share their visions:

> Smiling, for it was an admirable idea, that had flashed upon her this very second—William and Lily should marry . . .

In spite of the tauntings of that odious student of Mr. Ramsay, who kept muttering that women couldn't paint, women couldn't write, Lily finishes her portrait when she discovers what was missing from that purple triangle (one of its necessary angles or sides, the father in sympathetic relation to mother and son), and Mrs. Woolf finishes her novel in the same stroke.

But what is the story about? A trip to a lighthouse, Lily's picture, or Mrs. Ramsay's personality? Obviously, in one sense, about all three; but about none, in the same sense that Lily's picture is not about a mother and son, even as it is completed with the presence of the father. The novel must present, not represent its object: it too must be, not mean; and to do this the novelist must construct a single depth, and express it through a surface that is of some interest in itself.

Now that the main events of the story have been recounted, I may take the critic's privilege of constructing a hypothesis for giving a unified interpretation of the novel's depth. There are many hints to the structure, just as there are many cues for recognizing them. For example, the masculine and discursive intelligence of Mr. Ramsay, and of Charles Tansley, his student, is bound to evidence; and the evidential signs indicate to them that there will be no immediate trip to the lighthouse. This they know in their own manner of knowing. But the woman and the child feel or intuit more than they can conceptualize; the feminine intelligence that is close to instinct ignores the evidence and puts as indifferent the moment a given event is to take place. Tomorrow or ten years from now, what is the difference, if the event actually takes place? The time of the clock is indifferent to the matter—save for the deception in the feelings of a small boy, always given in an immediate "now." Yet time is of the essence, and if time is not to be measured by a clock, then by some other, more accurate instrument —human consciousness.

Thus the divorce between masculine and feminine intelligence is strengthened by the split between naturalistic and psychological time. The time of the clock, the measure of natural events, is scientific and conceptual; that of the psyche, given by the impressions of consciousness, value-laden and empirical. In the difference lie the worlds of Mr. and Mrs. Ramsay, respectively.

His time is objective (independent of the events occurring within), and single; it is continuous, with no breaks, and infinitely divisible. As infinite, it cannot end; nor does it have a first instant, and so has never begun. Further, it is homogeneous, i.e., everywhere alike (whether at the Isles of Skye or Timbucktoo); and lastly, it is isotropic, having the same physical properties in either direction. Time may occur as +t or —t in Mr. Ramsay's equations concerning the nature of the real world.

Mrs. Ramsay's time, psychological in essence, is relative, known through the felt changes in events: something could be added or subtracted without changing its essential character, even the death of its perceiver. It is likewise plural, allowing for differences in psychological make-up (as between hers and her husband's and between hers and Charles Tansley's or even between hers and Lily Briscoe's). Since one instant may be more interesting than another (Parts I and III are more humanly significant than II), its span can be broken into a discontinuous series to emphasize the importance of a given event. But psychological time must start and end, and does so within the limits of expectation and memory. It is therefore finite. Its instants are nonhomogeneous, since the now and the projected future are privileged moments, and the events themselves determine the length of the moments. Finally, psychological time is anisotropic: as a dimension of experience it flows unidirectionally from the future to the past.[8] Conceive this difference in temporal qualities, and you may perceive the difference between the personalities of Mr. and Mrs. Ramsay.

The last quality of psychological time, its flowing from the future to the past, enables us immediately to verify our temporal hypothesis. For psychological time to start, there must be an anticipated event; and with this event as an indefinite future, each succeeding moment will become present until there is attained that one moment of initial projection of time that is now definitely past and in relation to which all prior events are past anterior. I refer, of course, to the opening conversation between Mrs. Ramsay and James, the past of the narrative with respect to the future, anticipated event, the voyage to the lighthouse.

The symbol of the lighthouse, then, becomes luminously clear: it is an enduring physical object (in everybody's world), an anticipated event in the lives of James and Mrs. Ramsay and thus, in anticipation, the moment when psychological time begins its (backward) flow; it is likewise the value that ultimately fulfills James's life (and by extension that of his mother, who has already passed away in Part II of the novel) and that enables Lily Briscoe to relate the life of Mr. to that of Mrs. Ramsay through the will and achievement of James.

The beginning of time, it is likewise the measure of time (Mrs. Ramsay, recall, identifies herself with the third stroke of the rotating light), but that universe in which it is the beginning of time is different from that in which it is a measure. It is the beginning of time in the universe of Mrs. Ramsay and James; a measure in the one naturalistic universe shared by all the characters. As it rotates, the phases of its temporal passing are strictly analogous to the movements of all the timepieces, including the gold watch of Paul Rayley, though it be discreetly hidden in a wash-leather bag.

The two times of the represented events within the novel necessitate a further unification in a single time of the novel itself, as formed by the novelist and as performed by a perceptive reader. For this overall structure I may be permitted another hypothesis. In *Art as Experience,* John Dewey explains time as an organizing principle of an experience (remember that the experience I am interpreting is that of Mrs. Woolf's novel):

> Time ceases to be either the endless and uniform flow or the succession of instantaneous points which some philosophers have asserted it to be. It, too, is the organized and organizing medium of *the rhythmic ebb and flow of expectant impulse,* forward and retracted movement, resistance and suspense, with fulfillment and consummation. It is an ordering of growth and maturations. . . . Time as organization in change is growth, and growth signifies that a varied series of change enters upon intervals of pause and rest; of completions that become initial points of new processes of development. Like the soil, mind is fertilized while it lies fallow, until a new burst of bloom ensuies.
>
> When a flash of lightning illumines a dark landscape, there is a momentary recognition of objects. But the recognition itself is not a mere point in time. It is the focal culmination of long, slow processes of maturation. It is the manifestation of the continuity of an ordered temporal experience in a sudden discrete instant of climax. It is as meaningless in isolation as would be the drama of Hamlet

> were it confined to a single line or word with no context. But the phrase "the rest is silence" is infinitely pregnant as the conclusion of a drama enacted through development in time; so may be the momentary perception of a natural scene. Form, as it is present in the fine arts, is the art of making clear what is involved in the organization of space and time prefigured in every course of a developing life experience.[9]

It is no accident, of course, that Dewey's description of time as a formal organizational device corresponds, almost point for point, with Mrs. Woolf's novelistic structure. (Interesting to note, the same description gibes well with existentialist accounts of human being as "temporality.") He was describing the form of a well-constructed experience, and she was presenting her readers with an example of the same phenomenon. All that is lacking is a critic to be able to perceive the relationship and to disclose to others what his perception has already disclosed to himself.

Texturally, the depth of the novel is reinforced by the surface. Noting the impressionism of her general style (to capture the glimpses of experience each character contributes to the novel), I shall restrict myself to the significance of Mrs. Woolf's use of parentheses and brackets.

One entire section of Part I occurs within the parentheses indicating an abrupt breaking of the flow of events that mark off naturalistic time; they show the mind, like the soil, "fertilized while it lies fallow, until a new burst of bloom ensues." Other uses of parentheses mark switches in point of view, which indicate the multiplicity or plurality of (psychological) times of which the universe of the novel is constructed and through which the various characters live.

In Part II the more abrupt breaks of brackets are used to indicate the manner in which the naturalistic events of conceptual clock-time break into the psychological moments constituting the more significant events of the novel's context. How surprising, for example, to read in the middle of the novel:

> [Mr. Ramsay, stumbling along a passage one dark morning, stretched his arms out, but Mrs. Ramsay having died rather suddenly the night before, his arms, though stretched out, remained empty.]

But, this event too is only a new beginning in the realization of the first project to land at the lighthouse. United at last to her husband, in sympathy, some years following her death, Mrs. Ramsay lands at the lighthouse with him and their two youngest children; and one stretch of time comes to an end. The rest is silence.

The voyage, Mrs. Ramsay's portrait, and the novel are one and the same event; and with their completion time passes through temporality into timelessness. But this is in effect what the lighthouse has always symbolized as an enduring physical object in the rolling waves of the sea. The measure of time, itself timeless, the lighthouse is the point at which life passes over into art:

> Her horizon seemed to her limitless. There were all the places she had not seen; the Indian plains; she felt herself pushing aside the thick leather curtain of a church in Rome. This core of darkness could go anywhere, for no one saw it. They could not stop it, she thought, exulting. There was freedom, there was peace, there was, most welcome of all,

> a summoning together, a resting on a platform of stability. Not as oneself did one find rest ever . . ., but as a wedge of darkness. Losing personality, one lost the fret, the hurry, the stir; and there rose to her lips always some exclamation of triumph over life when things came together in this peace, this rest, this eternity; and pausing there she looked out to meet that stroke of the Lighthouse, the long steady stroke, the last of the three, which was her stroke. . . . Often she found herself sitting and looking, sitting and looking, with her work in her hands until she became the thing she looked at—that light, for example.

In this passage the roll of the sea, the phases of the light, and the rhythm of the prose are unmistakably one.

Mr. Ramsay finally redeems himself by coming toward her, in sympathy—the sympathy he could never give her, alive—as she stood there, rigid in death, a platform of stability for all who have sympathy enough to know or to feel. Although he is not permitted to see it, the reader knows what the essence of Lily's picture must be.

III

In sum, I have been maintaining that improvement in the teaching of literature depends at the least upon two considerations. First, that teachers, and *a fortiori* teachers of teachers, become aesthetically more knowledgeable. Until they are capable of giving to their students a workable methodological approach to a particular art form, there will be no way of determining when claims to artistic knowledge are warranted. The methodology of art criticism is the business of aesthetics. Secondly, until aestheticians themselves are capable of showing the bases for their own methodological prescriptions and of defending them in actual criticism, teachers in the arts are not apt to adopt their pronouncements. Literature remains the only one of the major art forms to be taught by non-practitioners of the art. We have many painters who teach painting, and sculptors, sculpture; but there are few successful writers who willingly take on the role of writer-teacher, or even of writer-in-residence. Until, and even when they do, the methodology and the method of criticism will have to become a prerequisite to education in the art.

I have tried to show that a contextualistic (or existential-phenomenological) aesthetics provides a viable methodology, enabling a fruitful critical approach to literary analysis, and I would like to argue for its inclusion in any program of education in the humanities. The other questions concerning the value of literature—its social importance, its value as a didactic tool, its "mirroring of the times in which it is written"—all seem to depend upon its validity as an artistic expression in the first instance. Training in aesthetic judgment is to the appreciation of the arts, whether by the artist or his audience, as the science of logic is to the making of sense in any field of discursive intelligence.

Whether professional aesthetic educators shall be prevailed upon to adopt a single method of analysis may, in the long run, depend upon our ability to demonstrate its applicability to several artistic media. In literature, the principal field of "art appreciation" taught the majority of our secondary and advanced students, the counters of aesthetic expression seem patently clear. The medium is "thick," and the value of the literary idea (its depth expressiveness) is clearly understood to be a function of the "manner" of expression, controlled ultimately by the artist's manipulation of the sensuous surface of words.

If Virginia Woolf's novel illustrates clearly that "time" may serve to structure the total literary experience, a clear interpretation of the existential significance of time as an aesthetic structural device would seem to be in order.

In pursuit of this idea, we choose, next, the medium of dance, in which the distinction between creator and thing created is singularly nominal: the dancer, moving to create, is both means and end of artistic expression. Time is still the measure of the experience, but is defined, in context, by the rhythm of the body's motion. The task we shall assume, therefore, is a phenomenological description of the genesis of an autonomous artistic medium from the human being's capacity to move itself through space. Our technique will be one of successive "bracketings." Beginning with movements of the human body as they occur in everyday life, we shall observe how kinaesthetic responses emerge as the surface counters of balletic expression.

NOTES

1. See Hippolyte Taine, *Philosophie de l'art* (Paris: Hachette, 1906). The first lesson in this course of aesthetics contained three rules: to relate one work of an author with the others; to relate the total *oeuvre* of an author with those of others; to relate the total *oeuvres* of the various authors with the general climate of opinion under which each had been written in the first place. This method, called "modern" by Taine, is the one which more or less permeated education in the humanities today. Call it "the historical method," or "aesthetic positivism," or, more honestly, "cultural history," and the results are the same: students are made aware of everything about a work of literary art except its own intrinsic values.

2. See David Ecker, "The Artistic Process as Qualitative Problem Solving," *Journal of Aesthetics and Art Criticism* 21 (1963): 283–90.

3. I borrow here the terminology of D. W. Prall. See his *Aesthetic Judgment* (New York: Crowell, 1929), pp. 57–75.

4. For the accounts each has given of his own creative approach to mathematics, see *The Creative Process*, ed. Brewster Ghiselin (New York: Mentor Books, 1955).

5. For some discussion of the use of connotations in the interpretation of poetry, see Monroe C. Beardsley, *Aesthetics: Problems in the Philosophy of Criticism* (New York: Harcourt, Brace, 1958), pp. 149–52. Dame Edith's remarks, which first appeared in the London *Observer*, were reported in *Time Magazine*, November 12, 1951, p. 31.

6. This, in opposition to George Santayana, who claimed that only the characters of literature were proper creations. See *Sense of Beauty* (New York: Modern Library, 1955), pp. 173–76.

7. Santayana's discussion contains the basis for the inclusion of plot and character as formal structures within an aesthetic context. Such an analysis vitiates the older distinction between "form" and "content."

8. For these characteristics of the temporal distinctions I am indebted to my former teacher, A. C. Benjamin. See his *An Introduction to the Philosophy of Science* (New York: Macmillan, 1937), pp. 281–96.

9. John Dewey, *Art as Experience* (New York: Minton, Balch, 1934), pp. 23–24. [Italics mine.]

5

BEING IN THE BODY: ON SIGNIFICANCE IN DANCE

I

When asked to justify the theory and practice of physical education, teachers of dance have sometimes responded with ideas of great generality and widespread social approval. Physical education has been said to "teach character," or to "develop leadership potential," or to make its adepts "better citizens, in a democratic sort of way." The trouble with such answers as these is that no one, not even those who offer them as justifications for their educational policies, believes them; and no one believes them because no one can.

We cannot teach character to our athletes while insisting that they win at all costs, or by turning them into underpaid professionals. Leadership in any field other than athletics has little to do with physical strength, endurance, or skill—the late President Franklin Roosevelt led this country admirably for more than twelve years from the restricted confines of a wheel chair; better citizens, I need hardly add, need more qualities than teamship. To work with others in pursuit of a common goal is precisely that quality instilled in the fanatical German populace by a power-mad dictator; the essence of democracy is another habit—that of considering in concert the desirability of a proposed common goal, and the maintenance of respect for those who cannot acquiesce in the choice to pursue one goal rather than another.

Each of these so-called justifications of physical education, including the dance, is conceived from an external point of view, and each is grafted onto the actual practice of education in virtue of an extraneous, albeit tangential, relationship to the development of the human personality by physical means. One might as well argue, within the restricted framework of physical education for women, that the end of our educational program is the development of more physically fit wives and mothers. If this is truly the case, then perhaps we have been working on the wrong sets of muscles.

The corrective to these abortive attempts to justify physical education is a return to the phenomena of our physical existence. We cannot, like Plotinus, continue to feel ashamed to be in the body; and we cannot, like some physical educationists, continue to cover over our shame by espousing the ideals of mind, character, or social utility as justifications of our interest in educating the body. It is true, of course, that in some sense we are aiming to educate the "whole person," and not just the body or the mind; but if this is so, we must, in order to convince our skeptical opponents, be able to show how the intrinsic development of the human personality follows naturally from what we do to it in our efforts to educate it. In other words, if we are to break down the false separation of mental from bodily activity, we must show the continuity of physical responses and intelligent responses to the set of stimuli playing upon the human personality by virtue of its relationship to an environment—physical, biological, and social—in which goals are first perceived, evaluated, and pursued in the business of continued life. And this is another description of what I have previously referred to as the "phenomenal field" of human existence.

Education of whatever sort must take place within this field, and its purpose is the enrichment of the lives of the individuals capable of this kind of existence. Education must start with individuals at the level of development where they are found; they are to be led out of their narrow preoccupation with self; they are to be put in a position to conceive and to build a newer environment of ever expanding horizons, always working with what is given and, within the limits of possibility, changing what is given into what is desirable, the significant into something more significant because it is more satisfying and, not least, the personal creation of men. The range of education therefore covers the full extent of human expression—from seeing an object at a distance, to feeling ashamed to be in the body; from the facts man constructs by his habit of seeing, to the values he conceives—and, with luck, turns into new facts—by his habit of feeling anything at all.

Existentialist philosophers refer to this enlargement of the horizons of human experience as "transcendence," and if education is to mean anything at all, it should help man transcend the limits placed upon his development by the raw facts of nature. He can do this, I am convinced, because within the structures of his experience (or existence, if you prefer) he is capable of taking on a second nature; he can and does develop habits of conduct we loosely refer to as intelligent, meaning thereby a comparative or superlative degree of adaptability to the conditions of an environment. The term being compared is, I suggest, "significant," a delightfully ambiguous word used to qualify any fact possessing a meaning to some organism for its continued life process, or transcendence. I need only add here that significance is not properly speaking something we "understand"; it is, however, always, whether understood or not, something we feel and with respect to which we must act. Since perception of significance starts with the body, and the body must be oriented to perform an action, it is no mystery why education must start with the body. Any further development of experience will likewise have reference to the body, in that further significance will be constituted by other, varying ways in which the body may comport itself.

Continuity between body and mind is thus one of the facts of human existence. The question arises, however, as to the best manner of expounding this relationship; and here we have a choice. Phenomenological (or existential) philosophers are fond of saying that we can take either the "natural attitude" or the "phenomenological." We can assume the guise of the physical or natural scientists, abstracting completely from our own feelings or values, and describe in total objectivity what takes place in the area of our concern; then, relating this area to others, we will eventually have described everything that is true of the natural world, including the artifacts of men, moving from quality to fact, to law, and finally to the law of laws or nature itself. The difficulty that goes along with this attitude is not merely one of knowing where and how to find our facts as they happen independently of our own deliberate intervention; our frustration goes much deeper than this. It is of a theoretical sort in that the natural attitude itself dissimulates the nature of the enterprise we should be investigating everytime man and his behavior are the subject of investigation. In matters of education, we cannot be "objective," in the sense that our own values would make no difference for the outcome of our inquiry; our own values are part and parcel of the very process of education, and to abstract from them is to emasculate the experience it is our business to inculate.

The alternative to the natural attitude is the phenomenological. According to the latter, a phenomenon appears when a given subject is undergoing some kind of experience, which of course may later be described. An art critic, for example, allows the experience of a work of art to take place; he allows the work to engage his attention as completely as it may. The work must happen first, and then it may be described according to the manner in which it has controlled the critic's experience. Edmund Husserl, who invented the method, called this technique "pure description."[1] In order for it to work, the subject must "bracket the world," i.e., suspend belief in the reality of the real, physical world and hold in check the propensity to appeal to facts or laws of the sciences describing the real world. Our belief in a real world, and our appeals to the physical conditions of having an experience of it, are merely two ways of prejudicing the experience we should be describing. Instead of recounting what has happened in the phenomenal occurrence, we appeal to what should have happened according to known or supposed scientific prescriptions. To proceed phenomenologically, then, we let ourselves go to the experience and, in a moment of reflection, describe what has happened to us as it has occurred. As a recently deceased American sculptor once wrote, men were lovers long before they became gynecologists; and all the results of the most sophisticated kind of gynecology has had no bearing at all upon their capacity as lovers. On the contrary, the abstractions of the gynecologist may very well have impeded that capacity. To get out of such a predicament, our scientist friends must reassume the phenomenological attitude.

That is what Martin Heidegger meant, in *What is Metaphysics?*,[2] when he snidely remarked that if you ask a scientific question you are likely to get a scientific answer. The pejoration he intended has never been understood by many Anglo-American philosophers who have been seduced by the scientism of our own age. The fact of the matter is that education is not a science at all, not even an applied science; it is an art, one of the useful arts, which of course, may well use the technological results of any science, but which do so in the pursuit of a specified human value. To show that the phenomenological attitude is a necessary part of a viable educational procedure, I shall in what follows describe the human body first in "natural" and then in "phenomenological" terms. My guide is Merleau-Ponty's account of bodily existence as it is expounded in *The Structure of Behavior* and *The Phenomenology of Perception.*[3]

II

Within the natural attitude, the body can be considered in its most simple form as a purely physical entity. As physical, the body possesses mass and occupies space and its matter is convertible into energy. Mass is the constant we know relatively as weight, which, like the space the body occupies, can achieve enormous and unhealthy proportions. The function of the mind is to keep this from occurring; of themselves, bodies can only continue to occupy space, each part related to every other part contiguously and coextensively. Like stones, chairs and tables, and marble statues, the human body has a contour, is bounded in a shape that cuts its figure into "objective" space, the three-dimensional container of all physical existents; and like stones, chairs, and the like, the human body, if it were nothing but physical, could not move unless it were moved by another thing. Plato was so struck with this last thought that he used it to establish both the existence and the immortality of the soul.[4] After all, the human body does move, and not necessarily by the action of another physical thing. Whence, the soul. The soul is not moved by another thing, so it is self-moving. What is self-moving must be eternal; so the soul will never die, even when it has left the body and given it over to rot.

In our own day of psychological enlightenment we may be shocked to hear stories of the body and soul. But why so? We often declare our passion "body and soul," for what purpose it is never clear. Like Socrates, who could not resist the physical charms of the young Phaedrus, we begin to discourse upon the soul whenever the body begins to feel uncomfortable at the sight of our beloved. And should we fail to communicate we could even use the same myth as that invented by Socrates to explain our misadventures: the wise charioteer and the good steed always find it difficult to control the evil but powerful steed rearing its ugly head. This was the reason Plotinus felt ashamed to be in the body, but legend has it that he succeeded in getting out of his body at least seven times in his career. To show that the myths of the ancients have not really been surpassed in our own time I need only refer to those instructors of dance who teach their students to express themselves, i.e., to feel something and then to make the movements that will convey that feeling to a sympathetic audience.

Feeling, movement, feeling; what could be simpler—and more misguided? It should suffice to point out that self-expression and artistic expression are different concepts, that whereas the latter is always the former, the former only rarely attains to the latter. I am expressing myself now, as I write (read) these words; I could do the same by scratching the back of my head, yelling at my wife, or shooting my mother-in-law. Each of these acts would be mine, but hardly a work of art. Walking across the street, kicking a ball, or dancing each engages roughly the same muscular structures of the human body; each may be preceded by an intention of the mind; and all, if continued long enough, are capable of producing another feeling—extreme fatigue. The lesson to be learned is that the feeling I have before or after moving my body is not the feeling embodied in a dance.

Can we say, for this reason, as Mrs. Langer does,[5] that the feelings of the dance are unfelt, and merely symbolized by the movements of the dancers, the patterns of which correspond to patterns of sentience? If so, we must explain how the dance seen by an audience becomes translated into kinaesthetic reactions, and how these present a feeling to be understood. Better, it would seem, to show that the feelings expressed in a dance *are* the movements of a body, felt in the first instance and only then by the dancers as they move, and by an audience that perceives the forms of the movements themselves. Such feelings are objective, or at least intersubjective, and can be described in terms of the spatial and temporal coordinates necessary to define the force expended by the body in movement. Let us then forget the romantic notion of expression for the moment and adopt the language of movement considered as the articulation of spatial and temporal forms.

The dancer works with the body as instrument, creating a dance *in* space and time, the two ultimate realities of everything physical. Given a space and a time, we could calculate the force necessary to move from here to there; or given the force, the direction, and the destination, we could calculate the time; and so on. This, I am told, is the way dance is taught in many institutions, and there is only one thing wrong with the approach: the dancer's body is not a billiard ball rolling down a polished inclined plane, nor is it freely falling from the leaning tower of Pisa. We shall see later that it is not even an instrument; for, who would be using the instrument? the soul? the mind? or another body? And the space through which it moves, and the time it consumes? Are these given before the dance, before the body moves? Or, on the contrary, does the body, by moving, create a unique space and a unique time in creating the dance? We must be led to think so, lest we continue to be misled by our concepts of the soul as feeler of feelings to be expressed, and thus as mover of the body; of an instrument without instrumentalist; of space and time without life; and of consciousness without the body, whether in pride or shame. Of course, all this can be avoided; we have only to insist that the only person to come into contact with the human body as a physical object is an undertaker. And only that profession is interested in embalming and burying its objects.

To move from physics to physiology is an interesting step. The phenomenon of movement no longer plagues us; the soul is dispatched to limbo or some other place, and the mind is explicable in terms of the reflex-arc or conditioned reflex.

The reflex arc poses a simple model: stimulus-organism-response, the incoming (afferent) nervous impulses transmitted to the central nervous system where connections are made and transferred into effective action of the body by means of the outgoing (efferent) paths. Stimuli, it is supposed, can be controlled; overt behavior can be observed, and measured. Lights, sounds, and pressures can be increased or decreased, reactions noted, and thresholds established. With all this scientific precision, what could go wrong? What, indeed, except the precision itself? Our figures may be exact, but what do they represent? Are stimuli the causes of responses? If so, they should have the same effect at least upon the same subject. But they do not. Even discounting fatigue, reactions to the "same" stimulus differ when that stimulus is presented along with another stimulus of the same kind. There seems to be no absolute, i.e., noncontextual, significance to a given form of stimulation.

Aestheticians have known this for a long time: a patch of red presented contiguously with an equally intense and saturated green is seen as a space tension, and no longer as a red plus the green. And what are we to make of the connections in the central nervous system? Are they made there as in a switchboard, a dialing system, or a transformer? All the mechanical models used to explain the arc of the reflex system fail to account for the fact that each species and each subject, to some extent at least, interpret what is to count for them as a stimulus.

The attempt to construct complex patterns of behavior in terms of additive functions of simpler reflex connections is to reduce the rhythm of life to the hygienic conditions of a laboratory, where all the selection of stimuli is made by the experimenting "animal," the psychologist himself. Under these conditions the experimental animal always comes off as sick, pathologically related to an unreal environment; but we have made a gain: in the physicist's universe, you will recall, he was pronounced dead and ready for burial.

The learning of complex behavioral patterns by the conditioning of responses takes away some of the pathology, even if it introduces some theoretical problems of its own. One of Pavlov's dogs, you may remember, exhibited what Pavlov himself referred to as the "freedom reflex,"[6] an expression he used to cover the case where an observed response was a rejection, on the part of an overstimulated dog, of the whole experimental situation. How human of the dog, and how cynical (or canine) of the little boy who, if not allowed to pitch, picks up his ball and goes home!

Conditioning allows for the transference of a response proper for one stimulus to another. It can and does take place under conditions of control, and in the ordinary life processes of living beings working out solutions of problems by trial and error. The transference of reactions to different stimuli allows the physiologist further to suppose a general law of irradiation, according to which any reaction whatever might follow upon any given stimulus. Whence, the superiority of the conditioning process over the simple connections of the reflex arc.

But whence, too, the necessity to suppose some kind of limit on irradiation. If, in the life of lower animals, anything can become, theoretically, a stimulus to any kind of response, then there must be some further law operative in order to explain the specific responses of some species. A toad, for example, will not snap at anything but a moving prey, and will continue to do so even if it butts its head against an invisible screen. It will even overcome any inhibition one would expect from having successfully nipped off a piece of moving paper, and go on to the other trials following this error. Obviously, then, excitation, conditioning, and/or inhibition do not successfully explain all the learning behavior of animals even of a lower order, although experimenters have succeeded in conditioning reflexes of creatures having no cortex, such as fish.

Enough has been said, perhaps, to understand that the doctrine of conditioned reflexes is not "scientific," in any but an extended sense of the term. Since one might always appeal to the law of conditioning to explain any positive results, and to that of conditioned inhibition to explain any negative, the theory is unassailable; but this means that it can be neither confirmed nor disconfirmed. Indeed, since the term "physiological fact" properly speaking is used for the observed processes of the nervous system, the so-called "laws of conditioning, irradiation, and inhibition" are not physiological facts in the same sense. They are theoretical concepts supposed by the experimenter to exist, and then imposed upon the facts of observed behavior.

Rightfully speaking, then, physiological laws are facts of the observer's symbolic behavioral reactions. How otherwise to explain the continued pursuit of many errors in the behavior of experimental animals? or the fixation of one successful trial as the reflex response to a given experimental situation? As in the simple reflex-arc behavior, the character of the stimulus is after all determined by what is meaningful to the organism being tested. This is why the toad continues on its merry way in spite of our efforts to condition its behavior.

Some stimuli, moreover, seem to change character. Animals have been noted to react positively to two negative (inhibitory) stimuli when they are presented simultaneously. He who would count on a double, or reinforced inhibition is sadly mistaken: all behavioral responses are *forms* of behavior, and are all occasioned by *forms* of stimuli that are detached from the environmental situation by the animal responding. This evaluation of a situation by an organism is of another order than the physiological, and leads us forward to descriptions purely psychological.

The psychology of formal behavioral structures was pushed to its highest development in the work of the gestaltists. It is tempting to indicate that the failures of physiological explanation of perception, even in lower animal orders, stemmed from the inherent difficulty of describing the full nature of a complex physical stimulus. There seems to be no way of compounding simple stimuli. If colors in juxtaposition appear as spaces, and two inhibiting stimuli presented simultaneously fail to inhibit response because when presented as a whole they constitute a qualitatively different sort of stimulus, the reason would seem to be that the least perceptible element in human perception is contrast, a most elementary kind of formal relationship. No contrast, no light; and here we are in the dark night in which, as Hegel has pronounced, presumably of Schelling's Absolute, all cows are black.

The gestaltists concluded that all reactions are to forms, defined as a complex stimulus having a character different from any of its components in isolation. A change in any one of the components radically changes the total quality of the stimulus, whereas total transposition of the complex into another that maintains the relative values of the components fails to change the character of the whole; a change in key does not destroy the unity of a melody.

Moreover, there seems to be no physical explanation of this phenomenon. The structure of any stimulus can be known only through the structure of responses to it. Hence, any attempt to explain the structure of a given response by reference to the structures of the stimulus is obviously an explanatory circle. Whatever description can be given to structured responses must therefore be phenomenological in character: the experience must first be had, and then described as it has occurred.

Whether the behavioral forms are "syncretic," i.e., determined by the "rhythm of the organism's life" and tied to a specific characteristic of its environment, as in the spider's reaction to a vibration of its web; or whether they are "mutable," i.e., transferable from one situation to another, as in the conditioned reflexes; or, finally, whether they are truly "symbolic," and capable of expression in the absence of any correlative stimulus, these responses take place within the organism in reaction to the things and other organisms found in its environment. The relationship between organism and environment thus defines the field in which phenomena make their appearance.

I shall maintain that walking across the street, playing a game, or creating a dance are merely continuous modifications of the phenomenal field. The modification is achieved by abstraction from "assigned" significance to "conventional" significance, and from there to "auto-significance." I shall not maintain, however, that only humans dance; if my account is correct, i.e., if I have not been misled by Merleau-Ponty, only those organisms dance which are capable of responding in symbolic forms.

III

If being in the body is a notion turning on the absurd, and physiological psychology flounders in its attempts to explain the "horizontal" and "transversal" connections of incoming and outgoing nervous impulses at the center of the nervous system, some other mode of explanation is in order for the psychic phenomena of the body. For example, some bodily movements are concrete, i.e., tied to a perceived object in an organism's environment. I move concretely every time I catch a ball and relay it to a first baseman. If, however, the batter has hit a lazy pop foul into the sun in the general area of the first baseman and I am playing third, my movements are abstract, in that they merely point to the ball.

Grasping is a concrete movement; pointing, abstract.[7] Both have meaning in that they are directed toward an object, which is the end of an action; and there is no other reference for our ordinary English word "there." "Here," on the other hand, always makes a reference to the body of the person making use of the word. In general, I exist between "here" and "there" as my body intends the object it is grasping or pointing out; and in this intention I create a space of unique significance for human action. Sometimes, moreover, I can point to or grasp certain parts of my own physical body. Without looking, I can scratch the mosquito bite whose itching is driving me to distraction—a phenomenon which indicates, incidentally, that kinaesthetic responses may be controlled by tactile sensations alone. All this activity, then, whether directed outward to an object in space or inward to a part of the body itself, takes place within the body proper, the body as experienced in a lived situation, and suggests another mode of conceiving bodily existence. Schilder called this entity "the bodily schema" (*das Körperschema*).[8]

Uniting the functions of seeing, feeling (tactile sensations), and moving (kinaesthetic responses), the bodily schema takes in more objective space than the physical body and it can be contracted into a mere portion of the same space. Watch the exploratory motions of a blind man's cane and you will understand how the effective space of the normal organism may be reduced to what is felt and how the afflicted person creates for himself a further space through which to move. We may refer to this existential concept as spatiality. Microscopic and telescopic instruments, horses, automobiles, and airplanes are so many ways at man's disposal for enlarging his basic spatiality.

Since Schilder conceived of the bodily schema as a system of associated images, interoceptive, proprioceptive, and kinaesthetic, as well as a means of correlating visual with kinaesthetic imagery, his concept is better rendered, perhaps, as the "body image." Like most theories of images, this one explains the whole by reference to the parts: stimulus 1-stimulus 2-association-response. What to do then with those cases in which a subject is stimulated by pressure in the left hand only to have the pressure felt in the right? If the body image is a whole in any significant sense, the global design (gestalt or style) of the body must govern the movements and affectations of the parts; thus right-left hand transference and the experience of a phantom member by an amputee would be explicable in terms of modifications of the global image, not of the afflicted members. Konrad has already indicated this revision of Schilder's notion,[9] by interpreting the body image as a global consciousness of an organism's presence to itself. From a loose association of separable images, the body schema became a true system of intersensorial space, or form, in the gestaltist sense of the word.

But here too the phenomena of movement, in expression or inhibition, tend to overflow the sense established in a fixed concept of the bodily schema: a paralytic feels nothing of existing members; his ability or inability to move certain parts of his body indicates that the body proper (as experienced) is related to the kind of tasks it can possibly perform. Thus there must be a relation between internal and external action where the latter is conceived in full (or restricted) dynamic terms. For the spatiality of the body we must find an existential equivalent to our sense of time.

Consider for example the phenomenon of "timing" in sports. This does not mean a synchronization of objective time with object time as one watch is set with respect to the time read from another. The pedestrian must synchronize the time of his personal effort with the speed of an oncoming vehicle, whether he wants to cross the street safely or commit suicide by throwing himself in the path of the car. The swimmer must "time" arm stroke with arm stroke, and both with the scissor or frog stroke of his legs, in order to propel himself through water. The batter must continually change his personal time to counter-effect the change of pace, or off-speed deliveries of a clever pitcher.

Existential time, or temporality, is the second basic structure of human existence. Within temporality, past and future are given in the present, in the moment of intending an object in existential space. The moment I step slightly out of my crouch, leaning forward with my weight on my right foot for power, each of these movements recalls the patterns of those immediately preceding: the crouching itself and the intent gaze at the pitcher's stance; and each foreshadows those immediately to come: the hesitation—to judge whether the pitch will break, slide, or jump—and the swing from shoulders to biceps to wrists, were a moment ago already intended as the living future of my crouch, which will have meaning only if I succeed in hitting the ball. If my timing is right, I will; my swing will become a follow-through—aimed at distance in my drive and balance in my body, and which, of course, cannot be so extreme as to inhibit my running to first base should I hit the ball into fielding reach of an opposing player. If this example is correct, past and future are given in intention the moment my task is clear.

Physical activity thus affords some of the best examples for understanding the existentiality of the human personality. If we observe how movements are performed we can readily understand how the body in action creates both space and time—not the empty containers of classical physics, but a space and time of unique significance to this act of motion. My position in any vital situation is lived as an intentional-arc, uniting the "here" of my body with the "there" of the object intended; and my present intention points to an expected future as growing out of my immediate past. In this way, bodily existence is a system of "meanings" in process toward equilibrium, the whole of which is felt as a qualitative experience, more or less tense, more or less well adapted to the conditions of life. Having motor skills allows me to avoid the necessity of "thinking" or "imagining" what must be done by me to my body or by my body to its world in order to achieve what I intend. Motor skills are for living.

Teaching motor skills purposes the enrichment of living; it has as its aim to speed the process of bodily equilibrium, not to set up its limits. There is no way in which this can be done artificially. Physical education cannot, therefore, impose goals upon this process. To do so would be to close the universe of the student and to hinder further creativity. Whatever goals there are for physical education must come out of ordinary life processes: walking across the street, to buy a newspaper or merely to relax; playing a game, to earn a living or to feel the sweet tension of fatigue; creating a dance, to express oneself or to communicate a new world of feeling to an audience. Each of these actions is an acceptable goal for physical education, and in the remaining section of this chapter, I shall relate them to my topic, which has become in spite of myself "being the body." By now it should be apparent that it makes little difference whether I say "being the body" or "creating a world."

IV

In order to show in what manner the human species transcends any limitations set upon it by the conditions of its physical and even biological environment by creating for itself a cultural and social environment, I shall once more follow the lead of Merleau-Ponty, whose metaphysics is sometimes called a "philosophical anthropology," centered around the notion of continuity. Educators have always pursued continuity in theory and practice out of fidelity to experience, which exhibits a continuous gradation between lower and higher animals, and, within the behavioral patterns of the highest, between the life of the organism and the processes of art. Theory and practice cannot be separated because art and life cannot be separated; and art and life cannot be separated because in living certain organisms have achieved an order of response of unique significance, an order of response no longer dedicated to the sheer purpose of continued life, but to that of enriching life by suffusing existence with human qualities, those which only a man can feel, only a man express. All this, to be sure, is already well known; what is not so well known is that man has achieved the heights of expression, not because he has a mind, but because he has learned to use his body in significant ways and in an increasing order of complexity. Whether physical or mental, conduct is intelligent when it is ordered to an end.

Consideration of the kinds of ends a man can intend will afford a means of measuring the degree of significance our species may import into its life. In a word, the more significance man achieves, the more intelligent is his behavior. If it is the purpose of education to inculcate the higher, more significant behavioral patterns of human conduct, it cannot pursue this end by derogating the less significant or by supposing that the higher have no relation to the lower. Indeed, a closer inspection of human existence reveals a continuity between man and nature, between mind and bodily response. Each higher order of response is the "mind" with respect to those responses of lower order immediately surpassed. The creation of a human, cultural environment is a product of a body's having transformed its signals into symbols; but the signalizing responses are themselves mind with respect to the reflex behavior of immediate response, and reflex behavior is mind with respect to the action and reaction of the physical body within the system of universal gravitation.

We must learn to trace the ascent of man from corpse to living thing and from a signalizer to symbolizer much in the same way as Plato and Plotinus envisaged the ascent of the soul. Their most grievous error seems to have been the supposition that the soul continues to ascend when it once has lost contact with the body. It matters little that the one imagined the ascent to be directed toward the Good, while the other saw the process as a return to the One. These notions are themselves symbols for the highest ideals of mankind, and, ironically, are understandable only in terms of the continuity between matter and life and expression.

For all his intelligence, and no matter how absent-minded, man cannot lose contact with his body. These very words call up imagery of infancy, in which the organism is notoriously incapable of controlling either end of its anatomy. The child's sucking reflex fails to lose its significance in adulthood, and even gains for having been transported into the ceremony of love. Muscular contraction and expansion, along with the action and reaction between foot and pavement, permit locomotion to both children and adults. But even our locomotion may achieve an added significance, as it may when we send our young ladies to finishing schools to "learn how to walk"—i.e., in style or with grace. The grossest kind of coquette does nothing basically different. She may slink, swing, jiggle, or bounce; every movement of her body added to the strict necessity of getting from there to here announces the advent of art: engaged in one kind of activity, the walker holds out a promise of still another, richer and more rewarding for signalizing an intent not bound to the limits of our physical space. Those actions which are so bound, the syncretic forms of human response, are usually taken for granted. We all know how to walk, or have learned to, and so forget the triumph of our infancy when we first stood erect, pulling ourselves up on a chair or our mother's knee; an injury or a virus may well cause us to have to relearn.

But even walking is not our first encounter with space; that occurred when we first saw an object, at a distance or near, a rattle or a hand, both our own, and what a joy to touch! Seeing, reaching, touching; consummation; the thing was ours, wedded to our corporeal structure. Our physical education, it can be supposed, began with the synchronization of these formal perceptual responses. A figure on a ground relative to me: a perceived space tension; coordination of muscle and movement: kinetic trajectory toward that fascinating object; contact and caress: the object yields over its form.

Thus, the bodily schema at this very low order of organization already contains three coordinated structures: visual reaction, anticipated tactile consummation, and kinaesthetic synthesis of the body in motion. In a higher order, each of these may become symbolic of the other; here each is linked to the other by the necessity of life. The significance of syncretic responses, then, is assigned, either by the structure of the organism or the nature of the environment. As the spider will approach anything that sets up a vibrating motion of its web in search of a fly, so a child is attracted to what he sees. What he can see, of course, depends upon the objects in his environment, those making their appearance in his phenomenal field. How he propels himself toward the object depends upon the structure of his anatomy. Imagine, if you can, the woman capable of throwing an overhand fastball; she cannot. But she can learn to walk in the most seductive of ways, throwing the most insidious kind of curve.

When she does, her responses have already left the realm of the syncretic and entered the mutable. Freed from the necessity of getting from there to here, she has room to play with her own responses. Her game is conventional, and its end is arbitrarily set up for a purpose of her own. In making this move, she has performed a kinaesthetic abstraction. Since the end (or significance) is no longer strictly dictated by the limits of her own structure or that of her environment, she has abstracted the movement for the sake of what it represents or suggests. Seeing her at a distance I can note her style visually, kinaesthetically, or in the other manner; but if I should do that, I will be playing her game, since that is what she intends.

Organized sports, again, are not basically different from this mode of significance. A terrain is set up arbitrarily; goals and movements ordered to the achievement or frustration of attaining the goals within the conventional terrain are likewise regulated by arbitrary decision. Just as above, where some affairs can be illicit, some pitches are illegal and some blows foul. Since the achievement of the goal measures the significance of the act, all niceties of movement over and above the necessary to achieve the goal are for the form. A pitcher winds up to prepare his muscles for the delivery of his pitch; his goal is to throw the ball past the batter—preferably in the strike zone. His follow-through is for balance and power or break, all action intending an object. Yet some pitchers have style, and others lack form. Warren Spahn's overhand left-handed delivery and Robin Roberts's fluid sidearm right-handed motion were prodigies of human grace; both cases are not unakin to the slower-motion grace of a cat stalking a bird.

A further abstraction puts all the significance of the movement into this characteristic of the kinaesthetic-visual phenomenon. Diving, skiing, skating, and the like, are judged for excellence in form, the figure of the body moving through space as a dynamic configuration. And at this level of abstraction (from locomotion) we are at the approaches of fine art. All that remains for the sports to become art is the symbolic response to the kinaesthetic form, i.e., for the visual form to call out the kinaesthetic feeling. When this occurs, movement is dance. The significance at this last level of locomotor abstraction is created by the movements themselves, i.e., by the dancer in motion. It is for this reason that I have referred to the rhythms of dance as "auto-significant." The dance calls attention only to itself.

A last point may be made by comparing this scheme to the dance theory of Susanne Langer.[10] For her, too, the dance is symbolic of a pattern of sentience. The symbolism is explained by the dancer's activity of abstracting physical movements, describable in term of space, time, and force, into a dynamic image of virtual power, which appears only to the attentive consciousness. Her theory runs aground, however, since the pattern of feeling cannot be ascribed as felt, to any one person, either to the dancer who composes the image or the audience who perceives its structure. If the feeling is not felt, however, it is said to be "understood," both by the dancer and his audience.

This theoretical appeal to the understanding of the dancer poses all the old problems of mind and body that have been the bane of philosophy and psychology since the inception of each. Langer's model for the explanation of mental behavior—a transformer—is as mechanical and as inadequate as the switchboard of the physiologist. To suggest that a dancer first understands a feeling, and then translates it into kinaesthetic imagery, is to suggest that a dancer dances before dancing; since the counters (Mrs. Langer says "elements") of the dance medium are movements, the dancer must already have made the movements in order to have gained his or her "idea." Outside the notion of a locomotor motif, which can be taken from any ordinary life situation and which must be developed in context as an element of the total dance image, the word "idea" has no application in the dance art—unless it be a reference to the finished dance itself. But this must be perceived to be believed. Like her model for the mind, her model for creative communication by means of works of art is seriously defective. The dancer communicates through her finished products, and she can "understand" its "import" only by making the movements presenting the image of a virtual power.

The same kinds of shortcomings are apparent on the other side of the communication process. If the dancer makes the dance kinaesthetically, the audience must take in the dance visually. The "form" of a figure skater or water skier fails to fulfill all the requirements of balletic expression because the athlete is perceived visually, and only visually. The configuration of the athlete's motion outlines a dynamic image in physical space; it may even achieve the status of a virtual power; but the connection between what we see and the feeling expressed remains a theoretical surd. What Mrs. Langer lacked in order to have achieved the most significant interpretation of the dance is a working concept of the bodily schema, of a body that "understands" before a mind has had the time to function.

It is not uncommon for dancers to respond to the question, "How does this dance feel?" by making an appropriate balletic gesture. It feels like this. They are not inviting us to make an overt expression of our own physical bodies in order to understand what "this" means. And they do not have to: we see how the dance feels because the feeling is the global kinaesthetic image, a modification of the dancer's bodily schema; and when we respond visually our bodily schemata undergo a similar kinaesthetic modification. This is possible because within the bodily schema seeing and feeling and moving are correlative structures of a single system, of a single human existence in transcendence:

> Vision and movement are specific matters of relating ourselves to objects; and if, by all these experiences, a unique function is expressed, it is the unfolding of an existence which does not suppress the radical diversity of its contents. For, it relates whatever contents it has not by placing them under the strict control of an "I think" [that such and such must be the case], but by orienting them towards the inter-sensorial unity of a "world."[11]

And this is how, by modifying her world, the dancer succeeds in modifying mine; for as long as I attend to her dance I am inhabiting her world. All the significance of the dance is to be found in this experience.[12]

If the very closeness of the dancer to her dance may get in the way of a clear perception of the dance's significance, especially in those cases where the dancer herself becomes the object of erotic desire or where we become lost in the futile attempt to interpret the naturalistic signification of her movements, the distance between the painter and his object almost exactly parallels that between the same object and its viewers. The reason, of course, is that the principle of a painting's structure is primarily spatial, with any dynamic properties of the organization of the context to be found in the phenomenon of spatial tension—that tendency of surface or depth counters to pull our attention from one to the other.

We move, then, to a consideration of the way in which the painterly medium, considered as bare visual markers, may "thicken" to express whatever is reducible to a visual "essence." But whether or not the context of the painter's creation is "figurative," his art is measured by the degree to which he presents a meaningful abstraction.

Our guide for reading the significance of visual abstractions is, once again, Merleau-Ponty.

NOTES

1. See Edmund Husserl, *Ideas,* Gibson trans. (New York: Collier Books, 1962), pp. 184ff.

2. In *Existence and Being,* W. Brock, ed. (Chicago: Regnery Gateway Editions, 1949), pp. 325–61.

3. *La Structure du comportement* (Paris: Presses Universitaires de France, 1942); *La Phénoménologie de la perception* (Paris: Gallimard, 1945).

4. This account is culled from the *Phaedrus.*

5. Langer, Susanne K., *Feeling and Form* (New York: Scribner's Sons, 1953), *passim.*

6. *Cf.* M. Merleau-Ponty, *La Structure du comportement,* p. 134.

7. Kurt Goldstein, "Ueber Zeigen und Greifen," *Der Nervenarzt* 4 (1931):453–66.

8. *Cf.* M. Merleau-Ponty, *La Phénoménologie de la perception,* pp. 114–16.

9. *Ibid.,* pp. 116–17.

10. Pp. 169–207.

11. Merleau-Ponty, *La Phénoménologie de la perception,* 160; translation mine.

12. For a fuller account of Merleau-Ponty's existential analysis of bodily perception see my *An Existential Aesthetic* (Madison, Wis.: The University of Wisconsin Press, 1962).

6

THE VISIBILITY OF THINGS SEEN: A PHENOMENOLOGICAL VIEW OF PAINTING

I

Roman Ingarden published the first quasi-complete phenomenological treatise on an aesthetic subject in 1931. Though it purports to be an investigation into the intellectual discipline defined by the overlap of ontology, logic, and the science of literature (*Eine Untersuchung aus dem Grenzgebiet der Ontologie, Logik und Literaturwissenschaft*), his *Das literarische Kunstwerk*[1] contains a theory of literature, in strict phenomenological terms, that is capable of modification (to suit other art media) and generalization into a workable description of the structures inherent in any kind of aesthetic experience whatsoever. He insists that the objects he describes are "purely intentional," i.e., nonexistent except for the consciousness that happens to be aware of them. Likewise, in keeping with his Husserlian inspiration, consciousness itself is described as exhausted in its intending, or reaching toward, the objects of its own lived world.

In order to avoid the clattering sound of needless jargon, I shall attempt to use ordinary American-English expressions, which seem to me to correspond to the meaning of the phenomenological terms still unfamiliar and barbarous to the majority of American philosophers, in spite of the long and now hoary tradition of continental philosophy. For a starter, "one's own lived world" still sounds odd enough even to a pair of sympathetic ears, and so is in need of elucidation. The "world" that is lived is for most individuals, except those scientists who successfully inhabit a universe of stable objects with fixed meanings and measurable dimensions of space-time, something other than the world of the natural sciences.[2] We enter into it merely by being born and continuing to live. As we interact with the objects of nature, other living things, and our own bodies to express our impulses, we may enlarge or restrict this world of raw human experience. Physical infirmities may restrict it, and by dint of compensation the infirmity may yet become a means of enlarging its scope.

But, to study this phenomenon, we must decide, quite arbitrarily, to "bracket the world" [of nature]: to hold it for naught, and to reflect on the acts of consciousness and their corresponding objects. This bracketing is the phenomenological reduction, and has been practiced in aesthetic disciplines many centuries before the creation of Husserl's own *Lebenswelt.* Ordinarily, the distinction between the knowledge of the natural world and that of the lived world is cast in terms of attitudes: we can look upon any physical object as physical, or we may concentrate upon the phenomenal characteristics of the same object in order to linger over the taste of its sensuous qualities, individually or related one to the other. On the one side, then, we have an object of the natural world; on the other, an aesthetic object. That the latter should be phenomenologically described as a noematic correlate of an aesthetic consciousness is of little import for the subject of this chapter. It suffices to remember that the attitude and the object are correlates, and that the consciousness and its object are simultaneous occurrences in a single vital experience. The attitude does not precede the existence of the object; there is no strait-jacket or mystical pair of rose-colored glasses we can put on to make something appear. If the experience is visual, all we have to do is look; but if the experience is one of verbal mediation, then we must be able to read.

Ingarden's work is thus the description of the objects appearing to an alert consciousness as it contemplates a work of fine literature. A construct consisting of four "strata" [*Schichten*], the literary work is perceived as it shows itself: a polyphonic harmony of sound and sense. So far, nothing new or astonishingly inaccurate. His insistence on the inclusion of the vocal materials, supplied by the words as read, accords well with contemporary approaches to linguistics, putting primary emphasis upon the phoneme as bearer of linguistic significance. What I have referred to above as "sense" is given in a three-fold modification of the sensuous surface, or organized sound patterns, of the literary work. If literature could be nonobjective, it would contain nothing more than its sensuous surface. But since phonemes in their structures intend structures of meaning, the surface of the literary work must thicken: first, into the unities of meaning given in sentences and propositions, where the latter are purely intentional correlates of the former; second, into the stratum of represented objects and their relations that constitute an "idea," metaphysical or other; and last, into an order of schematized images [*Ansichten*] that at times fulfill or concretize our apprehension of a represented object or idea and that at others may stand in the stead of the same.

The only distinction that may escape the careless reader of Ingarden's text is that between represented object and schematized imagery. Ingarden draws it out of reasons of necessity: in phenomenological theory, a real object appears in a series of phenomenal manifestations. A real object, such as a familiar city, may appear in a literary work as the setting for a fictional event; as such it is represented, but as phenomenologically reduced. The streets of Paris we know and love may, in the fictional context, be other than the way we know and love them; if so, so much the worse, in this context the depicted city is the one that counts. Its depiction is given in terms of "schematized images," which are responsible for the transformation of the "real" streets into their effective fictional counterparts. Moreover, the distinction between actual represented objects and their manifestations in schematic imagery allows for an explanation of figures of speech, like metaphors and similes, in which two different objects may appear in interchanged characters owing to a common manifestation of a single set of imaginal schemata.[3]

The advantages of Ingarden's scheme are apparent: he is true to his method in not importing anything to the work except what he finds in an experience of it, and there is good reason for making each of the distinctions he does. If there is a serious disadvantage to the theory, it is to be found in the slight treatment of the aesthetic object as a whole—the aesthetical idea, in Kant's terminology. Granted that in some sense the aesthetical idea is the total literary creation or construct, granted that the term "polyphonic harmony" is at least a suggestive metaphor for describing the effect of apprehending the total construct, phenomenologically something is still lacking: a description of the manner in which the various strata interact in our perception in order to determine the particular effect they have in combination. Ingarden's description of the "polyphonic harmony" is singularly inconclusive; it is a function, presumably, of the "value qualities" of the various strata out of which it is built; but these so-called value qualities are not given phenomenological treatment. Moreover, since Ingarden distinguishes between the work and its myriad "concretizations" (*Konkretizationen*; we should say "readings," I am sure), and the work is presented only through one of its readings, the literary structures are not in any sense autonomous. But, of course, the autonomy of an art-work is an aesthetic ideal, so why the bland admission of its heteronomy?

There are various ways of answering this question. My own attempts to sketch out an answer will be a bit fairer, I believe, than the attempt given by Mikel Dufrenne,[4] who claimed that Ingarden's position is "rationalistic," by which he meant that Ingarden had given too much emphasis to the depth of the work (the strata of sense, as described above). Dufrenne is correct, however, in suggesting that whatever meaning is to be found in a literary work, no matter how allegorical or symbolic, is strictly controlled by the structures of the words used to build up the sensuous surface. There is, then, some control on the associated meanings any one reader may find in a given text, and this is a move toward autonomy. Ingarden, less idealistic perhaps, may very well admit this point without destroying his thesis; for the control of the meanings to be associated with a given morphological interpretation of phonemic structures is never completed. People do read the same text in different ways, and often it is difficult to choose between two readings. There is good reason to accept heteronomy. And the fact that Ingarden has done so is indicative of his fidelity to his own method, as well as of his own intellectual integrity. But the matter cannot be ended on this note.

Given two different, but consistent, interpretations of a single text, how does one even try to decide between them? We may not want to; both may be acceptable for certain purposes. But what about an aesthetic purpose, the different qualities of the two readings? Obviously, this is not a question that can be answered without some elucidation of the notion of an aesthetic purpose, and there is no call for dogmatism on this point. How do people who usually pose the question as meaningful decide the matter? Putting aside the possibility of personal predilection, prejudice, or what have you, serious aesthetic investigators usually appeal to "the context" of the experience of "the work," according to its variant readings. The intention of the author is no help here, for that is the question to be decided. Moreover, even if the author is alive and capable of commenting on his work, there is no good reason to accept his comments as constituting the "true reading" of the work, if his comments either tend to contradict a more meaningful interpretation or give a less tense interpretation of the same. Thus, any decision on the relative merits of variant readings of a text are usually settled by an appeal to the clarity and the intensity of an experience controlled by one reading or the other. But please note, both the clarity of the vision and its intensity within our experience are controlled phenomena. They are controlled by the overall structure of the literary work—the polyphonic harmony.[5]

Consider, for example, the significance to be accorded to Rubashov's decision to confess to a crime he did not commit in Koestler's *Darkness at Noon.* Was it weakness of character, and defeat at the hands of the Neanderthaler, Gletkin? or last service to be rendered to the Party he had helped and whose revolution was being changed at the hands of the newer regime? Both interpretations are possible, and both are commented on in the context of the story itself: by old Wassilij and his daughter, Vera, in reverse order. Only Vera's way of seeing the outcome of Rubashov's decision makes the new Party triumph, whereas Wassilij's view shows Rubashov a martyr to the first revolutionary Party he had striven so hard to institute. In both cases there is a death freely chosen, but only one interpretation of the death's meaning gives maximum significance to the life thus ended. Both hypotheses must be entertained in order to motivate the characters of Wassilij and his daughter; but there is a greater intensity in the literary expression if one assumes that Wassilij's account is the "true" one, for then the pattern of life between the old man and his daughter can be read as symbolic of the relations between Rubashov and the Party. This last image, call it *eine schematisierte Ansicht* if you will, then serves not only as part of the surrounding action of Rubashov's death, but also as a succinct statement of its significance.

The point to be noted is that the richness and the clarity of the context give ample reason for choosing one rather than another interpretation. And this may have been what Ingarden intended by his expression "polyphonic harmony of aesthetic value qualities." If so, he could have been more explicit.

Lest some unwary reader assume that clarity and intensity are matters of sheer personal reaction (which would constitute a convincing case for a work's heteronomy), it must be maintained that both of these aesthetic values depend upon an objective (or at least intersubjective) factor: the manner in which the artistic context is structured. Clarity is a function of distinct determinations apperceptible in one's own lived world; and intensity, of the complexity of relations obtaining between the individual elements of each determination. I have no objection to having either of these qualities called "feelings," so long as such feelings are those felt in an immediate apprehension of the structural properties of the work in question. The feelings expressed in a work, or alternatively, the feelings of a work, are always those felt in the experience of some subject's lived world.

If I have lingered long on a phenomenological treatise on a literary subject, the reason should be obvious. Until something better comes along, Ingarden's work will remain a model of phenomenological analysis in matters aesthetic. Dufrenne's more ambitious work, entitled *Phénoménologie de l'expérience esthétique,* is a similar attempt to describe the phenomenological structures of works of art. Following the inspiration of Sartre and Merleau-Ponty,[6] it strives to show just how aesthetic significance occurs in the lives of an "informed" subject. But in Dufrenne's scheme, Ingarden's four strata are replaced by three emanating "worlds": that of physical presence, in which the aesthetic subject intends, or becomes aware of, the sensuous structures in a phenomenologically reduced act of perception; that of a represented universe deriving from the structures of the first, whether it contains a subject theme or not; and finally, that of expression, a distinct world of feeling, controlled by the relations obtaining between the first two worlds, and which brings into play the *a priori* (and presumably empty) affective schemata of transcendental subjects. It is difficult to render into acceptable American idiom Dufrenne's translations of Husserlian German.[7] He strikes one as having been unfair to Ingarden's efforts, and his appeal to the *a priori* is an inference from, if not a falsification of, experience. But to argue from the fact that one feels in such or such a way to the possibility of so feeling is as nugatory an inference as is one to the dormitive powers of experienced soporifics: Kant's transcendental deduction is still no substitute for phenomenological analysis. Finally, Dufrenne's contention that a work of art is a quasi-subject is a metaphysical confusion that effective analysis should obviate.

II

Since Dufrenne has claimed to be following the existential trend set up in France by Sartre and Merleau-Ponty, in the remaining sections of this chapter I shall attempt to apply what I have learned from a careful reading of these men to an analysis of the phenomenological structures of the visual art of painting. Before proceeding to the analysis, I should like to summarize the aesthetic view of the two Frenchmen.

The bulk of Sartre's work on the visual arts was done in his earliest, Husserlian, stage of development, when he was preoccupied with the problem of imaginary entities. In the conclusion of his *Psychology of the Imagination,* he describes an aesthetic object as an intentional object distinguished by its absence or nonexistence and intended by means of the physical analogue constructed by the artist.[8] In the nonrealizing attitude of the aesthetic contemplator, who perceives the physical analogue, or artifact, the aesthetic object appears on the margins of the real world. To use the example taken from his earlier text,[9] Dürer's etching, *Ritter, Tod und Teufel,* is a physical analogue affording a hyletic content for the imaginary consciousness apprehending the figure of a knight, accompanied by his faithful dog but hounded by death and harassed by the machinations of the Evil One. Death is a personification, and the evil exists only in the mind of the devout Christian knight: thus, two examples of schematized images, in Ingarden's sense of the term. But the knight is a real, represented object, one that might exist and that is cast into the usual environment of knights-errant, looking for good to do in an evil world. The form of the image, the manner in which the alert consciousness intends these objects, real or nonexistent, is supplied by the artist's *savoir imageant,* which could be exhausted by a conceptual description of the etching's representational world. In a word, the real, physical etching refers to an imaginary state of affairs, as described above, by virtue of the resemblance perceived between the representational structures of the etching and the image it calls out in the attentive consciousness.

This kind of analysis will run into trouble when the visual object perceived contains no figurative elements, as for example, in cases of nonobjective art. Dufrenne thought he had solved this difficulty by treating aesthetic representations as special cases of *Vorstellungen,* which need not resemble any other object than those they present. But this epistemological, and idealistic, gambit will not get us very far in aesthetic criticism, since the question may always be posed as to the function of the representational content of the figurative piece, and of the lack thereof in the nonfigurative piece. Dufrenne's insistence that a cathedral has as "representational" content the idea of a cathedral, although nothing is figured in the architectural structure, is blatant confusion. The idea of a cathedral is precisely what is presented in the "physical presence" of the object of concern. This same sort of aesthetic confusion is evidenced by the remarks of uninformed critics, for whom the epitome of painting had been reached in the realistic techniques of the Renaissance, after which there could be developed only the decadence of sensuous profusion called, pejoratively to be sure, "modern art." Recall former President Truman's remark about "ham and egg" art. The only way out of this confusion is a trip back to the facts of our perceptive experience.

Such is the prescription of the phenomenological method, and one that was followed throughout the philosophical career of Merleau-Ponty, whose *Phénoménologie de la perception*[10] is one of the really great philosophical texts of our time. In it he claims that the epistemological squabble between rationalists and empiricists rests upon a mistake, the assumption of the constancy of the objects of awareness, which is possible only because both empiricists and rationalists believe, unreflectively, in the primacy of the objective world; the same controversy may be seen in the development of art from the Renaissance to our own day. Realistic painters picture a universe of real objects in perspectival space; and where linear or aerial perspective does not suffice to give the image of space, objects will be foreshortened to create the illusion of a real space—cerebral and rationalistic, all this. On the other hand, perspective drawing was for the most part abandoned by the impressionists, who thought they had found a new basis for representing objects by placing small dots or strokes of primary colors in close juxtaposition, in an attempt to capture the sparkle of the first visual impressions made by light reflected off real objects—empiricistic and sensuous, all this. According to Merleau-Ponty, it was Cézanne who rediscovered what painting was all about. He did not try to represent space by geometric rule; nor did he attempt to show how objects impinged upon our consciousness by the effulgence of sensory impressions. His problem was to show how, in the first instance, there came to be objects in our perceptual field at all, a problem whose solution he doubted having discovered all his life.[11]

Cézanne's paintings accord beautifully with Merleau-Ponty's phenomenology of perception: the conceptual space of the Renaissance and the equally conceptual synthesis of sensory impressions are derivative epistemological phenomena, and they derive from an earlier relationship between organism and environment that is one's own lived world. In this prerational or nonreflective universe, the organism intends its objects physically or vitally, without even a thought to their contents: a rock in a path is something to be avoided, or moved, or used as a weapon merely because the impulse of life is to continue its outward movement into the organism's world. Intentions are, thus, first bodily phenomena, and they define a corporeal schema by the arc subtending the physical body and its preobjectively constituted world. So likewise is seeing a bodily phenomenon: at rock bottom, it is a tension felt without our phenomenal field of possible action. When a painter is successful, whether figurative or not, he succeeds in presenting on the sensuous surface of his work the same kind of tension produced in the organism's phenomenal field when it first becomes aware that an object exists. Cézanne's doubts were in vain; the experience of the tension in his paintings is sufficient evidence that he succeeded.

At the time of his death, Merleau-Ponty was aware of the shortcomings of his "thin" aesthetic doctrine. Where Sartre had placed all the value of paintings in the imaginal content, he had placed it all on the perceptual surface. His last aesthetic piece is dedicated to this very problem; significantly enough, as noticed above, the article is entitled "l'Oeil et l'esprit." This article on the eye and the mind recalls many of the problems he had discussed in his *magnum opus,* and contains at least one surprise. In the five-part essay he takes up his older distinctions between knowledge by description as it is garnered in science by the application of operational techniques to the data of experience and knowledge by direct acquaintance afforded in the first instance by the lived processes of the body proper; he establishes the bodily character of visual phenomena, noting the correlation between body movement and binocular vision (we can see nothing if we are not looking in the proper direction, and we orient ourselves with respect to what we see and what we see with respect to our own bodies, which are at one and the same time the seeing vehicle and one of the things seen); and he repeats his criticism of Descartes' rationalistic approach to visual phenomena:

> The body animated by the soul is not for it an object like all the others, and the soul does not deduce the rest of

> space on the basis of some kind of implied premise. The soul thinks according to the body, and not according to itself; in the natural pact uniting soul and body, space and external distance are stipulated in advance. If, for such or such a degree of accommodation and convergence of the eyes, the soul apperceives a given distance, the thought which deduces the second relation from the first is one immemorially inscribed within our internal fabric. . . .[12]

So runs Merleau-Ponty's new *Dioptrique*.

Since Descartes uses the sense of touch as a model for the visual act (his universe, you recall, is a plenum), an act of seeing could only be considered the occasion for thinking (concevoir) the object, already located in conceptual space existing *pars extra partes* as an indefinite continuum. This is the same "assumption," according to Merleau-Ponty, of Renaissance painting in *perspectiva naturalis*. Modern painting, on the other hand, made its appearance when painters became aware of the fact that color is form, not an accidental property of natural objects; colors and spaces are given simultaneously and, taken in juxtaposition, create a series of receding planes before our visual apparatus. The recession of the planes constitutes a space tension, which occurs in our visual field, but only in our visual field. Space tensions, therefore, are purely intentional objects; they are not, however, represented, but are presented to the man who looks. All this is a repetition of Merleau-Ponty's earlier work.

The surprise contained in the article is found in the metaphysical treatment of painting in its last section. For the first time I can recall, Merleau-Ponty used the word "Etre" with a capital E; and its inspiration is entirely Heideggerian. He declares that all the so-called elements of painting—depth, color, form, line, movement, contour, and physiognomy—are "ramifications of Being, and that each one of them can recall the whole cluster of the others."[13] That is why, as noted above, he claimed that the dilemma between interpretations of figurative and nonfigurative paintings is badly conceived: ". . . no grape has ever been what it is in the most figurative of painting and no painting, even an abstract one, can escape Being; Caravaggio's grape is the grape itself."[14] To understand this claim, it must be remembered that the visual object we usually refer to as a grape is presented to our bodily perceptors as a felt space tension. Thus, "vision is the meeting, as if at an intersection, of all the aspects of Being."[15] The subjective and the objective aspects of experience melt into a pure, unitary phenomenon.

In spite of its interesting historical ramifications, Merleau-Ponty's last turn of mind is disappointing for aestheticians, who may have hoped that he would continue to work on the problems in the philosophy of art. When he says, in commenting upon the art of Paul Klee, who described the process of seeing as a return to the eye and the beyond, that

> In this circuit, there is no rupture; no place where it can be said that nature ends and man or expression begins. It is mute Being itself that comes to manifest its own meaning.[16]

he has patently given himself over to the problems of philosophy in art. When he had earlier criticized psychologists for handling their problems like physiologists, or worse, physicists, he was arguing for a psychological discipline that would treat psychological phenomena on their own terms;[17] we may at the present time turn the tables on him, and ask for an aesthetic discipline that will do likewise for purely aesthetic phenomena. One shepherd of Being is enough. I can only conclude this review of Merleau-Ponty's latest thought on matters aesthetic with an expression of regret: *Dasein,* yes; *Sein,* no.

III

In my return to the phenomena of art, I propose to pass by the theories of both Sartre and Merleau-Ponty. Both of them are instructive for the mistakes they contain—Sartre, in the first place, for his reduction of the facts of aesthetic consciousness to a single function of the imagination. It is proper, of course, to submit that an imaginary object does not exist as we picture or visualize it, if in fact it exists at all in the sense that our perceptual objects may be said to exist. But if the work of a painter is to be judged successful, then that work must be able to be perceived when he has made his last stroke. I am saying only that Sartre has misplaced the emphasis upon a banal fact: that before the painter has begun to work his attention must be placed upon something that is absent, or nonexistent. But what is absent or nonexistent is precisely the work to be created. This is what Alain meant when he said that an artist's aim is to fix our imaginary experience; the artist can do this only by creating an object for our apprehension. Once the object is created, it is otiose for us to look for some resembling other to which "the physical analogue" stands in analogous relation. We are presented with a sensuous surface structured precisely the way it is. Thus, in placing the emphasis upon "the mind's eye," Sartre has clearly neglected what is there to be perceived by the body's two eyes. He has simply avoided the problem of visibility.

Moreover, if communication is the object of painting, the artist and his audience must at least perceive the same sensuous surface if they are to imagine the same "aesthetic object." And on the phenomenological structures of perception Sartre is ambivalent. In his first work on the imagination,[18] he indicates that he accepts Husserl's analysis of perceptual objects; and, indeed, in *l'Etre et le néant* he gives a version of Husserlian phenomenology that even a college sophomore can understand: the perceived thing is one and the same and exists as it is given in myriad manifestations of itself; but the perceived object is nothing more than the essence or *ratio* of the several perspectival appearances. The essence is the finite determination of an indefinite (theoretically infinite) series of *Abschattungen* (profiles). In their various reductions, the essence and its manifestations are experienced; and experiences, possessing no perspectival variation, are thus intuitions.

An analytic philosopher may experience some difficulty with this analysis. Since the notion of "essence" would add nothing to that of "object," each object would literally be its own essence and the expressions "essential object" or "objective essence" would be redundant. The crux of my criticism, however, is to show that an objective essence must be intuited in one conscious act in order that a second, imaginative, act of consciousness might be motivated; and if this is the case, it would make no difference to the perceived qualities of a given sensuous surface if the objects represented on the surface are imaginary and hence nonexistent or real and hence perceivable in some other context. On Sartre's own terms it would be difficult to distinguish imaginary from real objects in an aesthetic context, since both may be represented in a single work by the agency of conceptual foreknowledge (*savior imageant*); and whenever this happens the conceptual knowledge would take precedence over the sensuous intuition, and the work is not one of art but of industry (to use Kant's term) or technology.

But a painting cannot be reduced to the representation of objects, real or otherwise. The imaginary object that is of some importance to the art of painting is the real object constructed by painters, but before the object has been constructed. Having radically separated the acts of the imagination from those of perception, Sartre is left with a theory of aesthetic objects that makes it impossible for him to judge the value of a given sensuous surface (the sensuous intuition) for presenting whatever depth references a work may contain. In a visual medium it is death to ignore the visibility of what we see.

Merleau-Ponty was to have corrected all this. A painting, whether it is figurative or not, always presents a sensuous surface; and an aesthetic object is the object perceived. In effect, and in the last analysis, one always sees space (intentional and pre-objective, not scientific or conceptual space, which by definition can never be seen). In this sense at least, intuitive knowledge runs ahead of concepts. Ignoring the represented strata of aesthetic experience, however, he is hard put to explain why we judge some paintings to look like other things of our natural experiences when in fact they do; or why we should not, if we should not. In a word, he tends, for his part, to ignore the value of the representation in the total expression, or how we come to understand, in an act of precise vision, an "idea" in pictorial exhibition. All these questions, I maintain, can be explained within the context of phenomenological analysis. But here at long last we must turn to the facts.

I have chosen ten paintings, some of which are purely surface expressions, the others surface-depth expressions. Of the latter I have chosen three "realistic" and three "abstract" pieces. The purpose is to trace in some measure the gamut of visibility. I shall not maintain that the whole gamut is to be found in every painting; obviously, in the nonobjective pieces, there is no depth in the sense I have been using the term. Fuller explication of the same term will be given in my conclusion.

The paintings are:

Figure 1: Ecce Homo, Lucas Cranach
Figure 2: Christ with Cross, Rembrandt
Figure 3: Blue Fox, Franz Marc
Figure 4: Small Composition (IV), Franz Marc
Figure 5: Serenity, Ernst Wilhelm Nay
Figure 6: Black and Red Lines, Fritz Winter
Figure 7: Rhythm, Theodore Werner
Figure 8: Norway in the Sun, Giacomo Balla
Figure 9: Blue Dancer, Gino Severini
Figure 10: War, Otto Dix

Figure 1 is a depth-dominated piece in which we find not only the representations of Christ, the world, angels and the heavens, but the further representation of a religiously significant event for the life of all Christians: the torture of the Savior prior to his ultimate crucifixion. Indeed, in a piece of representational foreshortening, the wounds clearly visible indicate that this Christ has already been crucified, and the body we see, elongated to emphasize the effects of the passion, is that of the resurrected Son of God. As such, the figure spans heaven and earth. The feet seem to be straining to lift off the orb of the earth as the projection of the body moves upward into the heavenly vault. The vault itself is designated heavenly by the presence of the choir of angels, rejoicing at the return of the divine son. Behind the vault is the void, lit up and made significant by the figure of the sacrificial Christ, who seems to generate his own light, reflected onto the objects around. The historical dominance of Christ's role as Savior of mankind (an idea) is pictured in the dominance, within the structure of the represented universe of the painting, of the figure of Christ; and the second dominance, achieved by the size and detailed expressiveness of the central figure, is emphasized by the light-dark contrast of the surface. Easy symmetry is avoided by the canted head, still suffering for the sins of mankind; but symmetry there is. It may be taken to betoken another idea, the success of divine Providence as a unifying plan for the will of God and the actions of men. The symmetry of the design, the light-dark contrast surrounded by the muted blue-grey mist of the heavens, and the stance and gesture of the dominant figure all stand in harmonious relation to the depth content of the painting: Jesus Christ as God the Son uniting heaven and earth through the act of his sacrifice; through his sorrow there will be everlasting joy, as sung by the choir of innocents.

Every good Christian knows the story, so the question arises as to how much of the Christian myth is applicable to the painting. We may answer this question by contrasting Figure 1 with Figure 2. In the latter, we see the raising of the body on the cross, whereas in the former the cross appears only symbolically in the position of the arms. Instead of the redemption of man by God, we are led to concentrate on the relation of Christ to his crucifiers. The pyramid formed by the contours of the three figures rises to the cross itself, and the presence of the pulley indicates further the human instrumentality in Christ's death. The light, a dominant feature of the surface, is not generated by the figure of Christ itself, but comes into the painting's representational universe from the side and bathes the three figures in the awesome presence of God the Father. Here, then, we are faced with man's inhumanity to man, and the cause of Christ's sacrifice, while in the former painting we were presented with its effect.

The same story? Not at all. Each painting tells its own story, and the story it tells is decipherable in the style of the artist. Only that part of the legend is told which is thus readable on the sensuous surface of the painting in question. Nor is the difference describable in terms of "Northern Renaissance" and "Dutch Baroque," for each of these styles is qualified by *the aesthetic idea* expressed in the two paintings. Religious stylization and foreshortened perspective in the one, mystical illumination of human activity in the other, yes; but the aesthetic significance of each painting is the felt tension of this precise rendering of only one aspect of the well-known story.

Figure 3 is still an obvious depth expression. We see the figure of a fox and other forms of nature. It is not "blue," but the surrounding forms of nature are unnaturally blue and the reflection of the intense blue made still more intense by the contrast with the reds and browns casts a bluish haze over the reposeful form (oval or egg-shaped) of the sleeping animal. While the fox rests, nature is active (the attitude and direction of the flowing forms, the piercing triangles and pyramids of the surrounding objects, indefinite except in their brilliance of contrast). The light here is not from an unknown mystical source, nor does it stem from a single dominant figure; it comes, as natural light can only come, from the reflection of nature's colors as they play one upon the other. The space of the painting, unlike that of the two precedent, is created from the picture plane out—toward the viewer, where the picture jells into a unified expression of color relatedness. The blue fox is a biomorphic form reduced to its visual essence. The painting depicts nature, but emphasizes the sensuous quality of colorforms in whose contrast we experience the tension of life and the real dimension of a lived or perceived space. In effect, the nature we can see is the space we can perceive, and all life takes place therein.

Where Figure 3 is expressionistic in style but representational in content, Figure 4 is expressionistic in style and totally abstract in content. Indeed, in the conventional sense of the term, the painting has no content at all. The surface-depth relation of Figure 3, so precise and immediately perceivable, has here undergone denudification. The total expression is on the surface, but the surface gains in intensity for the lack of a depth to be associated with it. Curved twisting planes are interlaced in such a way as to utilize space above and below an imaginary horizontal plane. Some colored planes are brought out from the picture plane; others recede behind—but not in a strict linear progression, so that the universe of the painting is literally created in three dimensions of lived space. There is a point of deepest penetration, of closest progression, and holes permit the vision of planes behind planes as well as the central abyss, out of which, into which, or about which most of the other planes evolve. Even the lines of the painting are restricted planes, which, intersecting, form other lines. Their feeling? The phenomenal tension holding this gyroscopic universe in equilibrium. There is nothing of a general nature here that was not already in the foregoing example; in abstracting from representational content, the artist has merely intensified the surface.

Figures 5, 6, and 7 are further examples of nonobjective art, illustrating variations possible in surface tensions. Nay's "Serenity" (Figure 5) seems at first blush to be misnamed: the violence of color contrast and the almost ferocious activity of spiraling lines connote everything but peace and serenity; the serenity, then, is that following upon violent activity—the peace of youth, rather than that of old age; the peace that encloses, rather than excludes the bustle of life. The activity is apparent, but the enclosing peace and serenity is achieved in the balance of opposing counters of the surface: the reds by the greens, the yellows by the blues. The activity of the lines, darting in and out and around interstitial planes of the tension of contrast, bursts with energy—but not outside the bounds of balanced structure.

Figure 6, Winter's "Black and Red Lines," likewise bears a surface title. The lines form contours of shapes enclosing in negative space what is presented in the solid shapes of colored planes, some translucent and others opaque. They function, therefore, on two different levels: on one plane, as moving line and shaping contour, and, as shaped contours, against other planes to give the impression they do of airy lightness in the tension with the more solid planes. Where Figure 5 takes its title from the affective correlate of the surface's perception, Figure 6 takes its from the surface's "objective" correlate.

Figure 7, on the other hand, is entitled from a vantage

point between; rhythm may be objectively described in terms of the movement of lines or figures or of the effect such movement has upon our psychic apparatus. And in this painting, Werner's "Rhythm," both the figures (the wide brush strokes of the colored planes) and the pink, green, white, and blue lines are undulating in movement. The fixed points are controlled by the gold, blue, and green circles (or solids) and the gold triangle (or pyramid). The rest of the painting moves: the predominantly positive planes of the left side are balanced by the equally intense negative space formed by the lighter planes on the right. To help pull off the design, the gold, pink, green, and blue are thrown into the balance on the right.

Figures 8, 9, and 10 likewise form a group. They are all "abstract" pieces in which the element of depth content is controlled more closely than that of the first two pieces. What was taken as light and dark, suggesting properties of represented objects in the religious paintings, is presented in what follows as the light and dark of the objects themselves—not externally as a reflection, but internally as the interior space of the abstracted object. The colored planes of the nonobjective pieces also have their correlates here: they become facets of the abstracted objects. For all intents, the distinction between surface and depth breaks down in each of the following paintings; any statement about the surface automatically becomes one about the depth and vice-versa.

The majesty of Norway's mountains might well be the subject of Balla's "Norway in the Sun" (Figure 8), but if so, that majesty is nothing more nor less than the perceptual effect of the intersecting planes of color, the cold

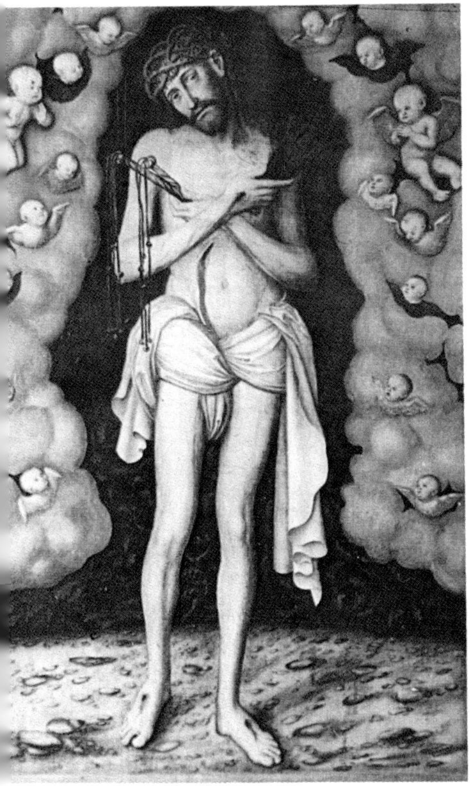

Figure 1 Lucas Cranach: Ecce Homo

Figure 2 Rembrandt van Rijn: Christ with Cross

Figure 3 Franz Marc: Blue Fox

Figure 4 Franz Marc: Small Composition, IV

Figure 5 Ernst Wilhelm Nay: Serenity

Figure 6 Fritz Winter: Black and Red Lines

Figure 7 Theodor Werner: Meter and Rhythm

Figure 8 Giacomo Balla: Norway in the Sun, or Mercury Marching Past the Sun

Figure 9 Gino Severini: Blue Dancer

Figure 10 Otto Dix: War

greens and blues struggling against the warmth of the browns, and all rising in concentric circular pattern to the white hot disc hovering above. Its rays, on the other hand, descend in straight lines through empty spaces or bounce off the sides of obstructions, to become lost in their own conflict with the shadows of the dark and blacker regions.

Severini's "Blue Dancer" (Figure 9) is not represented in rhythmical movement. Rather the rhythm of the dancer is cubistically presented in the relation of undulating planes, lighter and darker shades of blue; in the many-faceted presentation of the lace on her dress, up and down and around in the groups of circular black spots; and in the many perspectives of her moving face and hands. The warmer browns and reds give her a space, as background, in which to dance.

Finally, Otto Dix's "War" (Figure 10) presents a universe broken by the explosive power of man's war machines. Men themselves have become mechanized in their close connection with the instruments of destruction; the sanguine (the red colored heads) and the fearful (the ghastly blue) must all die in the ultimate holocaust. To describe the holocaust I would have only to describe the relation of the bursting planes of this mechanomorphically structured universe. If one looks closely, one will see a cannon in the upper central regions bursting out at the viewer himself.

IV

The foregoing descriptions are not given as exhaustive analyses of the various paintings. They apply only to the purely intentional objects of my own consciousness, and not to any physical object upon which paints have been spread. Since *Dasein ist je meines,* intentional descriptions could not be otherwise; and it is in this sense that aesthetic criticism must be phenomenological. The objects of criticism appear to the consciousness that lets itself be guided by the visual structures of the painter's universe. It would be a mistake, however, to infer from the phenomenal character of the intentional object we call "the universe of the painting," or the "object of criticism" (Pepper) that a single painting has many valid viewings. Obviously, there are empirically different interpretations of the same physical objects; but we need not, as Ingarden does for literary works, argue for the heteronomy of aesthetic objects. Ingarden's mistake, I believe, is to have viewed the various strata of an aesthetic object as independently existing (as single voices in the polyphonic harmony), without due consideration of the necessary connection between the strata.

If my analyses show anything, it is that the various strata in a multiply stratified object have their own intrinsic qualities changed for having entered into relation with the others, if in fact there are more than one stratum present. It is for this reason that I prefer the term "total expressiveness" to Ingarden's "polyphonic harmony." A nonobjective painting is exhausted by an experience of the felt space tensions set up in the colors. It is aesthetically insignificant to state that red occurs in a painting; its meaning depends upon a relationship to other colors and other spaces. All significance in a visual field is a differentiation, and the least differentiation perceivable is some form of color contrast.

It is fitting, then, to begin my account of the structures of a visual phenomenal field with the organization of the sensuous surface; at bottom, colored spaces. The tensions of the colored planes are the felt correlatives of the differentiations perceived. These are given in every visual phenomenon, and it is to Merleau-Ponty's credit to have located these experiences in the body proper of the perceiving individual.[19] However, when the space tensions are modulated in such a way as to depict objects, the surface of our phenomenal, or lived, universe thickens, and a depth is represented.

In contrast to what Sarte claims, and to some extent to what Ingarden indicates in his distinction between represented objects and fulfilling imagery, it makes no difference if the represented object has a correlate in the natural world or not; for the significance of any represented object is likewise exhausted by the system of relations set up in the universe of the painting. Not all crucifixions tell the same story, and the separation of the true from the false of a myth is of little consequence to the value of the painting embodying a legend. The meaning of the represented object is conveyed precisely by its manner of depiction, i.e., by the presentation of the object in the sensuous form constituted by the surface—a point made admirably clear in successful "abstractionist" paintings. This is the aesthetic concept that eluded Merleau-Ponty, and prevented him from solving the problem of the "eye and the mind"—or the relative aesthetic merits of figurative versus nonfigurative painting.

Ideas constitute the third and final stratum of the visual object; and these too may be traced back to the basic sensuous surface. They can be expressed, but only as a relationship between represented objects. And here again, there is no need to appeal to a realm of existents external to the system of relations set up within the universe of the painting; an experience of the painting is self-contained. As a relationship between represented objects, the idea will not exist if the objects are not represented; and the objects cannot be represented in a visual medium without a basis in color perception.

The gamut of visibility may thus be conceived as a series of emergent strands of experience: the organization of a surface is itself meaningful—as significance is felt in the qualitative differentiations perceived in a visual field. And in nonobjective paintings there is no other significance. But when surface tensions are set up in which represented objects appear, there emerges a second "stratum" or strand of the experience. The meaning of these representations is given in their manner of depiction. This is clearer, perhaps, in abstract paintings than in realistic representations, since in the latter, ideas usually emerge in the pattern of relations obtaining between represented objects. Beyond this third strand a painting cannot function: any attempt to push the painter's art beyond the presentation of an idea is risking the possibility of losing contact with the sensuous surface, and of lapsing into insignificance.

One last point: an apology to romantic aestheticians, like Dufrenne, who envisages a separate "world" of expressed feeling within the phenomenological structures of aesthetic objects. His error should now be apparent. The second world of represented objects does not occur in all paintings, and where one does not, there could be no further emanation of aesthetic significance. His world of expressiveness I can only take as a philosophical mystification. There are no *a priori* affective schemata, just as beyond the felt tensions of an organized sensuous surface there are no feelings nonsymptomatically expressed in art. Collingwood, as noted above, had this perfectly clear when he said that a painter paints to get his feelings clear.[20] I need only add that a painter must think with his brush—or some other instrument for applying color pigment to some surface. If I am right, all the painter's expression emerges from this (physical) act; but if it does, it emerges only in the lived world of some viewer.

In reducing the expressiveness of painting to the controlled structures of some sensuous surface, I am being consistent, I believe, with the work of those neopragmatists, like David Ecker,[21] whose methodology of art education is conceived on the model of controls introduced into qualitative thought. If the painter does control his expression as above described, it seems only fair that a critical viewer limit his associations or his effusive feelings by reference to the same set of controls. An aesthetic object, however intentional, is autonomously significant; its expression is self-contained. As Kant so rightly put the matter, in our aesthetic judgments we are given an intuition for which no concept is adequate. Therefore, to talk about our aesthetic intuitions we must always, in the very last analysis of painting, go back *zu den Sachen selbst*—back to the visibility of the things seen.

To whatever degree of abstraction a work of visual art may attain, the significance of the work is measured by the internalized responses of appreciators. Communication, it should be remembered, takes place when creator and appreciator express internally the same (or similar) response.

Perhaps the best means of understanding this "internalization" of aesthetic responses is to consider the medium of music: there, what we have referred to previously as "time" is clearly presented as something else. Existential phenomenologists refer to the phenomenon as "temporality."

NOTES

1. Halle: Max Niemeyer Verlag, 1931.
2. I am using the description of the *Lebenswelt* adumbrated by Merleau-Ponty in *La Structure du comportement* (Paris: Presses Universitaires de France, 1942), pp. 139–99.
3. Ingarden, pp. 272–73.
4. *Phénoménologie de l'expérience esthétique* (Paris: Presses Universitaires de France, 1953), 1:266–73.
5. For an elucidation of this concept, see Ingarden, *Untersuchungen zur Ontologie der Kunst* (Tübingen: Niemeyer Verlag, 1962), pp. 32ff.
6. 1:4n.
7. See Appendix A of my *An Existentialist Aesthetic* (Madison: The University of Wisconsin Press, 1962).
8. *l'Imaginaire* (Paris: Gallimard, 1940), pp. 239–46.
9. *l'Imagination* (Paris: Presses Universitaires de France, 1936), pp. 149–50.
10. Paris: Gallimard, 1945.
11. See Merleau-Ponty, "Le doute de Cézanne," in *Sens et Nonsens* (Paris: Editions Nagel, 1948), pp. 15–49.
12. "l'Oeil et l'esprit," *Les Temps Modernes* 17 (1961):211.
13. *Ibid.*, p. 225.
14. *Ibid.*
15. *Ibid.*, p. 224.
16. *Ibid.*, p. 225.
17. In *La Structure du comportement, passim.*
18. *l'Imagination.*
19. See *Phénoménologie de la perception,* second part.
20. *The Principles of Art* (New York: Oxford University Press, 1958), pp. 110–11.
21. See his "The Artistic Process as Qualitative Problem Solving," *Journal of Aesthetics and Art Criticism* 21 (1963):283–90.

7

TIME, TEMPI, AND TEMPORALITY

I

If it is true, as Pater assured us, that all the arts aspire to the condition of music, musical theory has been of little help to one seeking an understanding of either the condition or the aspiration. Consider a case in point. The following excerpt is taken from an introductory text discussing "the structural problems of a 'time' art":

> The fact that music occurs in time is of real significance to musical form. First of all, whereas the form of a painting or other space art is perceived initially as a whole and only afterward in more detail, the form of music is perceived bit by bit during performance and only afterward as a whole. Some hearers even report a kind of flashback of the whole musical form during the moment after its completion.[1]

Ignoring for the moment the comparison with paintings, I shall call attention to the concept of time implicit in the statement. More essentially than the other arts, music takes place in time; the perception of its parts is successive; and only when the time necessary for its execution has elapsed may one "hear" the piece in its entirety. No doubt one possessing a remarkable gift of aural memory can recall the entirety of a slice of his temporal awareness; and if one also possesses training in classical harmony, the phenomenon of tonality—direction toward a prefigured resolution of a harmonic tension—will aid him in the process of recall. The question one should ask concerns "the real significance" of music's occurring in time. Any physical process takes place in time; all doings and undergoings, all happenings and events begin and end in differing moments of universal time, even the act of attending to the value properties of a painting. What then is the "real significance" of *music's* temporality?

William S. Newman's other consideration may be more telling. He tells us, for example, that the perception of the whole of music depends upon memory to establish the beginning, middle, and end of the piece.[2] But on this score, too, memory is implicit in every act of meaningful awareness; for, if the present were discrete, it could be related only externally to a past and a future, where real significance is to be found.

His next two considerations are related. Climax, he says, will occur at the end of the temporal sequence; second, interest and boredom are managed in the production of the climax.[3] But surely the "climax" of any temporally developing sequential stimulus is reached the moment significance is apprehended and is found in any act of perception—aural, visual, tactile, or other—temporal processes all. And boredom and interest are relative matters, describable in terms of factors other than the moment of climax, or achieved significance, after which all else is anti-climax—silence or peace, as the case may be.

Lastly, the temporality of music is said to be responsible for the necessity of re-creation each time the music is to be enjoyed. If by "re-creation in time" is meant the necessity to perceive the musical counters in their relations in order to have the experience of music, this condition, too, hardly differentiates music from the other arts—or from many other activities not usually considered experiences of fine art, such as working or making love.

Still, the fact that all these conditions—taking up time, implicating the memory, reaching climax at the point of significance where the relative play of "live" and "dead" spots achieve a maximization of interest rather than boredom, and necessitating a fresh act of perception for the retention of the significance in the experience—apply equally as well to love-making as to listening to music does not deter at least one musical theorist from exalting this sense of time as the mark of musical excellence. Perhaps the *Liebestod* of Wagner is the perfect example of significant musical climax. At least one wag has been quoted as saying that after a performance of *Tristan and Isolde* not a single seat in the house was found to be dry.

The obscenity of this example must not dissuade us from further analysis. For interest and boredom properly managed through a temporally sequential stimulation do bring about both climax and significance. The aesthetic question to be solved is *how* music manages its points of interest and boredom, i.e., we must investigate the manner in which a musical structure achieves significance, and then describe the nature of this significance.

On this latter point experts have agreed only to disagree. For over a hundred years since the stirring debate concerning autonomy versus heteronomy of musical expression between Eduard Hanslick and Richard Wagner, musicologists, psychologists, aestheticians, and critics have been unable to come to a single conclusion. On the one hand we have the statement that music is only what it is, sound in motion, to quote Hanslick; on the other, that music, above all the arts, is what it does. It is the most moving of the arts because it does in fact move. The debate is all the more curious in view of modern analytical philosophy, which would brand as nonsense the true statement that a painting may move owing to the kinetic structure of certain visual counters, while accepting the more obvious fact that music can do nothing but move. Audition is not vision, they say, and auditory surface counters flee past the most attentive of listeners.

Yet acceptance or refusal of the obvious needs further explanation. If a painting is said not to move because it is a spatial construction in which a third dimension has only illusory status as a thing represented (as in projective drawing) or as a thing presented (in spatial tensions created by the juxtaposition of color-planes), only our assumption of the reality of the two dimensional surface stands warrant for our judgment. Yet, as some paintings begin to work, we perceive their kinesis, which transpires only for or within our act of perception. Even Matisse, the master of the "flat" technique, conceived of his constructions as moving in a rocking chair rhythm. And as a matter of fact they do.

The same analytical caution must be afforded the obvious movement of the musical medium. Indeed, Hanslick had already said it in 1854:

> Psychical motion, considered as motion apart from the state of mind it involves, can never become the object of an art, because without an answer to the query, what is

> moving, or what is being moved? an art has nothing tangible to work upon.[4]

Since there is no mobile object being displaced through space—the assumption equivalent to the reality of the two dimensional surface in painting, we are hard put to explain in these naïvely realistic terms what constitutes the movement of music.

Whether, therefore, we are dealing with a primarily "space art" like painting, or a "temporal art" like music, aesthetic pronouncements upon the quality of aesthetic objects based upon the assumption of naïve realism are misleading in their "obviousness." When the naïve realist states that a painting obviously does not move, he means that it cannot possibly move, given his assumption about the reality of the universe; but when he says that music obviously does move, he tends to forget that for motion to take place in nature there must be an object being displaced through space. From one point of view, then, music seems to our auditory perception to move, even though there is no relevant real space through which anything is moved. Thus, in this second case, what is "obvious" is the phenomenal characteristics of a purely perceptual object, not a deduction from a prior assumption concerning the real nature of the universe.

The feat of giving a meaningful interpretation of aesthetic experiences depends upon our ability to accept the seeming as real. Not even a "willing suspension of disbelief" is adequate as a description of our purpose, for, from the point of view of the ongoing experience there is no ground to assume that one thing rather than another constitutes a primary object of our belief. Phenomenologists refer to the aesthetic attitude as "phenomenological,"[5] and to its object as "intentional."[6] This means only that an aesthetic object appears to him who holds himself open to the working of a work. Heidegger in particular refers to "openness" as a constitutive state of a human being's being,[7] a claim not unlike the biblical pronouncement that unless one become like unto a little child he shall not enter the kingdom of Heaven. To let oneself be by holding oneself open to the conditions of experience is a promise of ultimate fulfillment, especially in matters aesthetic. And to "understand" a musical idea, Hanslick assures us, we need only listen and contemplate the successions and forms of sound that alone constitute the subject of music.

II

Vom Musikalisch-Schönen was first published at Leipzig in 1854, and attained to seven editions in 1885. First translated into English by Gustav Cohen in 1891, the book was brought back from oblivion by The Liberal Arts Press in 1957, with Morris Weitz as editor. Although Hanslick is widely interpreted as the most outspoken exponent of musical autonomy, it is clear, as Weitz points out, that his position comes down to a modified form of heteronomy, in that music is said to be capable in its moving structure of signifying the dynamic properties, and these alone, of an emotional experience.[8]

More recent treatments of the debate have not left the matter there. Consider first the psychology of music. Carroll C. Pratt, in 1931, took his cue from the aesthetics of George Santayana to divide his subject into three categoreal distinctions: materials, form, and "meaning."[9] Given the nature of the sensuous materials and their capacity to be articulated into larger dynamic forms, his task was to disclose the manner in which the articulated forms could be thought of as expressing human feeling. It will be remembered that for Santayana the aesthetic object was a formal intuition of various strata of characteristics: the primary, secondary, and tertiary properties of a substance were said to be unified into a single experience; the pleasure and pain associated with the other properties were equally to be thought of as belonging to a single "object," which in turn could be associated with any other meaning, the second term of aesthetic expressiveness.[10] Pratt was unhappy about this "pathetic fallacy." How can a feeling be a property of an object? Feelings may be aroused in any stimulus situation, and these are purely subjective, i.e., belonging to the subject and not to the stimulus object.

The question is further confused by a refusal to distinguish between feelings and emotions, especially by those who argue for musical expressiveness as a paradigm of "aesthetic emotion." William James himself, who, along with Lange, invented the famous theory that reverses the causal position of patterned human response and affective state, was guilty of referring to a putative aesthetic emotion as "an intellectual emotion." He hoped to express thereby the need of "distancing" our responses to organized aesthetic stimuli. When the pattern is familiar enough to be named, as for example in fear, love, hate, etc., we clearly experience emotions, and when the pattern is easily recognizable as under the control of an aesthetic stimulation, an emotion may be said to be experienced under the influence of the structures of a work of art. We are put into the state by our apprehension of the work, which apprehension is guided by the intellect, and the resulting emotion is the expressiveness of the piece.[11]

But, according to Pratt, to distance our responses is not sufficient to render objective what is essentially a subjective state. Although the causal relation between bodily posture and subjective response may be as James and Lange maintained, emotions are to be distinguished not only by their recognizable and repeatable patternings, their intersubjective structures, but by the nature of the stimulus object and their intensity as well. A feeling, he claims, is merely "a single dimension of experience ranging between two maximal opposites, pleasantness and unpleasantness, through a point of indifference."[12]

Emotions, on the other hand, are distinguished from feelings by their definiteness, if by no other characteristic. The specificity of an emotion derives in part from an association with an object that appears lovable, awful, fearsome, etc., such that when a vaguer affective experience is controlled by the perception of an aesthetic object, that response too is described as an emotion. It is in this way that many of our affective responses, which bear superficial resemblances to emotions, are not emotions at all, but become mistaken for them.[13] Pratt concludes, quite properly, that there are no specific "aesthetic emotions," no mark on any affective state that distinguishes an aesthetic from a nonaesthetic emotion:

> My own contention . . . is that if a work of art gives rise to emotion, the emotion is no different from any other kind of emotion; but that on account of their formal resemblance to certain subjective states, many truly objective properties are classified erroneously as emotions and included under the general head of aesthetic emotion.[14]

Failure to recognize this resemblance allows some theorists to confuse subjective and objective elements of a stimulus situation.

The purpose of Pratt's psychological investigation was to lay bare the similarities between certain subjective states and the mysterious "objective" properties of the musical stimulus. Since the psyche is moved (cf. the German "Gemütsbewegung") under the stimulus of moving sound patterns, an experience of music yields to analysis a double strand of kinetic processes. A formal isomorphism unites the movement of the music to the corresponding kinaesthetic reactions of a perceptive audience, and music merely "sounds the way moods feel."[15] The further question, whether this isomorphism between "music's moving tonal architecture" and a purely affective human experience is sufficient to constitute a language of the emotions, is difficult to answer.

Romantics are poorly served here; for, if by a "language of the emotions" is meant the ability of music as a significant experience to arouse certain subjective states, the answer must needs be no. Certainly music may arouse emotions, but for the most part they are irrelevant to the significance of the music itself.[16] Musical significance is internal to the psychological stimulus, and is fully controlled by our perception of the music's structural relations. On second thought, then, "language of the emotions—yes; but emotions removed from the sphere of bodily sensation and presented to the listening ear through the sensuous medium of moving, meaningless, wondrous sounds."[17]

Such, in Pratt's account, is the immanent expressiveness of a musical stimulus. So far he is in agreement with Hanslick.

But he has gone beyond the contributions of Hanslick by clarifying the latter's rather arcane statement, that the very form of music constitutes its substance or subject.[18] After all, where form is subject, there is no distinction between form and subject, and to state their equivalence is merely to deny the applicability of form and substance as aesthetic categories to the musical experience. On this question Hanslick is no doubt correct; but when he says,

> The most essential part [of scientific aesthetics], the physiological process by which the sensation of sound is converted into a feeling, a state of mind, is unexplained, and will ever remain so.[19]

he was clearly misled by the ambitious program of the reductionistic physiological psychology. He could have no inkling, of course, of the explanatory methods of *Gestalttheorie* used in Pratt's account of musical expressiveness since he wrote before the dawn of Gestaltist psychology.

What the autonomist, formalistic or expressionistic, denies is only that there are any *extra-musical* ideas or emotions expressed in a musical context. And on this score Pratt parts company with Hanslick. Analyzing musical structures into its dynamic features (variations in tonal intensities and effects of rhythm and accent), Pratt finds similar structures in the kinaesthetic patterns of movement. To musical dynamism there is a corresponding "psychological" dynamism, i.e., ". . . the active, personal, mobile character which seems to attach to most bodily sensations."[20] These two associated dynamic series may be taken as symbolic, one of the other; and when they are, we have a case made for heteronomous meanings in music:

> . . . these meanings just beyond the world of sound seldom reveal corporeal concreteness. The suggestion of personal struggle and effort, let us say, which music can so effectively convey, derives from the close similarity between skillfully manipulated accents, rhythms, tempi, pitch-differences, and movement (plus the effects of dynamism), and the actions and motions of those who in real life struggle and strive, so that the perception of one not infrequently evokes the state of mind which was responsible for the other.[21]

In short, the movements of music present, in the first instance, a moving pattern of significance to the human ear. These constitute the immanent meaning of a musical work. But the human body, in its reactions, is also capable of patterned kinaesthetic responses, controlled by the simple tactile qualities of tones, clangs, and instrumental timbres, or by the complex qualities of tonal combinations, measured in beats. These so-called "absolute" dynamic qualities are further modified by the "relative" dynamic values, attributable to melodic phrasing, harmonic intervals, and rhythmic accents. The time so structured reaches its maximal complexity, perhaps, in the polyphonic harmonies of the fugue, and is lived as a continuous series of dynamic tensions.

Heteronomy enters the picture when the felt psychological tensions of the musical experience are interpreted as representing a further idea: the expression of a will. One need only abstract from the fuzziness of Schopenhauer's metaphysics—by reducing "the Will" to a will and a "will" to its associated ideas of action and movement[22]—to understand how music can be understood as a direct copy of the will itself:[23] the musical experience is not objectively temporal first, and then somehow mysteriously colored by subjective expectation, fulfillment, and memory; it is a context in which dynamic tensions are immediately felt (its immanent or autonomous significance), giving rise, through association, to an idea of volitional action (its referential or heteronomous signification).

III

The original thesis of Pratt's *Meaning of Music* was reformulated in a later article, entitled "The Form and Function of Music,"[24] where he states: "No serious objection need be raised to calling music the language of emotion, provided one bears in mind that music is neither a language nor an emotion."[25] He maintains that music is not literally a language because it does not represent or symbolize anything beyond itself. Adopting Hanslick's peculiar semantics of the self-referring symbol, he attempts to clarify the above paradox with a repeated denial of the validity of "content" and "form" as interpretive categories of musical expressiveness: "Tonal form represents only itself. The form and content of music are one."[26]

His principal thrust is against an idealist aesthetic, which speaks of the language of music as the "embodiment" of feeling in sound. But closer attention to the properties of the musical stimulus, as well as to the character of emotional response, allows one to distinguish the part of feeling which belongs to the response and that which more properly belongs to the stimulus. Psychological studies have proved the falsity of empathy's claims; since music is tonal and emotion is visceral—two quite different areas of sensory discourse[27]—it is easy to understand the confusion in the description of music as the embodiment of emotions. Emotions can be embodied only in the corporeal structures of biological entities, and must remain there in spite of all our attempts to project them into an object, aural or visual, by any process of *Einfühlung*.

The truth of the matter is, music sounds the way emotions feel.[28] And the reason for this phenomenon is the functioning of "tertiary" qualities in the organization of an aural gestalt. Consider examples: agitation, pensiveness, longing, languor, and the like. Each of these properties is found to be a property of the musical stimulus, owing to the similarity in structure between these subjective states and the objective, formal properties of the stimulus itself. Since there is formal congruence between stimulus organization and typical patterns of psychic response, it is easy to understand the contention of emotivists that the content of music is a feeling. They only fail to recognize that this "content" is nothing more than (Langer will say) a "logical" projection of the formal properties of a response onto the similar properties of the stimulus. But this is only to say that the responding organism organizes its stimuli into familiar patterns. Thus when we call a certain passage of music "agitated," we mean that it is perceived in the same way that agitation is felt.[29] The "agitation," a tertiary quality, is an intrinsic quality of the formal stimulus.

When, in addition, the question of the function of music is asked, the answer is a bit more obvious: the human organism acts to fulfill specific human needs.

Music allows the imaginative fulfillment of emotional craving, not because we actually experience, say, Wagner's neurotic eroticism, but because his music presents the form of welling desire. In the very peculiar sense in which music may be said to be a language, or to communicate feeling, ". . . its tonal design is capable of releasing in vicarious fashion the emotions which in ordinary mortals are inexpressible. . . . The tertiary qualities of music exist in a realm of ideal and abstract sound. They are pure creation."[30]

Our joy or exhilaration in the experience of this emotional fulfillment may be further intensified by the contemplation of music's immanent expressiveness as a symbol of a universal will, but this emotional reaction has nothing essential to do with music's inner structure:

> The emotions and strivings of the will and desire are embodied in music not directly, but indirectly by way of tonal designs which closely resemble in formal outline the inner movements of the spirit, the *Gemütsbewegungen.* But here at last it may indeed be true that music becomes symbolic, for it seems to stand for and express the joy and sorrow of all mankind.[31]

Thus music is symbolic, if at all, only in heteronomous fashion.

Two more recent treatments of the structure and function of music have arisen to challenge Pratt's view. The first is the general symbolistic aesthetic of Susanne K. Langer, who would further specify in what sense exactly music may be considered a language; and the second, by Leonard B. Meyer, whose musicological method is derived partly from psychology and partly from semiotic. A brief discussion of each is in order.

Mrs. Langer distinguishes two kinds of symbols, the discursive and the nondiscursive, or presentational. The discursive symbols of mathematics and speech are defined conventionally and have fixed dictionary meanings, are capable of unification into larger complexes of meaning by formation rules, and are translatable into other, equivalent formulations.[32] Nondiscursive symbols, on the other hand, have no meaning outside of the context in which they occur; the counters of such symbols are united by our sensory apparatus into a significant gestalt according to the principle of *Prägnanz,* or maximal organization; and this significance cannot, in consequence, be translated into an equivalent expression in any other symbolic system. Thus, if music is the language of emotion, it is not significantly like any verbal construct.

Langer agrees with Pratt on still another account, that art and music do function as a fulfillment of a human need—not for emotional fulfillment, since the feelings of art are not felt, but only conceptualized, but for symbolically transforming experiences into maximal significance. If we continue to look upon the rituals of magic and religion as irrational and upon myths as only false, the reason is that we fail to see ritual, myth, and art as nondiscursive symbolism. As in the creation and appreciation of art, ritual performance possesses its own "logical form" of symbolic projection, and functions to transform human experience into a significance of a very different order from that of discursive symbolism. Where the primary function of discursive symbols is to represent or state a *signification* other than itself, that of nondiscursive symbols is only to present a *significance* on the very surface of the created work.

Music, we are told, articulates its meaning; it does not

assert anything. Having no fixed connotations, its symbols are "unconsummated":

> The actual function of meaning, which calls for permanent contents, is not fulfilled; for the assignment of one rather than another possible meaning to each form is never explicitly made.[33]

What enables us to speak of "meaning" at all in connection with presentational symbols is the "logical" congruence of musical and experiential forms.

Having studied the long tradition of musical psychology, she proclaims that "the upshot of all these speculations and researches is, that there are certain aspects of the so-called "inner life"—physical or mental—which have formal properties similar to those of music—patterns of motion and rest, of tension and release, of agreement and disagreement, preparation, fulfillment, excitation, sudden change, etc."[34] It is in this way, then, that music sounds the way emotions feel, and nothing prevents our taking the one as the symbol of the other. A composer does not symptomatically express his own feelings; nor does he arouse ours. His compositions present concepts of feeling which, indeed, may never be felt by anyone at all.

So runs the argument of *Philosophy in a New Key*. In a mordant review of the book, Ernest Nagel pointed out that Mrs. Langer had misinterpreted some of the properties of symbols, primarily in her assumption that the pattern of meaningful discursive symbols must be in some way analogous to the patterns of events symbolized.[35] This is to attribute iconicity to all meaningful discourse, and is patently false. Richard Rudner added that analogous structures between two events are not sufficient to constitute a symbolic relation.[36] Presumably something more is needed beyond mere isomorphism, some intention capable of seeing or interpreting the relationship as symbolic. Pratt's account of the immanent expressiveness of music is one way of describing the psychology of this intention.

In her later works, Mrs. Langer has tried to profit by criticism, and to modify her notion of the unconsummated symbol. She now speaks of symbols as having "vital import."[37] *Feeling and Form* is her major aesthetic opus. In it she generalizes her semantical theory of musical expressiveness to cover the entire gamut of the arts. A symbol is here called "any device whereby we are enabled to make an abstraction."[38]

The artist is said to make an abstraction by arranging the materials of his medium in such a way as to make an "unreal" object appear. Shoes, buildings, and machines are arrangements of material parts; statues, temples, and pottery are presented in abstraction from the material world and the self-contained round of practical utility. They are pure "semblance," in which material *parts* are transformed into functioning *elements,* as sounds are transformed in music to motives, phrases, and movements. Such objects are virtual, i.e., illusions—not to say "delusions"—created for our perception by the fusion of elements of the plastic medium into a transparent, and auto-significant "aesthetic object."

The primary illusion of the musical medium is time, the image of our own lived or experienced time, not the real time measured by the clock or even the regular periods of a metronome:

> Musical duration is an image of what might be termed

> "lived" or "experienced" time—the passage of life that we feel as expectations become "now," and "now" turns into unalterable fact. Such passage is measurable only in terms of sensibilities, tensions, and emotions; and it has not merely a different measure, but an altogether different structure from practical or scientific time.[39]

Such virtual time is created by the flowing forms of the musical stimulus. But to call it "unreal" reveals a peculiar prejudice for the "reality" of a purely scientific concept of a continuous, one-dimensional sequence of homogeneous instants forming a part of the multi-dimensional universe. One could call it "empirical time," if the physical scientists had not preempted that epithet; or, because they have, "temporality," as the existentialists in fact do.

The difficulty with Langer's aesthetic conception is that the intentional character of temporality—our consciousness of the passage of moments of meaning flowing one into the other—is taken as symbolic of a feeling other than itself. This is the brunt of Rudner's criticism of her semiotic aesthetic: the distinction between the symbol and the feeling symbolized, although he himself is somewhat confused on this matter. He takes the symbolic relation to hold between the physical art work and the aesthetic object, not between the aesthetic object and the feeling it intends.[40] For the purely intentional object, the physical substratum of its appearance is irrelevant; only the semblance succeeds in expressing feeling in the logical way Langer explains. His valid criticism is to have pointed out that to distinguish between the symbol and the thing symbolized is a mistake if the thing symbolized is treated as the bearer of aesthetic value.

Moreover, as Langer explains the matter, our experience of the image of virtual time—our own temporality—is already through and through emotional. In contemplation of the musical image our experience is completely colored by the tensions and releases of the musical forms; our kinaesthetic sense is not lulled to sleep by our auditory attention, but rather is activated by it. And if this is true, the feelings of music are felt and not symbolized at all. Indeed, if we were to claim that the virtual time of music merely symbolizes a pattern of sentience, only an experience of that pattern would persuade us to admit the congruent relation between the forms of the stimulus and those of the response. How can one write

> The phenomena that fill time are *tensions*—physical, emotional, or intellectual. Time exists for us because we undergo tensions and resolutions. Their peculiar building-up, and their ways of breaking or diminishing or merging into longer and greater tensions, make for a vast variety of temporal forms. . . .[41]

without having *the experience of* the creation and release of the psychic tensions in listening to music? The significance of music is in the stimulus because it is felt to be there; it is not an idea or concept of the composer or of his audience.

What keeps this deeply moving emotional experience from slopping over into the realm of sheer sentimentality is the controls built into the stimulus itself. Thus, what Langer needed to guarantee a distanced response was not the notion of a symbolic relation between aesthetic object and its feeling, but an explanation of "relevance" in aesthetic response. After all, if the music is sentimental, we have to hear it that way or be guilty of irrelevance in our response; and responding to all music as if by way of "understanding" is just one way of guaranteeing irrelevance in response. The image provided by music is not *of time* at all; it *is* our own temporality directed outward toward, and controlled by, the moving forms of sound.

The musical aesthetics of Leonard Meyer moves us one step closer to our phenomenological-existential conclusion. His own method may fairly be called "empirico-hypothetical." His purpose is to test the hypothesis that "emotion or affect is aroused when a tendency to respond is arrested or inhibited"[42] against our experience of musical affect, where music is considered primarily as a system of "embodied" meanings. Like Pratt he is to play the psychologist, and like Langer, the semiotician.

His first concern, following a consideration of the kinds of evidence available for the contention that musical stimuli and emotional response are significantly correlated, is to distinguish various kinds of meaning. Although all meaning structures exhibit a triadic relation between sign, referent, and interpreting mind (or between stimulus, that to which it points—its consequent, and the conscious observer),[43] some are only designated by their signs, while others are embodied in a single, developing, stimulus-response context.

Designative meanings arise when the stimulus points to something else, or has an interpretive consequence of a kind different from itself. Embodied meanings are apprehended when the initial stimulus is fulfilled by a consequent of the same kind, and is experienced in a continually developing stimulus situation. The requirement here is not that sign and consequent possess isomorphic structures or be analogous in any other way—only that an initial stimulus call out responses to anticipate further stimulus objects of a like nature. Quite obviously, the vast majority of meanings in music are embodied in this sense, as autonomists have always argued:

> From this point of view what a musical stimulus or a series of stimuli indicate and point to are not extramusical concepts and objects but other musical events which are about to happen.[44]

Some such meanings are "hypothetical," in so far as they create expectancies for consequents to follow. And if such expectancies are fulfilled, the complementary sequence is referred to as an "evident" meaning. The total moving complex of hypothetical and evident meanings, once brought into final resolution, is termed a system of "determinate" meanings.[45]

It is clear here that we have an alternative description for the immanent expressiveness of music's moving surface. The trick to be turned is to show ample evidence from the experience of music to substantiate the traditional claim that it does embody emotion, or affect, in a system of determinate meanings. And Meyer's musical knowledge is sufficient to pull it off. The "law of good continuation" is applied to melodic continuity and to rhythmic organization, and that of "completeness and closure," to melody, rhythm, and harmony, as well as to the "principle of return." The weakening of shape is discussed as a means to prevent easy closure, as is the effect of texture, polyphonic organization, chromaticism, and ornamentation in the creation and release of musical tensions. Nor are his examples limited to classical Western music. Oriental jazz and folk music, as well as atonal composition, yield to the principles of simultaneous and successive deviation from the perceptual norms set up by gestalt apprehension.

Yet Meyer is modest in his claims. "This material," he states, "has consistently demonstrated the connection between the inhibition of tendencies (deviation) and the affective aesthetic response. And while this evidence is not exhaustive, it is clearly representative."[46] He would like to avoid, of course, the charge of Pratt, that "embodiment" is a misleading metaphor for the experience of musical significance; and at the same time to avoid Rudner's criticism of semiotic explanations of that embodiment: viz., that two aspects of an aesthetic sign-situation, one apprehended immediately and the other mediately by the act of reference, fail to yield a consistent interpretation of aesthetic objects as consummatory experience since they are, by hypothesis, only mediately apprehended through the physical work of art.

It has already been pointed out that Rudner seems to have won the argument only because of the naïvely realistic interpretation he gives the expression "art-work." If the art-work is what it does to our attentive consciousness, there is no distinction to be drawn between "art-work" and "aesthetic object." The only reality of aesthetic experience is the intentional object—the working of the work; and our intentionality spread throughout time is temporality. There is no confusion of "mediacy" and "immediacy" in the experience of aesthetic value; any apprehension, by any means whatsoever, of an object has its own peculiar intentional feel. The aesthetic question is whether this apprehension of semantic meanings may find its place in a larger intentional consciousness.

This is what Meyer has succeeded in pointing out—to an extent; for, having concluded his analysis of the immanent expressiveness of musical compositions, he proceeds to discuss possible designative meanings—images, connotations, and moods—associated by sensitive individuals with the experience of musical form. No doubt for many "unmusical" listeners, such referential expressiveness is the only affective response experienced in connection with music, now reduced to a stimulus for private reverie. It is for this reason that formalists like Hanslick, Pratt, and Langer either exclude, or place a restriction upon the relevance of, associative responses.

But there is evidence for the communication of nonmusical ideas in the musical experience. Everyone has experienced natural events, and is capable of associating musical passages with contiguous or similar natural happenings; it suffices that the musical occurrence be recognizable *in its connection with* the nonmusical event for the association to be relevant. In the same way, everyone lives in some culture whose conventionalized patterns of behavior are clearly known; and everyone is capable of learning the patterns of behavior of another culture. Even a mood—the general qualitative feel of a given psychic state—may be expressed through musical form. To play a musical composition with expression (*mit Gefühl*) is to perform it in a specific manner, with emphasis, accentuation, or stress upon a specific phrasing.

The difficulty with the expression of images, connotations, and moods, of course, is the ever-present danger of attending only to these, and not to the expressiveness of the sensuous vehicle. But this is likewise the case with the experience of literature, where no one doubts the relevance of nonverbal objects or events as present in signification. As long as the associated meaning is continually referred back to the embodied meanings of the piece, there can be no cogent reason for doubting its relevance. True, images, connotations, and moods tend to set up their own sequence of psychic continuance, and hence may diverge from the meaning of the piece, but for this reason many composers indicate with greater or less specificity the program being interpreted.

Whenever communication takes place simultaneously on two levels of significance there is a problem—but for aesthetic categorization, not for the comprehension of the experience. Meyer appeals to the principles of gestalt psychology to explain the immanent expressiveness of music, and to those of associationistic psychology to explain the occurrence of referential expression. He is aware that the total musical experience is somehow unified within the consciousness of the listener, for he states

> . . . in so far as music is able, through connotation, mood, or the use of a program or text, to designate situations similar to those existing in extramusical experience, such designations will tend *to color and modify* our musical affective experience.[47] (Emphasis mine.)

And, although he claims that the principal function of a text in program music is to provide "the causal connection between the successive moods or connotations presented in music,"[48] he likewise asserts that the understanding of the referential meanings "may play an important role in the actual shaping of our affective experience."[49] In a word, he believes that designative *expression* is as capable of controlling aesthetic *expressiveness* as the more direct process of "embodying" affect in musical forms.

The only step remaining in this historical survey of musical aesthetics is to attempt a phenomenological description of the manner in which music controls a single, complex, value-toned response; how, in other words, time and tempi—the temporal organization of music—affect the conscious temporality of human transcendence, of the human being's being in the world.

IV

Since 1928, the chief proponent of phenomenological aesthetics has been Roman Ingarden, whose *Das Musikwerk* was originally published in Polish and then in German, along with three other articles on painting, architecture, and the film. The latter book, entitled *Untersuchungen zur Ontologie der Kunst,* has been available since 1962.[50] The problem, like that of his *Das literarische Kunstwerk,*[51] is to describe the structures of an aesthetic object as the intentional correlate of consciousness.

Unlike literary objects, however, a musical work cannot be defined as a many-leveled or stratified structural whole. In proof of the point, Ingarden reiterates the conditions necessary and sufficient for an aesthetic object's "stratification" (*Schichtenaufbau*): (1) that it contain heterogeneous elements, such as the word-sounds, significations, images, etc., of the literary piece; (2) that each of these groups of heterogeneous elements be composed of homogeneous parts capable of organization into higher orders of significance, as words joined together form sentences; and sentences, paragraphs, etc., (3) that each of the homogeneous strands retain its perceptual unity, and (4) that all the strands be experienced in a single, unified "polyphonic harmony" of total literary significance.[52]

Music lacks this stratification, having no superintendent layers of nonmusical signification or imagery, and so must be considered, in spite of the misleading metaphor used to describe the relationship between literary strata, to organize its significance in a different way. Consider, for example, the tonal "materials" of music. There is a serious question whether the individual acoustical sensations of which tones and tonal imagery are constructed are themselves ever heard in musical context.[53] And the reason for our hearing something other than the sensuous materials is our tendency to group sounds into tonal patterns: individual chords give way to the perception of motives; and motives, to melodic sequences against a harmonic background. Although these higher perceptual orders of experience are homogeneously ordered, and can be associated with the corresponding homogeneously ordered sequence of sensory data, the two orders are never *experienced in relation* for the simple reason that we never perceive the discrete sensory "data" of the whole gestalt, but only their manner of functioning in the presentation of the tonal image. We can, of course, listen "abstractly" and attend to the component, purely "psychical" contents of our intentional act, thereby separating the significant perceptual objects into sensory "data"; but then we no longer have an experience of the working of the work. We can, for example, reflect upon an intuition of a melody in any given work and then discover the "unintuited" psychic content of the consciousness we had of the performance in question as it was played.[54]

The point being made here is the familiar Husserlian thesis that a conscious act is describable in terms of a psychic matter and an intentional form, and that the whole psychic complex intends some external and "purely intentional" object. When we attend a musical performance, we can arbitrarily pick out the characteristic style of a performer's virtuosity, listen to the sounds without hearing the music, or apprehend the structure of the musical object itself. So, performances are not works; they are *of* the works, and may be better or worse, depending upon how our listening to them permits us to intuit the essence of the piece.

This distinction between the performance and the work is of the essence. Each performance of a musical work is an individual, real, temporal, and unrepeatable process. Each is solely acoustical, and may be objectified within a certain spatial locality; each is given in a series of overlapping tonal images that constitute a peculiar "coloring" of the consciousness at a given time; and, finally, each is univocally determined by a specific manner of playing, or the presentation of tonal qualities not capable of further differentiation.[55]

Once it has been created, however, the musical work, as distinct from its performances, persists through time. It does not depend upon any real physical or psychical processes; it cannot therefore be located in a single space or time; and, if there is a relation between the overlapping acoustical images and the perceptual essence of the piece, these images are determined by a relationship *inter se,* and not by a process of successive addition. Indeed, it is with respect to these internal relations of constitutive acoustical imagery—the true individuality of the piece—that each performance is perceived as "correct" or "false," "good" or "bad." And, as for the separable tonal qualities, such as tone color, tone fullness, or intervalic character, which in each performance are determined by the particular instrument or technique of playing and tuning, these are in the actual work only vaguely determined through imprecise musical notation.[56]

But the score cannot for this reason be considered the work either. As a real entity, it is nothing more than marks on paper—of an entirely different order from aural perception. Interpreted, the score is a system of "imperative symbols," i.e., signs for the reproduction of the piece; and, although it serves a useful function in the production of music, it can be ignored for the purposes of aesthetic contemplation of the tonal individuality of the piece.[57]

As intentional, a musical work is an individual, determinate object independent of localization in space and time. It can exist only as the object of someone's consciousness—which is not the same as to say "in someone's consciousness." If by "individual" is usually meant that the thing so qualified is determined with reference to spatial and temporal coordinates, then some other term is more appropriate for the musical work's essence. The term "essence" is here used in the Heideggerian sense: the manner in which something comes to be and persists as it is. Ingarden uses the term "supra-individuality" *(Überindividualität)* to suggest the nonactuality of the work.[58]

A construct of the aesthetic properties of sensuous stimuli, the musical object is a single strand of organized processual qualities. Within its context, the tonal qualities of the continuous image delineate a pattern or shape at the same time they set up an "environment" *(Umgebung)* for the appearance of the tertiary qualities of experience —the expressive or value-laden complexes Leonard Meyer referred to as "affect." It is within this musical environment or context, considered as a whole, that the musical piece is to be discovered.

Since in music the aesthetic object creates its own time and its own space through the internal relationships of its tonal qualities, its temporal process is clearly extra-scientific and our knowledge or experience of intersubjective time is irrelevant to aesthetic analysis. Thus, rather than describing or pointing out the spatial and temporal coordinates used to determine scientifically the "real" existence of entities or processes, the critic must examine the musical context to show how aesthetic properties emerge from our awareness of the immanent temporality of the music itself. It is these aesthetic properties that determine the music's aesthetic individuality.

Although "supra-individuality" is a barbarous mouthful, it does serve to point out the nonactuality of the essence of a musical piece. If it helps avoid the errors of naïve realism, such as those committed by Newman, linguistic barbarity is a small price to pay. It also avoids the unsavory connotations of Langer's "illusion." Yet it remains to be seen whether this barbarity may be reduced to simple, understandable English.

The first step in the reduction is to consider the purely temporal character of the musical process. And here once again we must distinguish the properties of scientific or conceptual time from the radically empirical sense of "lived" time.

A real temporal event, for example, takes place *in time.* The moments of this temporal slice, which as a whole is an unrepeatable span of history, may be experienced as a sequence of qualities or properties unfolding before our perception. Experientially, then, time is not a sequence of "befores" and "afters." Within experience each moment may be characterized by a specific temporal *quale* that "colors" the homogeneous point-instants of universal time, making them heterogeneous, and possibly discrete,[59] moments of awareness. In reality, of course, this process of time determination is reversed, since we normally "abstract" from our lived temporality to construct the scientific concept of time as a uniform dimension of successiveness—a continuum of infinite, homogeneous point-instants. If we begin with the scientific notion, the explanation of our consciousness of time must proceed by a description of the process by which this infinite homogeneous series is "filled in" by a successive accumulation of interest-laden moments into a finite unit of felt expressiveness bound at one end—the beginning—by memory, and at the other—the end—by anticipation.

The moments of every really developing process, on the other hand, may be considered as determined by earlier phases of its development, as well as by those immediately preceding the beginning moment. This is true even of a musical performance. As distinct therefrom, the musical piece has its moments determined not solely by reference to past moments—either within or without its own temporal span—but most importantly by reference to its own future development: expectancy, frustration, further development, and fulfillment, which, considered as temporal process alone, "fill out" the temporal image, bring it to completion, and determine its "individuality." Only upon completion does the beginning become known as such, and this by memory.

The universal time continuum overlaps our psychic temporality, which motivates the appearance of a uniquely defined "supra-temporal" entity. In Ingarden's words,

> If an individual concrete tone image fills out a longer temporal division, then its own parts, which go together to fulfill the corresponding phases of this temporal division, are characterized by the appropriate temporal qualia of these phases through which the whole of the concrete tonal image becomes specifically colored, achieving thereby, in its individuality, a certain unrepeatability.[60]

Hence, where the unrepeatability of a real temporal process depends upon the ineluctable pastness of its happening, that of the nonactual musical essence is the uniqueness of its qualitative determination in which future and past are joined in the significance of the present moment.

The reason for confusing the two processes is readily apparent: aesthetic contemplation takes place in time, and usually on the occasion of a given musical performance that is itself a really developing temporal process. To make his distinction stick, Ingarden must adequately distinguish the performance from the work, and, if possible, distinguish it by a description of the process by which the aesthetic object appears on the basis of a successful performance. For the musical enthusiast, the trick is to listen to the music and to intuit the "time" of the piece—which time has little to do with the signature, pulse, measure, or even rhythm (in abstraction from melody and harmony).

Our listening is to be guided by what we hear, the tonal image as it unfolds. The individual sounds, however, form only the "psychic matter" of the image, which must be "informed" by our manner of intending the object of the image. As informed, the image becomes concrete.

This concrete image is often confused with the specific temporal quale of the physical performance even though there is not even an iconic sign relation between the sounds we hear and the qualitative "feel" of the piece. The performance is a tonal phenomenon, but the quale is not. There is, of course, a specific qualitative feel to each differing performance; and each is strictly determined by the way in which the performance affects our attending consciousness. In an act of aesthetic contemplation, however, we are forced to project beyond any particular moment, to anticipate, and hence to change, the actual psychically determined temporal coloring with reference to an as yet unresolved future. We must be trained, then, to "perceive" beyond what we have heard *(überhoren);* for only by refusing to hear the immediate present as present can we achieve the significance of the piece.

The musical composition possesses all its parts simultaneously in each moment of its structural process.[61] No real temporal process has this property. Although it may be argued, as Sartre has, that the significance of any real past event is to be gauged by its relation to some determinate future, no real temporal process exists in such a way as to be determined by a future.

By projecting the actual into the nonactual in an act of intention, and by avoiding all irrelevancies, we can attain to the temporal significance of the tonal image as a whole:

> In this way we come to the work and apprehend it in a gestalt which is totally free from the temporal colorings determined by a relationship to the concrete filling-in of our living present. This and nothing else shall be taken

> to be the meaning of the statement that the musical work is, in its import, "supra-temporal": that it is not determined, via the score, by the temporal colorings of its own separate performances.[62]

Performances, after all, are real; and the qualitative whole which is a musical work is not. It is only intended by the consciousness motivated by the successive tonal moments of the performance.

Many musical scores indicate similar "temporal colorings" in their opening phrases—otherwise variations on a theme would be impossible; yet each beginning, considered as a real process, is further modified by an as yet unreal future, which we must be trained to "hear," and the significance of an opening is supplied by the manner in which it is remembered: i.e., qualified by what has followed. That we should be "surprised" by a given resolution is only further evidence that the time of music is immanent to the musical temporal structure, and not a transcendent phenomenon at all. Music, more so than any other art, is other-worldly; but the reason for this is only that the musical context constitutes its own world, to the exclusion of all "nonmusical" values.

It would be easy, at this juncture, to criticize Ingarden's account of the aesthetic object on the grounds that it employs a "normative definition" of the term—formal consistency, internality of relations, or organic unity—to describe the very existence of every musical work. And his words could be twisted to mean that every work that is recognizably *a work* is necessarily a good work of art. The temptation is great, especially since he has eliminated all but the purely formal conditions of musical expressiveness as irrelevant to the issue. Then, describing the ideal state of affairs—maximal interpenetration of parts in the determination of the whole, he presents this normative judgment as descriptively valid.

Except for the almost insurmountable ambiguities in the notions of musical "form" and "content," this charge may have been allowed to stick. For what is the "content" of a piece of absolute music? and what, the "form" of a piece of program music? Considered as separate entities or elements within musical context, neither the content nor the form may be considered in isolation:

> The eventuality must be taken into account: no universal directive [for judgment] is to be set up; one must seek out with care the separate "formal" or "material" moments, or their contextual togetherness along with the harmonic relations growing therefrom, in order to discover the aesthetically valuable moments which lay a foundation for a determinate aesthetic worth.[63]

In other words, aesthetic judgment is a response to the contextual qualities of the musical experience; nothing considered out of context possesses an absolute significance. A dissonance may be either positive or negative, depending upon its function in context; and "sweet," erotically toned melodies, may likewise be either positively or negatively valued within context, as all "emotional qualities" may in one way or another be expressed in a purely banal fashion.[64]

The aesthetic categories that avoid the ambiguities of "content" and "form" are "surface" and "depth." Both may be applied to the musical object, even though it be described as a finite developing gestalt of a single stratum of sensuous significance. Analysis will show how.

Let us begin with the surface, or tonal substructure of the musical work.[65] Gestalt descriptions (as of 1928) had left unclear just what more was implied in the perception of a whole than "a mere summation of its parts." Ingarden stipulates a double criterion: (1) that the whole has a peculiar harmonic quality which unifies the various parts into a single characteristic nature, and (2) the whole constitutes a "pure form," which, constituting a new type of objectivity, may become the subject of further properties capable of further organization. To one trained in harmony, a triad or diminished seventh chord is heard as a unit; and this unit may be heard as part of a developing progression.

Melodic, harmonic, and rhythmic gestalten are workaday materials of the musician's craft. Add to these the effects of dynamism (as described by Pratt) and those of chromaticism (by Meyer), and we obtain a clear idea of the surface expression in music. The surface "thickens," however, with our perception of the second-order gestalt organizations. Not all of these are the "tertiary" qualities mentioned by Pratt. One of the first effects of musical dynamism is to call attention to the temporal structure of the work, which itself is not tonal at all. As explained above, it is the extrapolation beyond a given psychically colored temporal span that allows the listener to grasp the immanent qualities of the work itself, in which the expressiveness of the qualities (temporal qualia) is controlled by their manner of being interrelated. It is not a particular duration of so many successive moments, but a single pervasive quality of many funding moments whose interpenetration modifies further the initial coloring of each of them.

Since this "supra-temporal" or "quasi-temporal" object

—the epithet is defined with reference to the qualities of universal, intersubjective time—is nonactual, it has nothing to do with the particular feeling tones of either the composer's or the listener's actual state of consciousness. "Tertiary" qualities are, however, attachable to the musical object as temporally constructed. "Pretty," "soft," "harsh," are so many terms used to describe the feel of relatively simple sounds or groups of sounds; "languid," "sad," "stirring," of relatively more complex tonal images. But the significance of each of these nonacoustical phenomena (called "aesthetic value qualities" [*ästhetische Wertqualitäten*] by Ingarden) may be experienced as positive or negative within the total musical complex. They are therefore to be distinguished from the aesthetic value *per se* of the complex itself.

The reasons for maintaining the term "value" for the emotional componential moments of a larger musical work is a mystery unsolved by Ingarden himself. He maintains that when such figures appear within the work and are ultimately experienced as "positive" or "negative," the explanation of these positive or negative evaluations is exponential: within context a "soft" tone may yield a "bland" or superficial affective expression. But this raising to a higher power is not always the case; for sometimes we give the "exponential" judgment without being able to point out the component "aesthetic value qualities."[66] He is aware of the problem, and admits it; and he calls for further phenomenological analysis of both phenomena to determine which of our overall judgments are dependent on, and which are independent of, our experience of "tertiary" qualities.

The means for such an analysis is, however, sketched out in his description of the immanent temporal structure of the total tonal image. It is clear, for example, that at any moment of a real performance, only a given portion of a tonal image is presented as an acoustical phenomenon; the rest of the structure is, and must remain, nonactual. Thus, our actual temporal awareness, colored by memory and expectation, may yield a significant object only when memory has revealed the significance of the opening. What must be held in memory, however, is not the time of the performance, but the temporality of the piece.

The rate of playing the notes of the piece—its tempo—remains strictly a device for establishing dynamic significance, and hence of "coloring" our psychic temporality. The fact that we cannot be aware of all its constituent moments simultaneously indicates only that the ultimate aesthetic worth of the temporal object cannot be concretized within consciousness at any one moment of its development. Within its own temporal context, as a remembered whole, each moment is determined by its own future and past coloring.

Value judgments are another matter. Like the overall aesthetic value of any other perceptual object, the value of music is a property of the organization of its context. Whether the object of our judgment, the intuitively apprehensible perceptual organization, is based upon the funding of component affective qualities or more directly upon the sensuous structures of the tonal image,

> The true aesthetic value of the musical work is not dragged in from the outside; it is also not an abstract form which merely corresponds to an intentional value judgment; it is something intuitively graspable within the work itself, a concretely-characterizing something.[67]

The value must be there to be an object of our intuition; it is not created by our intentions; and our perception of it *is* our judgment. Any question concerning this ultimate value of a musical composition must be solved by an experience of the music in its context.

If this analysis of the musical context is valid, our awareness of a musical "surface" thickens in a dual sense. The first higher-order significance beyond the acoustical phenomena is understood in the appearance of the music's temporality—the continuously flowing, but nonactual, and finite temporal scheme. This temporal scheme is composed of the interpenetration of its several determinant moments in such a way that the total image determines the significance of each of the parts. Some of these parts may be further characterizable with reference to the tertiary qualities—or aesthetic value properties—which are themselves gestalt wholes funding into further significance. But the greatest depth of our aesthetic awareness is the value structure of the total musical context. It may be uniquely determined by the further organization of the component aesthetic value qualities, or more directly through the organization of the tonal substructures themselves. In this latter case, "nonmusical" imagery may obtrude upon the work, as it does in programmatic music. But even here there is no cause for value skepticism. A program may be used to guide the association of nonacoustical images,[68] and the affective or value qualities of these may be experienced as a nonmusical form of temporal "coloring."

Two possible interpretations may be given the admission of programmatic imagery. One is to admit the stratification of the musical object—a gambit that Ingarden declines on the ground that to do so would be to give up all claim to the autonomy of music, and hence to place the control of its significance within the consciousness of the hearer. This move, however, is a violation of the phenomenological method, which should describe and not theorize. Is musical heteronomy an unforgivable sin?

The other possibility—more in accordance with the dictates of Husserl's method—is to admit heteronomy, the consideration of nonmusical imagery, but to reduce its significance to an affective coloring of our psychic temporality. After all, if we hear a program, it forms a legitimate part of the musical experience; and we must still refer this psychic matter to a contemplation of the now more complex musical temporal scheme. All we would have done is admit a new level of "depth," but the control desired on the unbridled pursuit of visual or intellectual "content" would be guaranteed by our experience of the total expressiveness of the piece.

In short, for anything to be a valid part of a musical composition, it must be traceable to the developing tonal image and its qualitatively unique temporal scheme. And, as in any other contextual judgment, the total significance would be determined by the interrelationships between funding counters—none of which is ever significant in itself. The phenomenological problem of program music is to hear the program, not to explain away its effects.

V

In the preceding, I have been concerned with some of the theoretical difficulties arising around the conception of music as "an art of time" as opposed to, say, painting, "an art of space."

Both space and time, when used in the ordinary scientific way, may be useful for describing the physical object hanging on a wall, as well as for a given stretch of successive duration necessary to play the notes in the score of a musical composition at a determinate tempo. But if these objects are to exhibit any aesthetic properties in addition to their physicality, they must enter into the experience of a conscious appreciator, where their sensuous properties are organized in perception according to the principle of maximum significance.

Newman's musicological treatise called "Understanding Music" (1952), in particular, was found to contain the misleading presupposition of naïve realism; not that a musicologist is expected to be a metaphysician, but that any musicological reference to "time" as the organizing principle of music needs buttressing by a further analysis of the manner, precisely, in which time is thought capable of organizing experience.

The problem becomes more complicated when it is taken into account that human experience is, after all, the substance being organized through temporal forms—a substance that is more accessible to knowledge through responses of a notoriously subjective nature than through stimuli of an objective, physical nature.

The connection between musical stimulus and psychological response constituted the principal research problem of Pratt's *The Meaning of Music* (1931). He was disturbed by the work of earlier psychologists, who attempted an explanation of "an aesthetic emotion" in terms completely foreign to musical experience—either through empathy (discredited by observational research) or through the intellectualization" of the emotional response (discredited in theory).

If music is, as tradition has had it, a language of the

emotions, it does not express the real emotions felt by either the composer or his audience; but, rather, since real feelings and musical forms have congruent structures, sensitive listeners are said to organize the stimuli of music into the familiar patterns of affective response; so much so, in fact, that for them music actually sounds the way emotions feel. And if we understand the functioning of the "tertiary" or affective qualities in the organization of stimulus pattern, we can likewise see that music so organized in our attentive hearing is capable of being taken for a "symbol" of acts of the will itself. All one need do is to reduce the notion of "the will" to its associated ideas of movement and action; our kinaesthetic responses to the music will suffice to supply the meaning of the music.

Music, then, is capable of "expressing" feeling in both an autonomist's and heteronomist's sense. In the first of these, the feeling is embodied within the musical structures themselves; and in the second, the dynamic patterns of the musical image are referred to appetencies, impulses, and conative expressions of any living organism in general.

Langer (1942, 1953) was similarly critical of the traditional doctrine of musical "expression." Taking that response to music which evinces or evokes a feeling to be a symptom of the actual condition of composer or hearer, which has nothing essential to do with the affective significance of a composition, she argued for her own notion of expression as the symbolic transference of meaning.

For her, the organized stimuli of music become interpreted as a "presentational" or nondiscursive symbol, which allows one to transform the complexity of human experience into units of emotional significance through its abstractive power. The form of the symbol, as Pratt had argued, is congruent with the form of a "pattern of sentience"; and so one may be considered the "logical" projection of the other. What is expressed in a musical composition, then, is the idea or concept of a feeling, not a feeling actually felt.

Central to Langer's doctrine is the creativity of the artist. He is said to manipulate materials in such a way as to transform their physical properties into plastic elements, which function to create a "virtual" object. It is this virtual object—or illusion—which serves as presentational symbol. Thus, the composer presents an image of time, of "lived" or experienced time, as opposed to the concept of the universal or intersubjective time of history.

Critics of her theory have been quick to point out that the symbolic connection between the image of time and the actual pattern of sentience could hardly be "understood" if the feeling of this pattern were never truly experienced. For this reason, Leonard Meyer (1956) conceives of musical expressiveness as the embodiment of actual feelings within the moving structures of the developing composition.

These feelings are "signified" in the sense that they are *consequents* of an initial stimulus object, or *sign*; they are *interpreted* so as to resolve tensions set up by the tendencies of sound to achieve significance in maximally organized patterns. In this way, the triadic relation of sign, referent, and interpretant is meticulously preserved.

Once resolved, the tensions felt in music constitute a set of "determinate" meanings; in our initial response to them, they become interpreted as "hypothetical" meanings. Hypothetical meanings may, of course, have various resolutions; a tension may anticipate one manner of resolution only to have this expectancy frustrated—in which case the "affect" is only the more intense. Immediate resolutions are called "evident" meanings, and the totality of these constitutes the determinate, embodied meaning of the piece.[69]

Although Meyer's account of the embodiment of musical affect is more convincing than Langer's theory of "logical" expression, since it allows for the direct experience of the emotional tensions, it fails to give a clear picture of the effect of time in the organization of musical response. He discusses the dynamics of music in terms of tendencies, and gives a clear distinction for the related, but distinct, concepts of pulse, meter, and rhythm, but we no longer have a clear distinction between the dynamics of the music as it is heard and the dynamics of our own responses to the musical stimuli. In short, we are again faced with the inability to distinguish the properties of the stimulus from those of the response, or to distinguish between those of a performance and the musical "essence" of the piece. Pratt had already rejected the notion of "embodiment" as uselessly metaphorical on much the same grounds.

For there to be a distinction between a performance and the musical work, these objects must exhibit a different set of phenomenological properties. Performances are generally judged to be adequate or inadequate on the basis of their relative fidelity to the piece itself, and if these judgments themselves are to be found adequate, there must be some characterization of the differences between them. Roman Ingarden (1962) finds these differences in the "ontological" properties of each.

A performance is a real temporal event, which can be naïvely measured by the time required to "play the notes."

But playing the notes—or even hearing them—does not make a composition. What we perceive when we hear the notes is a developing tonal image that poses its own time structure, following the patterns within the organization of significant moments. Since every real event takes place in universal, intersubjective time, we receive no information from this fact for interpreting the temporal structures of music.

Real temporal processes have their particular moments determined by past instants. What one does now is determined by what one has done just before; but listening to music projects the hearer from the plane of the perception of the real processes of the performance into another, the imaginary, in which each moment is determined not only by what has preceded, but by what is to follow as well. Meyer called this phenomenon "anticipation," or tendency of a felt tension toward resolution, which must be "heard" just as well as what has already been played. The gestalt summation of these mutually determinant future and past moments—in that order—constitutes the individuality of the musical essence.

The affective "content" of these individual successive moments is referred to as "aesthetic value qualities," but the significance of each of the qualities, like that of the sounds proper, follows the law of gestalt organization: the significance of each is determined by the quality of the whole. Outside of pure duration of interpenetrating moments, the temporality of music is perhaps best conceived in terms of this continual affective psychic "coloring."

Time enters into the interpretation of music, consequently, in various ways. First, and most insignificantly, is the universal, intersubjective time of all natural events.

Each performance of music is a specific slice of this temporal dimension of real space-time, and is experienced as a specific "coloring" (length, measure, accent, and qualitative figure of the moving patterns of sound). These are what constitute the sensuous materials of musical perception, which reflects a similar structuring of individual organismic response within the consciousness-body of the attentive listener. In perception, the temporal qualia of the performance must be reflected in the temporal qualia of each listener's ongoing awareness, or one simply cannot be said to be hearing the music. To this point, then, we have one universal temporal dimension, and two parallel developing temporal processes, to which we may refer as the "dynamism of the performance" and that of our organismic reactions. Both are real.

The temporality of the music itself comes into existence only through the imagination; it is an intentional, non-actual, object. When an expectancy arises and is frustrated or fulfilled, the imaginative order of experience has intercut the time sequence of the performance, and the qualia of our psychic responses are thereby changed. New meanings are projected upon the evident meanings already embodied, with a consequent modification of the temporal qualia being presented in the performance and responded to in the audience. As soon as the embodied meanings become "determinate," by completion of the performance, the significance of the opening is for the first time "understood," for the significance of the opening is only prefigured in an end not yet having appeared when the initial chords are sounded. In the same way, the significance of the end is immediately felt in the manner in which it resolves some prior "hypothetical" meaning.

For this reason, it can be truly said that memory is responsible for the significance of the beginning or opening, just as expectation is responsible for the significance of the end of a musical piece. Memory and expectation constitute the terminal points of music's finite temporality, whereas the actual moments of expectation and memory specify the time span of the musical performance.

Our experience of the significance of music, then, shows temporality as the organizational structure of the musical experience, not time, with its ineluctable movement from the past into some indeterminate future, but temporality, with its organization of significance out of a movement from a determinate future to a "hypothetical" past. With respect to the infinite, homogeneous, forward-progressing sequence of "real" *time,* this psychological time—or *temporality*—is an anomaly. It is finite, heterogeneously structured, and "backward" moving. Beginning at a real moment of expectation, our experience of this temporality can be had only in the imagination—by the projection of some future; music merely projects us into a determinate future, from which all other significance devolves, including that of the opening chords. But surely this is what C. I. Lewis and Ingarden have both meant by referring to the "nonactuality" of the musical work.

But to call something "nonactual" is not to imply that its experience is any less immediate than that of an actual perceptual object. This is what Rudner failed to comprehend when he wrote his "On Semiotic Aesthetics" (1951). Either he lacked the requisite aesthetic categories, or he failed to understand that what we perceive motivates what we can imagine and that both may take place within a single temporal spread. The experience of the qualities of our own ongoing temporality has always been called "immediate." That the aesthetic object be intentional, rather than real, has nothing to do with the immediacy of our response. Unimaginative listeners are as common, perhaps, as other "nonmusical" appreciators of the musical art, and some of these are also unimaginative aestheticians.

As Ingarden intimates, there is no aesthetic problem that an adequate experience of an aesthetic object fails to solve. We must merely jettison our theories and get back to the things themselves. In any temporally organized aesthetic structure, the significance of an opening can be given only in memory when its resolving sequences have been realized, where that of an ending is already prefigured in the expectation created by the beginning measures.

It is this property, no doubt, that has led some mystical critics to refer to the "timelessness" of an aesthetic object. For any object that generates its own temporality is surely not defined by the positivistic limits of scientific time. Nor is this "timelessness" a value-making property of a work; it is only the immanent temporality of the work's generative structure.

From the visibility of painting's space to the audibility of music's thickly sensuous time, attention may be brought once again to the entire gamut of human experience. For, anything that may be formulated into words is a proper subject of poetry—from the single image of Japanese *haiku* to the ponderous epics and mock epics of heroic proportions, from songs and incantations to the brooding dramas of the Greeks and the urbane suffering of the seventeenth-century neoclassics, from explanations of the ways of God to men to—an explication of the ways of men to the gods.

For Heidegger, whose interpretation of the poetic experience follows, poetry is simultaneously a way of living and of giving name to faceless Being. His method is still phenomenological, though less systematic than the one outlined in Chapter 4, and is designed to show, by example as by precept, that thinking has as its end the "dis-covery" of truth.

While we were concerned in Chapter 1 with a description of the sensuous surface of poetry, Heidegger's analysis of the medium shows how imaginatively profound the poetic voice may be. Characteristically, he will let the poet speak for himself.

NOTES

1. William S. Newman, *Understanding Music* (New York: Harper & Bros., 1952), p. 125.
2. *Ibid.*, pp. 125–26.
3. *Ibid.*, p. 126.
4. From Eduard Hanslick, *The Beautiful in Music,* translated by Gustav Cohen, copyright © 1967, by The Liberal Arts Press, Inc., reprinted by permission of The Bobbs-Merrill Company, Inc. P. 37.
5. Cf. Edmund Husserl, *Ideas,* Gibson trans. (New York: Collier Books, 1962), pp. 99ff.
6. See Ingarden's use of this term for purposes of aesthetic theory in *Das literarische Kunstwerk* (Halle: Niemeyer Verlag, 1931), *passim,* and *Untersuchungen zur Ontologie der Kunst* (Tübingen: Niemeyer Verlag, 1962), viii, 16–23, 27–51.
7. In *Sein und Zeit* (Tübingen, Niemeyer Verlag, 1957), pp. 133ff.
8. See the Cohen trans., *The Beautiful in Music,* pp. 36–37. The editor, Morris Weitz, comments on Hanslick's "modified" heteronomy in his Introduction, p. xii.
9. Carroll C. Pratt, *The Meaning of Music* (New York and London: McGraw-Hill, 1931).

10. George Santayana, The Sense of Beauty (New York: The Modern Library, 1955), pp. 191ff.
11. Pratt, *The Meaning of Music,* pp. 177–78.
12. *Ibid.,* p. 177.
13. *Ibid.,* p. 178.
14. *Ibid.,* p. 192.
15. *Ibid.,* p. 203.
16. *Ibid.,* p. 202–3.
17. *Ibid.,* p. 204.
18. P. 92.
19. From Eduard Hanslick, *The Beautiful in Music,* translated by Gustav Cohen, copyright © 1967, by The Liberal Arts Press, Inc., reprinted by permission of The Bobbs-Merrill Company, Inc. P. 83.
20. Pratt, p. 221.
21. *Ibid.,* p. 239–40.
22. *Ibid.,* p. 244.
23. *Ibid.,* p. 245.
24. Reprinted from the *Journal of Aesthetics and Art Criticism* in Beardsley and Schueller, eds., *Aesthetic Inquiry* (Belmont, Calif.: Dickenson Publishing Co., 1967), pp. 219–28.
25. Beardsley and Schueller, p. 220.
26. *Ibid.*
27. *Ibid.,* p. 221.
28. *Ibid.,* p. 225.
29. *Ibid.,* pp. 224–25.
30. *Ibid.,* p. 228.
31. *Ibid.*
32. *Philosophy in a New Key* (New York: Penguin Books, 1948), pp. 76–79.
33. *Ibid.,* p. 195.
34. *Ibid.,* p. 184–85.
35. In the *Journal of Philosophy* 11 (1943):323.
36. In his "On Semiotic Aesthetics," reprinted from the *JAAC* (1951) in Beardsley and Schueller, p. 102.
37. See her *Feeling and Form* (New York: Scribner's Sons, 1953), pp. 31–32.
38. *Ibid.,* p. xi.
39. *Ibid.,* p. 109.
40. *Ibid.,* p. 102.
41. *Ibid.,* p. 112–13.
42. See his *Emotion and Meaning in Music* (Chicago: The University Press, 1956), p. 14.

43. *Ibid.*, p. 34.
44. *Ibid.*, p. 35.
45. *Ibid.*, p. 38.
46. *Ibid.*, p. 254.
47. *Ibid.*, p. 270.
48. *Ibid.*, p. 272.
49. *Ibid.*, p. 270.
50. Tübingen: Niemeyer, 1962.
51. Halle: Niemeyer, 1931.
52. "Das Musikwerk," pp. 33–34.
53. *Ibid.*, pp. 16–23.
54. *Ibid.*, p. 22.
55. *Ibid.*, pp. 7–11.
56. *Ibid.*, pp. 11–16.
57. *Cf. ibid.*, pp. 23–27.
58. Compare the treatment of C. I. Lewis, *An Analysis of Knowledge and Valuation* (LaSalle, Ill.: Open Court, 1946), p. 478.
59. Compare Sartre, *Being and Nothingness*, Barnes trans. (New York: Philosophical Library, 1956), pp. 107–70. The original "upsurge of consciousness" breaks the continuity of universal time by an original act of "nihilation."
60. "Das Musikwerk," p. 41:

"Wenn ein individuelles, konkretes Tongebilde einen längeren Zeitabschnitt ausfüllt, dann sind seine einzelnen Teile, welche die entsprechenden Phasen dieses Zeitabschnittes miterfüllen, durch die zugehörigen Zeit-Qualia dieser Phasen charakterisiert, wodurch das Ganze des konkreten Tongebildes spezifisch gefärbt und dadurch in seiner Individualität zu etwas Unwiederholbarem wird."

61. *Ibid.*, p. 43; we should be reminded of the "Gleichursprünglichkeit" of the three temporal ek-stases in Heidegger's treatment of temporality. See *Sein und Zeit*, pp. 404ff.
62. *Ibid.*, p. 42:

"Auf diesem Wege gelangen wir zu dem Musikwerke selbst und erfassen es in der von den auf die konkrete Ausfüllung unserer lebendigen Gegenwart relativen Zeitfärbungen ganz freien Gestalt. Dies und nicht anderes soll es bedeuten, dass das Musikwerk in seinem Gehalte 'überzeitlich' ist: Es selbst ist durch die Partitur nicht in der Zeitfärbung seiner einzelnen Ausführungen bestimmt."

63. *Ibid.*, p. 88:

"Man muss mit der Eventualität rechnen, dass überhaupt gar

keine allgemeine Direktive aufzustellen ist und dass man mühsam die einzelnen 'formalen' bzw. 'materialen' Momente bzw. ihre Zusammenstellung und die sich daraus ergebenden harmonischen Beziehungen suchen muss, um die ästhetisch valenten Momente, die einen bestimmten ästhetischen Wert begründen, zu entdecken."

64. *Ibid.*, p. 91.
65. *Ibid.*, pp. 53–62.
66. *Ibid.*, p. 95.
67. *Ibid.*, p. 98:

"Der echte ästhetische Wert des Musikwerkes wird nicht von aussen her in dasselbe hineingetragen, er ist auch nicht ein abstraktes Gebild, das bloss einem Werturteil intentional entspricht, sondern er ist etwas im Werke selbst intuitiv Fassbares, es selbst konkret Charakterisierendes."

68. See Meyer, pp. 269–72.
69. A later essay by Meyer, "Some Remarks on Value and Greatness in Music," originally appearing in the *JAAC* and later in Beardsley and Schueller's *Aesthetic Inquiry* (pp. 260–73), attempts to describe, on the basis of information theory, the value of a "great" work of art. That work which communicates the larger amount of musical information—the greater number of tonal complexity consistent with a final resolution of the initiated tendencies—is the better work. He regards here as "syntactical" all the determinate meanings of the musical piece. The sensuous and the associative-characterizing aspects of music may be thought of as "content" of the syntactical forms. Truly great music is said to convey more information of every sort than that which yields an immediate gratification of the senses, or represents a nonmusical program. Thus Debussy's *Afternoon of a Faun* is judged excellent, but Beethoven's *Ninth Symphony* as great; Mozart's C-Major Piano Sonata, whose information is conveyed only by syntax, is good, but not as good as Debussy's *Faun*.

What Meyer is looking for is an appropriate manner of explaining how contextual value judgments may be compared, once the original judgments are made on the objects of comparison. He does not imply that we make our original judgment by comparing one work to another. And his notions of "syntax" and "content" closely parallel those of "surface" and "depth."

8

POESIS AS PARABOLIC EXPRESSION: HEIDEGGER ON HOW A POEM MEANS

I

In a simulated dialogue with a visiting Japanese scholar,[1] Heidegger summarizes the direction his thought has taken from the dissertation, published in 1916, on Duns Scotus' doctrine of metaphysical categories and general theory of meaning to his own most recent speculation on the essence of language as it is exhibited in the creative activity of poets and philosophers. If, before, language was described as the "house of Being,"[2] Heidegger has more recently taken a step back along his own previous path in order to show how human beings arrive at an understanding of Being by following the paths of others—those of philosophers and poets whose *Erschlossenheit* (or openness to experience) is now described as being "underway to language."

Along the way there appeared *Sein und Zeit,* which attempted to tie hermeneutics to ontology;[3] a number of opuscula dedicated to the *Seinsfrage,* among them a letter, *Über den Humanismus,* defending his philosophy against its "vulgarization" in France by Sartre; and numerous other essays and lectures on poets and poetry.[4]

Careful scrutiny of these comings and goings will show a constant preoccupation with the problems of categorizing reality—or if one prefers, of describing the meaning of Being itself. This is the same project attempted by the late Merleau-Ponty, who died before having worked out the necessary analytical tools for its successful completion.

Heidegger's latest major work (1961) is a two-volume exegesis of Nietzsche's philosophy. It follows the plan, laid down in *Was ist das, die Philosophie?*[5], of a two-man dialogue between himself as questioning interpreter, whose task is to reveal the "unspoken" truth of the earlier philosopher, and this same philosopher, whose work is said not only to gather together the significant trends of traditional Western philosophy but to constitute its very completion.[6] Although the Nietzsche study was not published until 1961, the lectures forming its nucleus were delivered at Freiburg from 1936 to 1940, and the accompanying essays were added to the lectures from 1940 to 1946.

The themes of this philosophical corpus are already well known: the analytic of human existence (*Daseins-analytik*) as being in the world; man as a being always at a distance from his true self, but still living in the nearness of Being, that openness on the ground of which the essences of existent things are revealed; and truth as this revelation. All three have by now passed into the history of contemporary European thought.[7]

If *Sein und Zeit* laid down the method for current existential psychiatry, it also sketched out the basis for textual criticism of the written word, illustrating the method by which things themselves are grasped in the completion of the "hermeneutical circle."[8] In the later works much less emphasis is put upon the completion of an explanation, and the technical apparatus of existential analytic has all but disappeared. Since the publication of the humanism letter, man is described simply as "the shepherd of Being," whose main concern has become in our time the overriding necessity of keeping the openness of the world open.

As a philosopher, man no longer writes philosophic disquisitions of interminable length, or creates strained systems of thought that close in upon themselves; in strict Heideggerian fashion, he merely asks questions about what he does not know, but about whose existence he has an inkling from the hints and clues found in what he does know. Thinking in this way becomes an activity of opening paths, of showing a way.

The greatest danger to the freedom of man's mind stems from the very human desire to live in the comfort of a closed systematic universe, where nothing, unfortunately, can be learned. Logic, which was discourse before it became elaborated into a technique by Aristotle, has become in contemporary "logistic" a technique for elaborating techniques, and is itself currently in need of serious reformulation if it is to fulfill its claims of being final arbiter of what is, or is not, reasonable. Heidegger's *Was Heisst Denken?*[9] presents an alternative to logical logistics, along with some acute remarks concerning the relationship between thinking and creative speech (*Denken und Dichten*), a topic not without interest to contemporary aesthetics.

His main contention is familiar: both thinking and speaking are linguistic phenomena, each revealing the essence of language in its own way. Only one caution is in order; philosophers and poets do not use language, at least at their best, so much as they create it. Thus Heidegger claims,

> Language is neither only a field, nor only a means of expression; nor only a conjunction of the two taken together. Poetry writing and thinking are not processes in which man uses language in the first instance in order to be able to speak out; they are rather in themselves the original, the essential (and hence likewise the last) speech acts that language achieves through man.[10]

There can be no mistake here; the claim is that, ultimately, language comes to fulfillment through men, not men through language, and original speech acts are those in which a language-user discovers what he meant to say in the act of speaking.

To reject this statement as a "linguistic oddity," or as a violation of the logic of the concept of "language," is as futile a move as the earlier rejection of the *Seinsfrage* as meaningless. For what constitutes a workable concept of language or norms for its use is precisely the matter in question, just as the question of meaning itself was posed in Heidegger's earlier formulation of the doctrine of Being.

The only reasonable alternative to out-of-hand rejection—or acceptance—of his thesis, therefore, is to follow the argument where it leads and to accept or reject whatever does not accord with our raw experience of the phenomena described. For those who still hesitate to follow his path, the concept of a living language, one that no particular person speaks because no one has complete command of its possibilities or even a hint at its future changes, should constitute sufficient a priori grounds for the plausibility of Heidegger's reversal of the generally accepted linguistic hypothesis that man first has an understanding of what he wants to say and then formulates the "thought" in the verbal symbols of an ordinary language.

His first step is a rigorous denial of linguistic naturalism, traceable to Aristotle's *De Interpretatione*.[11] The study of language is not primarily concerned with words (*Wörter*) but with words-in-context (*Worte*). Without the addition of the context of their use, the distinction is hard for an English-speaking philosopher to grasp. However, the French have become accustomed, at least since Bergson, to distinguishing between *la parole parlée* and *la parole parlante* (compare the German *Gerede* and *Rede*), between a thought already expressed, comprehended, and repeated (by teachers of philosophy and others) and a thought that comes to be for the first time in an original expression. Such is the word that speaks. For how can it be understood that a single word with a pre-fixed dictionary meaning comes to take on a new sense, unless it be by association with other words, such that the relationship itself between the words creates the novel meaning?

What good, then, to trace meanings to phonemes or graphemes, these to the morphology of sounds or marks on paper, and these latter to raw sensuous impressions?[12] We can only see or hear "abstractly," i.e., out of context and hence without comprehension of any meaning at all, if our attention is placed upon the sensuous character of verbal counters. Words are not containers into which meaning may somehow be poured, and poems are not sounds on which meaning has become mysteriously grafted.

Modern linguistics, like any other body of scientific

knowledge, must reduce its phenomena to objects, and so remove from them their essential connection with the creative purposes of mankind. It is for this reason that Heidegger likens the search for a consistent and empirically operable metalanguage to the development of technological science:

> The scientistic philosophy which attempts to elaborate a superlanguage is understood consequentially as a metalinguistic. That sounds like metaphysics; not only does it sound so, it is so. For metalinguistics is the metaphysics of the thoroughgoing technicizing of all existent languages into a single functioning interplanetary instrument of information. Metalanguage and sputnik, metalinguistics and rocketry are the same thing.[13]

In his earlier, more directly ontological approach to the problems of philosophy, Heidegger had already condemned the Russian and American technocracies as "metaphysically the same," ruthless and rootless in the lives of the people.[14] Since the point of this condemnation is metaphysical, not political, it is of no point to engage in *ad hominem* arguments—personal or circumstantial—in rebuttal. The last citation was written in the late fifties, and could be read, if true, as confirmation of the approaching metaphysical dangers of the technocracy Heidegger perceived in the middle thirties, when the condemnation quoted above was written.[15]

To speak against the supremacy of logic, science, and technology as decision-making procedures is not necessarily to be illogical; but if a thinker chooses to be a-logical, as Heidegger does, then he must come up with a viable alternative for the interpretation of the meaning phenomena experienced in life. Although in his later works he has abandoned the method of existential analysis, Heidegger does come up with two related solutions: creative speech and thought, traditionally the respective provinces of poets and philosophers. In a word, he indicates a return to the humanities for an understanding of human speech acts.

To think is merely to regulate one's reactions according to things,[16] to what is, and to the conditions for the existence of things. In the remainder of this chapter, I shall attempt to show how Heidegger has practiced this profession as he allowed his own reactions to be guided by the creative speech of poets. If his thesis is correct, as I believe it is, the essence of poetry is to be revealed in the attention we pay to words, not as they are sounded, but *as they speak* and so adjust the hearers' responses to a novel universe. "Dichten," we are told, means to create in and through the word;[17] but to understand this contention we must harken to the poet's voice: "Voll Verdienst, doch dichterisch wohnet / Der Mensch auf dieser Erde." (Deservedly, yet poetically, man lives on this earth.)

II

Heidegger's aversion to contemporary aesthetics is rooted in the same attitude that led him to reject logistics, philosophies of science, and technology in general. Logic without ontology, science without values, techniques without knowledge are three facets of the same stone; yet another is art without creativity. His thesis is clear: each of these human activities has become a technique in an already overly technological age, and harbors an expression of contemporaneous *Seinsvergessenheit* (forgetfulness of Being), in which language, separated from its ground, and mistaking itself as autonomous, has come to be the unique domain of philosophical inquiry, itself employed as a second-level technique of meaning analysis. Logic, ethics, and aesthetics in our time have become meta-logic, meta-ethics and meta-aesthetics, more often than not at the expense of knowledge by acquaintance (or encounter)[18] with the first-order experiences we have always called "logical," "ethical," and "aesthetic."

Aesthetics, conceived on the same model as logic and ethics,[19] comes to us from the tradition as knowledge of the sensuous. Whether this field is described generally as a "transcendental aesthetic," and hence a branch of epistemology, or as the more restricted area of sensations that are pleasing in themselves, the results are the same: loss of contact with that original experience in which meanings are established, the "worlding" of an individual world.

Consider the term in its most restricted sense, as a theory of beauty. Before the liberation of art from the yoke of representation and the establishment of independent expressive fields in the exploitation of sensuous surfaces by modern artists, beauty was thought to be the traditional concern of art considered as imitation of nature. The representation of ugly objects was thought to be shocking, distasteful, or obscene. Although there were beautiful objects in nature, the beauty of the artistic construct was such as to afford controlled, intersubjective experience of the objects of aesthetic inquiry. And in describing these experiences, aestheticians were led to the philosophy of art.

A crisis occurred within the philosophy of art, however, when a change in the aims of artists necessitated a concomitant change in descriptions of their work. They began more and more to ignore nature. The same crisis occurred in epistemology when ideas, conceived as representations, were found to be inadequate as descriptions of empirical knowledge. After Berkeley and Hume, ideas could be nothing more than presentations of organized sensuous "data" arising within the subject's perceptual field. Aestheticians should have known this all along, since at least one art, music, has always been chiefly "nonobjective," i.e., a presentation constructed through the expressive values of the sensuous medium itself. It is to this condition, if Pater is right, that all arts continually aspire.

Heidegger's analysis of the origin of a work of art achieves the generality necessary to cover poetry, painting, and architecture, and so neutralizes the restraint put upon earlier aestheticians espousing the mimetic doctrine of art.[20] He describes a work of art as a tension between expressing surface (which he calls the "earth") and expressed depth ("the world"), the perception of which shows truth, as an unveiling, in the making; and on the basis of this description he rejects aesthetics conceived of as the "science of taste":

> For us today the [experience of the] beautiful is a relaxation of tensions and a tranquilizing agent; it is therefore, intended for enjoyment. Art belongs, then, to the domain of the pastry baker.[21]

This condemnation is repeated in the short history of Western aesthetics contained in *Nietzsche I*.[22] If aesthetics is the science of the beautiful, it leaves its essential object untouched.[23]

Whether the ontological analysis of art objects is sufficient to bring man back into essential contact with objects of beauty, however, remains an open, and different, question. If to remember "Being" is to forget a work of art, one would have reason to suspect that even Heidegger's subtle analysis is doomed to failure. The question will be answered in his favor only if valid aesthetic categories are derivable from Heidegger's ontological descriptions of Being as the ground of experience, as the openness of the universe to which human beings may accede in their ordinary existence.

Heidegger's Japanese student was discouraged from his attempt to apply European aesthetic categories to the experience of oriental art because of the diversity of the conditions under which Being comes to light in Western and Eastern cultures.[24] The genius of the native language should suffice for an explanation of works generated in a given culture. The assumption is that the method of the philosopher of art is no different from that of anyone else who would appreciate a work of art: he must leave himself open to the working of the work. In the case of poetry, he must enter into dialogue with the creative poet. And if the poet happens to be speaking about how a poem is made—of how words take on meaning in the universe of the poet, and hence of his society and culture—the result of the dialogue will be a philosophy of poetry. Hölderlin is such a poet, and Heidegger became a philosopher of poetry by commenting on the former's works.

III

The attempt to describe "the essence" of poetry would seem at first blush to be as impossible as that of describing "the essence" of a work of art; for no one work of art, no one poem, could possibly contain a sufficient number of characteristics to be taken as a valid paradigm for all works of art, all poems. This charge is true, as long as aestheticians continue to hold to a doctrine of essence, valid for the natural sciences, as a single general description holding for a manifold of particular exemplifications. As he had distinguished between "essential" and "inessential" essences in his treatment of works of art, Heidegger will reject the notion of "essence" as a single general description in favor of a depiction of the manner in which a thing comes to be and remains what it is. In the self-conscious awareness of his own activity, Hölderlin has given such an "essential" account of the poetic act.[25]

Heidegger assembles his description from five different sources: from a letter by Friedrich Hölderlin to his mother, describing poetry as the most innocent of all human transactions; from the prose sketch of a poem, which was never written, qualifying poetry as the most dangerous of all human possessions; and from selective passages from three poems, as follows:

(a) Viel hat erfahren der Mensch, Der Himmlischen viele genannt, Seit ein Gespräch wir sind Und hören können voneinander.	(Man has experienced much, Named many of the gods, Since we are a conversation And can hear one another.)
(b) Was bleibet aber, stiften die Dichter.	(What remains, however, is brought about by poets.)

(c) Voll Verdienst, doch dichterisch wohnet Der Mensch auf dieser Erde.	(Deservedly, yet poetically, man lives on this earth.)

The essence of poetry, it is claimed, will be revealed in the elucidation of the connection between these five pronouncements.

The difficulty in following Heidegger's "explanations" is here, as elsewhere in his later period, occasioned by his use of metaphor to enlighten metaphor; and if the essay, "Hölderlin und das Wesen der Dichtung," were not accompanied by the rest of Heidegger's philosophical corpus, it would remain as mysterious as the poetry being explained. Correlation of texts, however, does throw some light on the meanings intended. Since what is claimed to be a revelation from the successive consideration of the five "parables" (to use the only English equivalent of *Worte* in an archaic sense) can only be understood by considering their sequence, I shall follow the method indicated, collating texts where necessary.

(1) *Poetry, the most innocent of all human transactions.* The making of a poem gives all the appearances of a play with language in which the poet dreams of a world other than the one in which he lives. Freudians and idealists agree with this proposition, as do a great many other aestheticians for whom art is the expression of a human value, a value realizable but not necessarily realized in any context other than the language of the poem itself. Thus, the harmlessness of poetry, even of a beatnik's *Howl,* is owing to its lack of effect on the events of nature, and thus on the history of a people. The truth of this "parable," however, is only the barest hint: the

values realized in poetry are presented in a linguistic context, and must remain there for the poem to continue to exist. The aesthetic object is autonomous, and the words used to create a poem contain all the significance there is to it. This is the doctrine we know as "contextualism."

(2) *It follows therefore that whatever significance we find in the poem must be related to the structures of the words themselves.* How can the ability to create such an autonomous linguistic context be considered the "most dangerous of human possessions"? Innocence can be dangerous—as every parent of a college coed knows; but if the innocence of poetry stems from its lack of effect upon the lives of its practitioners, how can the writing or the reading of poetry be dangerous? An answer may be forthcoming from a consideration of the nature of the goodness of language.

Heidegger divides the question into three facets: what good is language to men? To what extent is the use of this good dangerous? And in what sense is language in general a good?

Hölderlin himself gave an answer to the first: "Darum ist der Güter Gefährlichstes, die Sprache dem Menschen gegeben . . . damit er zeuge, was er sei. . . ." Language is given to man so that he may testify to what he is. Neither plant nor animal, but like them a part of nature, living with them on the same earth, but in a hut surrounded by what is his, man has become the inheritor of the things of the earth, watching over them and thereby learning their natures as he does his own. Thus, man—on the earth in the midst of things. For Hölderlin, heartfelt concern (*Innigkeit*); for Heidegger, care (*Sorge*); and beyond this nothing describes the being of human existence. Language enables man to express his care by inventing a world of words where nothing need be lost. The word names, and naming creates what is to remain as the history of man:

> Being witness to his own belonging to the universe of existent things constitutes man's history. However, in order for history to have begun to exist man was first given language.[26]

Such is the good of language.

How then can it be dangerous? The same word that may create can destroy. Owing to this possession of language, man may stand in the openness of history, detached from the force of things. But if it can reveal the existence of existent things (*das Seiende als solches*), language can also be used to repeat the commonplace. The quasi-divine power that is creation is addressed through language to men: "Indeed, in order to be understood and thus to become the common possession of everyone, the essential word must itself become common."[27] If speech is his pride, idle talk is the fall of man into inauthenticity.[28]

What then is the nature of this good? A power used authentically or inauthentically, a tool of communication, but more: ". . . language it is that gives the first general guarantee of the possibility for man to stand in the openness of existent things. Only where there is language is there a world . . . ."[29] In short, language permits the "worlding" of a world. This world may be the context of meaning relations lived by the individual man; it may be the more restricted world of a common history, or the still more restricted universe of scientific discourse. In each case, it is the imaginative use of language that permits the "breakthrough," if one may be permitted this unscientific scientific term to describe the opening of new avenues of thought and action, new directions, and hence meanings, to the life of man.

Thus, in answer to the third and final question concerning the good of language, Heidegger concludes: "Language is a good in a more primordial sense. It stands good for, i.e., guarantees man's possibility of, becoming a historical animal."[30] Man has a history insofar as his language opens up a world, and his historicity is what makes him different from plants and lower animals.

(3) The third parable stems from an unfinished poem. In it Hölderlin continues his discourse on man as the historical animal.

> Viel hat erfahren der Mensch.
> Der Himmlischen viele genannt,

Men hear many things in their earthly experiences with one another, and freely give names to the gods; and many have been the communications since the conversation has started:

> Seit ein Gespräch wir sind
> Und hören können voneinander.

The symbols of this quatrain are anything but luminously clear.

The men could be those who harken to the poetic word, and the heavenly being, the poet himself; or the men could be the singing poets, while the heavenly one is a divinity. But which? The unnameable one of Judaism;

the heavenly Father of Christianity; Zeus, the thunder-thrower; or Apollo, the god of light, bringing images through the darkness of Dionysus' drunkenness? All or none, for each is only itself an image for the ground of all that is.[31] The conversation that we are[32] links all men, poets or otherwise, with the highest of ideals, with the openness of the universe, which is the ground of all distinctively human experience.

Thus, in two pages of commentary on Hölderlin's poetry, Heidegger recalls the essential message of *Sein und Zeit*. For to be in a conversation, two minds must consider the same content. Each selects a single event from the flux of his worlding world, thus producing a single shareable world in which something comes to exist and remains as it is. Time, in its original three dimensions, breaks through the whirling confusion. What is, is seen for the first time as what has become, hence as what was, viewed on the horizon of what is to come.

The moment of awareness englobes all three of these dimensions simultaneously, as Being communicates itself to man:

> . . . the presence of the gods and the appearance of the world are not primarily a result of the occurrence of language; they are rather simultaneous with its occurrence.[33]

But to be able to speak, i.e., to communicate, man must be able to hear; and what he hears or fails to hear is what is to be said. In the dialogue that men are, Being is underway to language.[34] The explanation of this statement is the ultimate fruit of Heidegger's later philosophy, and must be viewed as a conclusion of the premises now being laid down.

(4) The fourth parable describes the result of the poetic dialogue: *Was bleibet aber, stiften die Dichter.* (What remains, however, is brought about by poets.) Once again the explanation is metaphysical. And here Heidegger recalls his earlier "Der Ursprung des Kunstwerkes."[35] To remain is the same as to have an essence (*wesan, wesen*). The ground of beings comes to light in essences, through the naming power of the poetic word:

> What the universe of existent things carries within itself, what it governs, must be brought into the open. Being itself must be opened up, so that beings may appear.[36]

The essence mediates the ontic and the ontological, but it must be made to appear. Grounded in Being, it must be revealed in human experience. This is the force of "stiften," a magical German word used by Heidegger in all its meanings at once; the poet, he claims, *establishes a foundation* for meaning, calling attention to the one noteworthy thing or event, which becomes *placed* in history as a *free gift* of man to men.[37] Meanings so created may then pass into the common language.

(5) The last parable summarizes the estate of man: *Voll Verdienst, doch dichterisch, wohnet / Der Mensch auf dieser Erde.* (Deservedly, yet poetically, man lives on this earth.) So convinced was Heidegger of the force of this poetic statement that he dedicated an entire lecture to its message.[38] I shall avail myself here of the exegete's privilege of collating texts.

First, the parable as the concluding step in the revelation of the essence of poetry. If it is true, as was explained in *Sein und Zeit,* that the being of human existence is care and that the existential explication of man's being (*Da-*

sein) in the world contains three basic human structural principles—affectivity, understanding, and discourse, Hölderlin has already described this existence. Man exists in a dialogue between Being, the ground of all existence, and himself as watchful caretaker. The poet creates by naming things, and so bequeathes to his fellow man the gift of novel meaning.

The inquiring mind of the poet comes to reside in that area of human experience which is neither purely ontic (of things on or at hand) nor purely ontological (of Being itself), but ontic-ontological (of things understood on the ground of their being, the pre-existent meaning complexes, or worlds, already available in the poet's past culture). Being, it will be recalled, is historical. Giving a name to the gods and a new twist to the history of mankind by opening and closing an epoch, the poet achieves the highest development of man: to be a creator.

Whatever else he may do, by force of will or dint of effort, is earned (*Voll Verdienst*); yet to achieve the fullest of his potentiality he must build his abode.[39] He can do so only on this earth, which is to say under the heavens (as horizon of the earth)—before the gods, and with his fellow men.

Although in his *L'Existentialisme est un humanisme*[40] Sartre had classed Heidegger with the atheistic school of existentialists, Heidegger has never given reason to doubt his theism, and has always rejected the term "existentialism" as a rubric for his philosophy. His "Gott ist, aber er existiert nicht"[41] could be mistaken for a proclamation of atheism only by one who failed to understand the difference intended in the two verbs, *sein* and *existieren*. And Heidegger himself has never confused them, employing the latter for the "ec-static" character of man's being, standing as it were outside itself, i.e., transcending itself toward its own possibilities. God has no possibilities, being pure act, and so does not "exist." But there is Being (*Es gibt Sein,* or *Es* (*Sein*) *gibt*), which we know as the Ground of all experience. As the groundless ground of all experience, Being expresses the metaphysical nature of God.[42]

Heidegger composed the letter on humanism and *Identity and Difference* to set the matter straight. And his excursus on Nietzsche's parable "Gott ist tot"[43] gives a clue for an interpretation of Hölderlin's onto-theo-logical poetry. God no longer makes a difference in the lives and the culture of people, and so, for all purposes, is dead. Hölderlin experienced a similar disenchantment with his early pietistic theological training and turned to the classical religion of the Greeks for clarification of his religious experience. His poetry in this sense pronounces the presence of the gods.

It is for this reason that Heidegger can proclaim: "We now understand poetry as the creative naming of the gods and of the essence of things."[44] And as if to give the conclusive hint that his metaphysics, like Hölderlin's poetry, is an onto-theo-logical doctrine, he repeats:

> Poetry is *the creative naming of Being* and of the essence of all things—not any random spoken word, but that through which everything we later come to discuss and negotiate over comes into the open for the first time.[45] (Italics mine.)

Living in the presence of the gods, however, is a dangerous business: Zeus's lightning flashes and Apollo's light-bringing images can be blinding. Hölderlin's madness is proof enough that poetry is a very dangerous occupation,[46] even though its creations must remain within the context of the dialogue men are, and thus appear as innocent word games. In the innocence of playing with words, in the original language game, poets must run the risk of losing their own mental stability. Too near the gods, yet among men, as voice of the people, there lives the poet, harkening to the call to authenticity.[47] Conscience of the people, and their only link to certainty, he stands between men and the gods.

The poetic symbols of a self-conscious poet translated into the metaphysical thought-structures of a self-conscious philosopher may be said to fail in communication, unless the ontological references are made applicable to the ontic experiences of ordinary human beings. But this is not extraordinarily difficult, if one brings to bear the necessary imaginative effort.

Heidegger's call for the remembrance of Being was poetically expressed in Hölderlin's "Andenken,"[48] where the poetic act is described as a passage, from home abroad to foreign lands and back home again—from the familiarity of our ontic experiences to the ontological and back to our everyday concern with things, now at last understood. According to Heidegger, "The historicity of history takes its essence from the return to one's own, which can only be at first a voyage out into foreign places."[49]

Nothing is so apparent as a stranger in a foreign land, but without this voyage there can be no homecoming; without a step out of the ordinary round of human experience, no true appreciation of what that experience promises, a glimpse into the source of things:

> But the actual world to which we have been accustomed by everyday experience does not permit the openness to

> remain as it is. Only the unusual can throw any light on the openness of Being, and this only in so far as it takes its hidden measure in the once-in-a-while appearance of simple things, whereby the actuality of the actual, habitual world itself becomes hidden.[50]

To live in the realm of the unusual, where the openness to novelty is the rule, is to incur the risk of madness in which there are no rules.

But without this risk there is no discovery, and the person or the society that fails to uncover the grounds of its existence is doomed to go under for other reasons. To be fully human is to be able to cope with the crises provoked in our pre-formed opinions and beliefs. The task of the poet is always to "épater le bourgeois"; of the scientist, to break through the limitations of previous knowledge codified in scientific discourse. Such, if Heidegger is right, is the promise of the imaginative life: the enrichment of culture, by the foundation of an epoch. The question of who is madder, the creative thinker or smug scientist, only history itself will decide.

But since madness is contemporaneously described as an inability to adapt oneself to the "real" world, and the real world is always in question in truly creative thought, the poet or the scientist who would break through cannot help appearing mad. It is a question of where, and how, he lives. The ontic madness of creative thinkers—poets or philosophers, a Hölderlin or a Nietzsche—has an ontological ground; and to him who understands, nothing is clearer, however unreasonable it may seem. Heidegger's philosophical dialogue with the poets of his culture shows that he has understood. His call to a serious reconsideration of the role of creativity is indeed a reason to take his work seriously.[51]

His life and his work, however, do not encourage serious philosophical attention. He could mistake the foundation of the German National Socialistic state as a creative act of statesmanship;[52] his own language comes closer and closer to pure poetry, the symbolic transformation of reality into poetic images, as in "Bauen Wohnen Denken," where human experience becomes the "mirroring of the square": each "thing" showing the cross-section of the four poetic symbols—earth and heaven, the divine and the human, the latter expressed in Hölderlin's term, *die Sterblichen,* which recalls Heidegger's earlier description of human existence as *Sein zum Tode.*

Nonetheless, to refuse his explanations as metaphorical is to give up the game. For when the question of the reality of the "real world" is posed, metaphor is the only language we have. The universality of scientific discourse must go by the board (*pace,* Mr. Snow), with the question of the reality it purportedly describes. Moreover, ontology itself must be rethought. And in *Zur Seinsfrage* the word for Being itself comes to be "~~Sein~~," to denote the free-floating locus of the "mirroring of the square."[53] By now the experiential grounds for this move are apparent: breakthroughs do occur. Scientists change their methods and procedures to accommodate and exploit the fertility of a new concept; writers do succeed in changing the common man's language. Both may go mad, and for no other reason than their insistence upon living in the openness of the universe: "Dichterisch wohnet / Der Mensch auf dieser Erde." (Poetically man lives on the earth.)

If there is a lesson to be learned in this "madness," it is that language itself must enter into question—as it has in philosophical circles, at least on one side of the Atlantic.[54] In the other departments of the humanities, it has always been in question on both sides. That this question be posed in the area of the humanities rather than in that of the technologically developed sciences can be considered a weakness only by those for whom "philosophy" is equivalent to "philosophy of science." But this is an uncritical attitude, if not an outright prejudice, that has retarded long enough the progress of the philosophy of art.

IV

The preceding section is based upon Heidegger's lecture on Hölderlin's conception of the poetic act delivered at Rome in 1936. Its five-point description of "the essence" of poetry was later to be tested in two further philosophical-poetical dialogues between Heidegger and the poet he interprets. The one is again with Hölderlin, and the other with Rilke. Both are interesting, not only for the interpretation of the poetry given, but for the illustration of Heidegger's hermeneutical method.

"Wozu Dichter?" was composed to commemorate the twentieth anniversary of Rilke's death. The title of the piece is taken from a poem of Hölderlin, and the aim of the essay is the judgment of Rilke's status as poet in needful times. He died in 1926, and the commemorative essay was read before a limited group in 1946.[55] As in the case of Hölderlin, the needfulness of the times is described in terms of the disappearance of the gods, and the resulting lack of permanency in the values of human beings.[56]

Poetry, it is claimed, fills in the lack, and points the way toward an experience of the holy.

This theme is sharply put in the song, taken from Rilke's *Sonnets to Orpheus:*

Wandelt sich rasch auch die Welt
wie Wolkengestalten,
alles Vollendete fällt
heim zum Uralten.

Über dem Wandel und Gang
weiter und freier
währt noch dein Vor-Gesang,
Gott mit der Leier.

Nicht sind die Leiden erkannt,
nicht ist die Liebe gelernt,
und was im Tod uns entfernt,

ist nicht entschleiert.
Einzig das Lied überm Land
heiligt und feiert.

[Translation: If, like the forms of clouds, the world too changes itself quickly, everything that has completed its round comes back to the oldest of the old.

Over the noise of the coming and going, your primordial song, O God with the lyre, can be heard.

Our suffering we fail to recognize, love we have not learned; and it is not unveiled to us what separates us in death. Only your song over the land hallows and consecrates.]

The effect of these lines on a people having experienced the destruction of its cities, the loss of its national identity along with a good proportion of its population, and facing the prospect of rebuilding from "the abyss up," obviously would be great; and most of the audience would not be psychologically prepared by the conviction that the war in the first place was to a large extent Germany's own doing. On this point at least, non-German historians are agreed.

Moreover, it would be snide of his interpreter to point out—if it would also be unperceptive of him to overlook—the fact that Heidegger had already described the establishment of a new State by direct political action in the same terms as the creativity of poetry and "sacrifice."[57] With the third German Reich, the "creativity" of a group of thugs began an epoch that ended in an entire nation's sacrificing itself—not for a lost cause, but for a chance to live closer to that openness of the universe which is Being itself. And we non-Germans can hardly forget that this Reich was to last a thousand years!

Since poetry is one activity admitted to be creative by Germans and non-Germans alike, it does not run the risk of misinterpretation from partisan motives. The Rilke essay shows an intelligent reader of poetry confirming a hermeneutical hypothesis in the context of Rilke's creative work. That this hypothesis stemmed from a reading of Hölderlin is no accident, for Heidegger had claimed to glean the essence of poetry from Hölderlin's philosophical poetry, and Rilke was found to have lived through the same poetic experience. The "proof" is contained in Heidegger's brilliant analyses of Rilke's poetic symbols.

It is likewise no accident that a creative philosopher is driven to the study of poetry in a time of crisis, since the pursuit of poetry appears to him as the most innocent of all human transactions, capable in the end of producing that same equanimity[58] which is the fruit of viewing the development of things as the destiny of Being *(Geschick des Seins)*. What remains throughout the fateful turns of history, we have been told, has been created by poets, so it is not amiss to search out the more permanent human values in a poetic context. In the warp and woof of poetic symbols, man is presented with a lasting image of himself, the creator. If we choose to pursue this matter in Hölderlin's poetry, rather than Rilke's, the reason is primarily the economy to be gained thereby. The source is Heidegger's "'. . . dichterisch wohnet der Mensch . . . ,'"[59] the lecture referred to in parable form above, delivered in 1951, when some of the passions fomented by the losing of a cause had passed into partial forgetfulness.

The method is everywhere the same. Heidegger poses a question—as always, a question of meaning—and then seeks an answer by analyzing the context that had occasioned the question in the first place. What does it mean to claim that the human habitation of the earth is grounded in creative speech? Insofar as creative speech is equated with poetry, poetry with word construction, and word construction with the play of the imagination, Hölderlin's fifth parable harbors a paradox: the earnestness of toil *(Voll Verdienst)* at least on the surface of things seems to contradict the innocence of verbal play. And the poet seems not unaware of this apparent contradiction, for he employs "doch" (yet) to reinforce the awareness of this paradox. "Voll Verdienst, doch dichterisch wohnet/Der Mensch auf dieser Erde." The parable returns like a leitmotif in Heidegger's thinking.

If this paradox is to be reduced, moreover, the interpreter must give a preliminary statement of its probable meaning, and then reinterpret the entire context in which it first occurred to test the workability of the suggested meaning. Accordingly, what follows will be an examination of the suggested meaning, and a subsequent test of its workability in context.

The essential connection between the earnestness of toil is found in the etymology of "bauen," not only the apparent "to build," but a more primitive "to preserve" *(hegen)* and "to care for" *(pflegen)*, whence the German derives its name for a peasant or farmer, "Bauer," occupied originally with the preparation of his field *(Acker bauen)* and with the cultivation of its harvest. Ultimately the farmer's care-filled toil must produce the buildings necessary to preserve both the fruit of his earlier labors and an abode in which to live *(wohnen)*. And where a man lives, there he is at home.

In an earlier essay, *bauen* is linked to the old high German *buan*:

> . . . bauen, buan, bhu, beo are our word "bin" in the versions: ich bin, I am, du bist, you are, the imperative form bis, be. What then does "ich bin" mean? The old word bauen, to which the "bin" belongs answers: "ich bin", "du bist" mean: I dwell, you dwell.[60]

The purpose of the essay from which this quotation is taken was to show the essential connections between the ordinary concepts of building, living, and being as these activities are exemplified in human thought (*Denken*). True to his conviction that thinking and poetizing are alike, both human activities of harkening to the saga of Being (*die Sage des Seins*), but each in its own way, Heidegger adopts this hypothesis—gained from his own attention to the consoling voice of Being—to interpret the meaning of Hölderlin's fifth parable. He states it succinctly, "Poetizing, as a letting dwell, is a kind of building."[61]

How then is the double exigency of thought—to interpret human existence as dwelling (*Wohnen*) and poetry as the creation of a living space (*Wohnenlassen*)—to be accomplished? How indeed, other than by listening to what is said by the language itself? In the first instance, it is language that speaks; man listens, and by listening adjusts himself to what is being said: "Man speaks first and only insofar as he responds to language, by listening to its appeal."[62] It is impossible, of course, to translate the word-play between "sprechen" and "entsprechen" contained in this Heideggerian parable, unless our "to speak" is rendered as "to respond."

But the author has presented another essay in explanation of the reversal of the roles of language and speakers in his "Die Sprache,"[63] containing a metaphysical—or what is the same—a phenomenological, linguistic analysis of a poem by Georg Trakl. Language speaks insofar as it names i.e., calls things to the attention of the self-adjusting hearer. And poets learn what they had intended to say only by attending to the expressive contexts they have created in their literary "response." This is, of course, to say no more and no less than that whatever meaning there is to be found in human expression must be found in context. Jurists are already familiar with this inversion, since they distinguish between the "intent of the law" as it is opposed to "the intent of the lawmakers." Why then should humanists hesitate to make the same distinction?

The meaning of human living is to be found in the context in which it has been expressed: not in caring for and preserving nature's harvest, and not in building a physical abode, but *dichterisch,* in the creative use of language. The location of the human abode, on this earth (*auf dieser Erde*), moreover, is no redundancy,[64] since its explicit statement is equivalent to a denial of the usual assumption that poems exist in the imaginations of poets alone. If it is to be a work of art, a poem must like other works of art reveal the essence of truth itself. According to Heidegger, this poem does more: it exhibits the manner in which truth comes to be a question for man at all; not truth about things, but truth about truth itself. But this had already been stated, when Heidegger maintained that Hölderlin's poetry was philosophical in an essential (ontological) sense.

V

The final test of an interpretive hypothesis being its application to the original context from which it was taken, the final step in our demonstration of Heidegger's thesis will be a rereading of the source from which Hölderlin's fifth parable was derived. Lines 24 to 38 of the poem beginning "In lieblicher Bläue blühet mit dem metallenen Dache der Kirchturm . . ." read as follows:

Darf, wenn lauter Mühe das Leben, ein Mensch
Aufschauen und sagen: so
Will ich auch seyn? Ja. So lange die Freundlichkeit noch
Am Herzen, die Reine, dauert, misset
Nicht unglücklich der Mensch sich
Mit der Gottheit. Ist unbekannt Gott?
Ist er offenbar wie der Himmel? Dieses
Glaub' ich eher. Des Menschen Maass ist's.
Voll Verdienst, doch dichterisch, wohnet

Der Mensch auf dieser Erde. Doch reiner
Ist nicht der Schatten der Nacht mit den Sternen,
Wenn ich so sagen könnte, als
Der Mensch, der heisset ein Bild der Gottheit.
Giebt es auf Erden ein Maass? Es giebt
Keines.

[Translation: Is it permitted, since life is nothing but trouble, for man to look up and say, "I too will be so?" Yes; as long as friendliness remains pure and heartfelt, man measures his existence not infelicitously against the divine. Is God unknown? Or is He revealed like the heavens? This latter I rather believe; it is man's measure. Man lives on this earth in full desert, yet poetically. Nonetheless, the shadow of the night with its stars (if I may say so), is not purer than man, who is called an image of godliness. Is there a measure on earth? There is none.]

These lines pose the ontological question, Where is man to find his measure, he who once was vaunted as the measure of all things? In the fruit of his toil? By toil he truly lives (*Voll Verdienst*), and as laborer is worthy of his hire. But is this fatigue all a man has to look forward to? Is it permitted for him to look up to where the stars shine and ask, Can my life be so, a fulguration of the divine?

The answer follows immediately: yes, so long as "die Freundlichkeit" is kept pure and sincere man can measure his being by reference to the scale of the divine. "Friendliness" is the usual translation of "Freundlichkeit," but is a strained rendering of Hölderlin's meaning, which has the felicitous effect of humanizing the relations between man and the gods. Heidegger points out that the poet had used the word to translate Sophocles' "charis," usually set into German by "Huld," our "favor" or "grace."

The friendliness intended, then, is the grace of the gods, the friendly gift of favor that man may receive, if only, and only insofar as, he lets himself open to its working. The poet must respond. The grace is referred to as "pure" (*die Reine*), i.e., unmixed with something it is not, such as human pride or prejudice. To reinterpret the answer to the ontological question, then, it is permitted for man to measure his existence by reference to the light from above, as long as he does nothing to distort that light. Even light-bearing poets must, in order to bring their images to clarity, collaborate with the source of all light.

But the light implies darkness. The stars are visible only on a background of the invisible. And too much light blinds, and in reflection distorts the nature of things—as Lucifer, the light-bearer, came to know through the pride before his fall into Hell, where he rules as the Prince of Darkness. How then can one fail to wonder, Is God forever unknown? The Ground of our being forever forgotten, known, as St. Thomas claimed, only through His effects, those beings we encounter? But even so, His existence is manifest, like the heavens. The poet confesses to his faith in the divine epiphany, and names it the measure and truth of man's existence. Man may return to the Ground of Being through his encounter with beings, if only he can be led to understand the distinction,[65] the difference Heidegger calls ontological.

God's revelation in things, in the shadows even of the night with its stars, opens a world for man to inhabit, "dichterisch." And if man ever attains to the fullness of his essence, to live by creating on this earth, he himself has been correctly called an image of God, purer perhaps than the stars themselves.

We are in a position now to understand the structural function of Hölderlin's parable: man lives on earth, but can find no measure, no guide for his existence there. The work he engages in produces only fatigue; but as he looks up, measuring the distance between himself and the heavens, he finds what is lacking on earth—a measure. And in poetry, as in life, the heavenly must be made to appear.

Heidegger refers to the distance between the earth on which poets live and the heavens toward which they aspire as the "dimension,"[66] which he purposely leaves unnamed. That dimension it is which allows man to surpass his earth-bound existence:

> Man's dwelling depends on an upward-looking measurement taking of the dimension, in which heaven belongs just as well as the earth.[67]

Man's life, in a word, is lived between heaven and earth.

Yet for the dimension of this "between" to be grasped, there must be consciousness of the essential measure; and poetry, an act of creative language in which the word becomes flesh, is the taking of this measure (*Massnahme*):

> In poetizing there occurs the taking of measure. Poetizing is the taking-measure, understood in the strict sense of the word, by which man first receives the measure for the scope of his essential being.[68]

It is the taking of this measure that allows action coordinated to an end (*Mass-nahme*), i.e., to take measures to any other end.

Two mysteries, however, remain to be cleared up: the nature of the gods, and the manner in which poetry, like the heavens, may be said to reveal their existence. And here, as before, the philosopher lets his thoughts be guided by the poetic image.

The Biblical divinity proclaimed Himself as that which is (I am who am); as such, He remains qualitatively unknown. Whence the poet's question, Is God unknown? It is not given to men to know what God is, even if His existence is revealed in things. What then of the measure? Answer: "The measure consists in the way in which the God who remains unknown is manifest as such in the heavens."[69] Pursuing this visual metaphor further, Heidegger continues: God's appearance through the heavens consists in an uncovering (*Enthüllen*), which allows the concealed truth to be seen, not by forcing it out of its concealment (in context), but by preserving the very context which is its concealment.[70] "The unknown God appears as the Unknown by way of the manifestness of the heavens. This appearing is the measure against which man measures himself."[71] The most imperceptive reader may recognize here Heidegger's onto-theo-logical concept of Being as "die Lichtung des Da," the light pervading the poet's "worlding" world.

The remaining mystery is the nature of poetry itself. But Hölderlin's image is clear. Poetry is a way of life: *poesis*, a doing, making, building; and Heidegger capitalizes on the point: "We attain to dwelling, so it seems, only by means of building."[72] "Bauen" with its marvelous cluster of meanings, such is poetry: cultivating, caring for, preserving nature's harvest; building an abode; constructing a universe in which to move, to live, and to have one's being.

The poet, however, must build with words; and in doing so, constructs a universe of unique significance: *ut natura,* revealing the essence of man and the nature of things entrusted to his care, not by describing or imitating the wonders of Nature, but by allowing the truth to appear; thus

> the poet does not describe, if he is a poet, the mere appearing of the heaven and earth. The poet calls into the aspects of heaven that which, in its self-disclosing, precisely causes the self-concealing to appear, and indeed to appear *as* the self-concealing.[73]

But when it does, there occurs that unveiling of an essence, the meaning of existent things (*das Seiende als solches*), which opens the way to an understanding of the meaning of Being itself, as the openness of the universe on the ground of which all things appear. It is this way that poetry is the taking—better, the making—of a measure. It opens a universe in which man may live.

A final caution is nonetheless in order. Heidegger underlines the condition mentioned by Hölderlin in lines 26 and 27 of the poem cited above. As long as the "friendliness" of the gods is taken to heart it is permitted to man to measure his existence against his knowledge of the divine. The poets can speak only insofar as they have heard, and thereby adjusted themselves to the gestures (*Winke*) of the gods. This means only that they must be guided by what is (*das Sein*), as indicating what is to be said (*das Zusagende*).

In his usual dithyrambic fashion Heidegger expresses

this thought, in a later study on the essence of language, simply as "the essence of language: the language of essence."[74] Language speaks in showing the essence of things, and so truth is "underway to language," where poets and philosophers live together in the nearness to Being.

VI

As the foregoing indicates, any serious criticism of Heidegger's ontological poetics must follow a tortuous path. It moves from his analysis of the essence of an artwork in "Der Ursprung des Kunstwerkes," through the description of creative speech in his commentaries on Hölderlin's poetry, to the summary of his position on the essence of language itself in *Unterwegs zur Sprache.*

In the first of these sources we find the working of a work of art described in terms of a tension between "earth" (sensuous surface) and "world" (imaginative depth). We have followed Heidegger's steps along the path in order to examine his claim to have brought the perceptive and imaginative aspects of human experience into a significant theoretical relationship, as each occurs simultaneously within an experience of a poem as an autonomous work of art. We are now in a position to evaluate this claim.

The first criticism brought to bear is perhaps the easiest to fend off. It is said that any criticism of poetry in general is doomed to failure; and so it is, if by the essence of poetry is meant a single description valid for all poems —past, present, and future. Such an essence would be constituted by a list of all the conditions necessary and sufficient for the recognition of a successful poem. Heidegger avoids this criticism by not attempting to give any such description. Instead, he searches for a revelation of the structures of an experience going together to make up an act of creative expression. Realizing that his own word on the matter will not be accepted on authority, he intensifies his search within the limited area created in the first place by a successful poet whose work consists to a large extent in a description of the act of writing poetry.

But this procedure allows a second criticism. The way in which Hölderlin describes his own creative processes may very well not fit the work of other poets, especially those not concerned with the description of poetizing, but with writing poetry. Against this charge Heidegger has two defenses.

In the first place, it is not true that he has limited himself to Hölderlin's self-conscious writing. An essay entitled "Die Sprache"[75] is built around a poem by Georg Trakl, *Ein Winterabend,* a simple poetic description in three stanzas of a winter's evening. Heidegger analyzes the poetic images for their human significance, showing how each of the quatrains presents an insight into the metaphysical structure of the universe: a thing, a world, and their belonging one to the other. Other poets he had commented on show a wide range of subject matters: Stefan George, R. M. Rilke, Gottfried Benn, C. F. Meyer, Johann Peter Hebel. Even the sermons of Abraham a Santa Clara, seventeenth-century German Augustinian monk, were not without interest for one seeking the secrets of linguistic creation.

His second defense is almost as simple as the foregoing. Nothing prevents one writer's presenting a description of the process of creation that is to be found exemplified in the writings of others. It suffices that the description be true, and that the other writers be masters of their craft. Moreover, since Heidegger measures the success of a work of art on its capacity to reveal the truth, the same test is being applied to Hölderlin as to the other poets, each independently of the other. What lies in question here is poetry's claim, as an art form, to reveal truth.

But "truth" is an ambiguous term, even in the writings of Heidegger. So runs the third criticism. The term may refer to the truth of beings or to the truth of Being. The distinction covers roughly that made above between poets writing about writing and others simply writing poems.

Those critics who claim that Heidegger's aim in the analysis of poetry—or human experience, for that matter—is solely to expose the meaning of Being, forget his earlier explanations of the relatedness between ontics and ontology: what is ontically the nearest is ontologically the farthest away from human accessibility.[76] We would have no ontology if there were no beings to encounter. In an aesthetic context this means that there could be no ontological analysis of poems without a prior explanation of the basic meanings of poetic images.

Moreover, to limit the explanations of poems to the first-level meanings of the poetic symbols is unnecessarily to restrict the human imagination, and, it may be added, is to take away one of the means for gauging the ultimate significance of poetic descriptions. Only a reading of the poetic text, with or without the suggested ontological hypothesis, will enable a third person to judge whether the original critic was justified in his interpretation.

The fact that Hölderlin had such a tremendous influence on the thinking of Heidegger himself is certainly beside the point. The extent of this influence is yet to be fully measured. But when Heidegger renounced his earlier hermeneutical method, it was to adopt this view of the world as a play of four forces: the human (*die Sterblichen*), the divine (*die Göttlichen*), earth (*die Erde*), and heaven (*der Himmel*).[77]

Hölderlin and Rilke were found to be "poets in needful times" in that each pictured a world from which the gods had flown, and wrote poetry showing a way back to a conception of the divine, back to an understanding of the Ground of human experience. Again in aesthetic terms, this means that each had produced poetry revealing ontological truth. Far from falsifying the account of poetry, Heidegger's ontological interest contributes to the understanding of the limits to which the human imagination may soar. Poets whose symbols are restricted to ontic descriptions are not lesser creators for their preoccupation with first-order significance. They too open a way to reflective thought.

The only lasting criticism, therefore, is the one that would invalidate any theoretical claim, that is false if it fails to accord with our everyday experiences—here, those of poems—and true, or acceptable, if it does. Heidegger's initial account of the working of works of art as a tension (*Streit*) between expressing surface and expressed depth will be accepted here as a workable standard by which to judge his later claims as to the essence of creative speech. Granted that the one is the earth and the other the world, what sense does it make to say that the earth (sensuous surface) of the poem is "inessential" to the creative act?[78]

One sense is obvious. Word sounds without meanings are not poems; nor are marks on paper. Yet, it is one thing to inveigh against the overly technical explanations of versification: rising and falling meters, consonance and assonance, internal and end-stopped rhymes, and the like; still another to say that a poem could exist without being expressed in some "earthly" fashion. This interpretation of an aesthetic surface is the strictest nonsense. We experience poems as artistic constructs of sound and sense. Some kind of sensuous surface, then, is a necessary but not a sufficient condition for poetic communication.

When in the same article, however, Heidegger sketches out the metaphysical structures of the imaginative content of the poem not as the parameters of space and time, which considered as a whole are not moved, but as "das Gegen-einander-über," the setting of one thing over and against the other in such a way as to open a possible experience of their nearness (*Nähe*), he compounds the problem; for, in his account, the mirroring of the four corners of the "world" is soundless:

> The saga [myth], as path opener to the four regions of the world, gathers all things together in the proximity of their relatedness over and against one another; and indeed without a sound: as silently as time comes to fruition, and space makes place—as silently as the play of time through space plays itself out.[79]

Language from the point of view of the sounding word (*das Sprechen*) is not the same as from that of what the words give sound to (*die Sage*). The one is composed of sounds (*Lauten*); the other, of silence (*das Geläut der Stille*).

The theoretical trick is to show how sounds and silences constitute the significance of a poem. They do so, if Heidegger is right, by setting up a tension in the experience of a skilled reader. And the only thing that can produce a tension with a sound is another sound—or a silence.

The "sound of silence" is a paradox only to someone who has missed one of the basic phenomena of music. Sounds, like any other perceptible phenomenon, are perceived on a background. And the background to an individual sound is a relatively unsonorous field of aural perception. Musical pauses are heard when the background comes to the fore, and they can be as eloquent as the loudest of chords. Effective orators use the same device, pausing when necessary to reinforce significance or merely to allow it to resonate in outgoing waves. Some sleepers accustomed to the rhythmical beat of their professor's voice are shocked into attention when he pauses to reinforce his point; other would-be sleepers are kept awake by the silence of a stopped clock.

According to Heidegger, language presents the same phenomenon:

> We call the soundless, summoning, collecting together which constitutes the saga (myth), and which as such opens the paths into the world-relation, "the sounding of silence." It is the language of the essence.[80]

The poetic word points in silence—to the presence of the essence of a thing, but it can do so only because the poet has spoken. In the words of an American critic, poetic language is gesture;[81] and we may add, a significance-laden vocal gesture.

Thus, whether or not the universe as we experience it is correctly described as the intersection of the four regions of the "world" in play, Heidegger's account of poetry describes a set of conditions under which it is possible to experience the sensuous and the imaginative aspects of a poem in a uniquely defined universe—that of sound (and silence), which must be experienced to be understood.

The greatest weakness in the written accounts of his thoughts is the seeming precedence he gives to the "sense" dimension of a sound-sense artistic medium. This impression could easily be changed, however, in the oral delivery of the lectures, where the poems cited would be fully performed, i.e., inflected as the sense indicates. The same American critic of poetry cited above refers to the "per-formance" of a poem as the completion of the poetic gesture.

To complete this account and to illustrate Heidegger's claim that poets and philosophers inhabit the same universe, language as the temple of Being, we may close this chapter with a presentation of a typically Heideggerian linguistic gesture.

In *Der Satz vom Grund* the same sentence was given a second meaning merely by emphasizing different words: when we read "*Nichts* ist *ohne* Grund" we have Leibnitz's formulation of the principle of sufficient reason, but when we read it as "Nichts *ist* ohne *Grund*" the sentence changes character from one of ontic, to another of ontological significance.[82] The fallacy of accent? or the essence of creative speech?

Only a per-formance of the gesture will disclose the answer. When both readings of the sentence are grasped simultaneously, the reader will have had that experience of the tension between expressing surface and expressed depth which is the lived significance of creative speech.

Hypothesis formation, whether it be "scientific" or "hermeneutical" (interpreting the significance of the poet's very being as human creator), is a way of laying out what one has already understood on first contact with a range of data too vast to be comprehended in a single act of perception. In poetry, prose fiction, drama, and other "depth-dominant" arts media, it constitutes the first grasp of the intent of the piece. When the experience of a poem comes full circle, when on second look the reader's supposition is borne out as the essence of the structure is uncovered, he may be assured that his "reading" is correct.

For the film, whose surface is composed of sight and sound—each moving, and moving possibly in counterpoint—hermeneutical hypothesis formation is a necessary part of our phenomenological method: it allows us to see the depth of an expression as a single field of conceptual schemata.

In Chapter 9, we shall consider Siegfried Kracauer's case against phenomenology as an interpretation of films, and counter his argument with two examples of phenomenological criticism.

NOTES

I

1. "Aus einem Gespräch von der Sprache," *Unterwegs zur Sprache* (Pfullingen: Neske, 1959), pp. 83–155). A work currently being translated for Harper and Row, who have given permission for me to publish my own translations throughout the text.

2. See *Über den Humanismus* (Frankfurt a.M.: Klostermann, 1947), pp. 42–43.

3. For a comment of his later period on the aims of *Sein und Zeit,* see *Unterwegs zur Sprache,* pp. 95–98. (Hereafter, *Unterwegs*).

4. In particular on Hölderlin; see *Erläuterungen zu Hölderlins Dichtung* (Frankfurt a.M.: Klostermann, 1951 [Hereafter, Hölderlin]; and Georg Trakl and Stefan George. See *Unterwegs, passim.*

5. Pfullingen, Neske, 1956.

6. Pfullingen: Neske, 1961, see Vol. 1, pp. 12–13.

7. See Werner Marx, *Heidegger und die Tradition* (Stuttgart: Kohlhammer, 1961) and Max Müller, *Existenz-philosophie im geistigen Leben der Gegenwart* (Heidelberg: Kerl, 1949). For my criticism of Merleau-Ponty's failure in this project, see Conclusion, below.

8. See *Sein und Zeit,* ninth printing (Tübingen: Niemeyer, 1960), pp. 152ff., 314–16.

9. Tübingen: Niemeyer, 1961.

10. *Ibid.,* p. 87:

> Die Sprache ist weder nur das Ausdrucksfeld, noch nur das Ausdrucksmittel, noch nur beides zusammen. Dichten und Denken benutzen nie erst die Sprache, um sich mit ihrer Hilfe auszusprechen, sondern Denken und Dichten sind in sich das anfängliche, wesenhafte und darum zugleich letzte Sprechen, das die Sprache durch den Menschen spricht.

11. *Unterwegs,* pp. 203–5, 243–45.

12. *Was Heisst Denken?,* pp. 87–90.

13. *Unterwegs,* p. 160:

> Die wissenschaftliche Philosophie, die auf eine Herstellung dieser Übersprache ausgeht, versteht sich folgerichtig als Metalinguistik. Das klingt wie Metaphysik, klingt nicht nur so, *ist* auch so; denn die Metalinguistik ist die Metaphysik der durchgängigen Technifizierung aller Sprachen zum allein funktionierenden interplanetarischen Informationsinstrument. Metasprache und Sputnik, Metalinguistik und Raketentechnik sind das Selbe.

14. See *Einführung in die Metaphysik* (Tubingen: Niemeyer, 1958), pp. 28, 34–35. (Hereafter, *Einführung*).

15. See *Vorträge und Aufsätze* (Pfullingen: Neske, 1954), pp. 13–44, 45–70. (Hereafter, *Vorträge*). This work is currently being translated by A. Hofstadter for Harper and Row. English citations from it given with permission.

16. See *Was Heisst Denken?,* pp. 125–30.

17. *Hölderlin,* p. 38.

II

18. Compare J. F. Taylor, "The Art of Encounter," *Arts in Society* 3 (1965):249–55.

19. See Heidegger, *Nietzsche,* I, p. 92.

20. See my "Notes toward an Understanding of Heidegger's Aesthetics," in Lee and Mandelbaum eds., *Phenomenology and Existentialism* (Baltimore: The Johns Hopkins Press, 1967), pp. 59–92.

21. *Einführung,* p. 101:

> Für uns Heutige ist das Schöne . . . das Entspannende, Ausruhende und deshalb fur den Genuss bestimmt. Kunst gehört dann in den Bereich des Zuckerbäckers.

22. See pp. 91–109, especially p. 99.

23. The relationship between the sciences, especially the behavioral sciences, and their objects is the theme of "Wissenschaft und Besinnung."

24. *Unterwegs,* pp. 86–89.

III

25. *Hölderlin,* pp. 31–32.

26. *Ibid.,* p. 34:

> Das Zeugesein der Zugehörigkeit in das Seiende im Ganzen geschieht als Geschichte. Damit aber Geschichte möglich sei, ist dem Menschen die Sprache gegeben.

27. *Ibid.,* pp. 34–35:

> Ja das Wesentliche Wort muss sogar, um verstanden und so für alle ein gemeinsamer Besitz zu werden, sich gemein machen.

28. See *Sein und Zeit,* pp. 167–80.

29. *Hölderlin,* p. 35:

> . . . die Sprache gewährt uberhaupt erst die Möglichkeit, inmitten der Offenheit von Seiendem zu stehen. Nur wo Sprache, da ist Welt. . . .

30. *Ibid.:*

> Die Sprache ist ein Gut in einem ursprünglicheren Sinne. Sie steht dafür gut, das heisst: sie leistet Gewähr, dass der Mensch als geschichtlicher sein kann.

31. See *Identität und Differenz* (Pfullingen: Neske, 1957), pp. 51ff.

32. See *Sein und Zeit,* pp. 160–66.

33. *Hölderlin,* p. 37:

> . . . die Gegenwart der Götter und das Erscheinen der Welt sind nicht erst eine Folge des Geschehnisses der Sprache, sondern sie sind damit gleichzeitig.

34. The destiny of Being, to be revealed through language, is the principal theme of *Unterwegs.* This linguistic emphasis is the distinguishing mark of Heidegger's later works. Fundamental ontology has

given way to linguistic phenomenology, without, however, Heidegger's having lost interest in the meaning of Being.

35. In *Holzwege* (Frankfurt a.M.: Klostermann, 1950), pp. 7–68.
36. *Hölderlin,* p. 38:

    Jenes muss ins Offene kommen, was das Seiende im Ganzen trägt und durchherrscht. Das Sein muss eröffnet werden, damit das Seiende erscheine.

37. *Ibid.*; compare *Holzwege,* pp. 62–64.
38. See *Vorträge,* pp. 187–204.
39. See "Bauen Wohnen Denken," *ibid.,* pp. 145–62.
40. Paris: Nagel, 1946.
41. *Was ist Metaphysik?,* eighth printing (Frankfurt a.M.: Klostermann, 1960), p. 15. Original, 1929.
42. *Identität und Differenz,* pp. 69–70.
43. In *Holzwege,* pp. 193–247.
44. *Hölderlin,* p. 39:

    Dichtung verstehen wir aber jetzt als das stiftende Nennen der Götter und des Wesens der Dinge.

45. *Ibid.,* p. 40:

    Dichtung ist *das stiftende Nennen des Seins* und des Wesens aller Dinge—kein beliebiges Sagen, sondern jenes, wodurch erst all das ins Offene tritt, was wir dann in der Alltagssprache bereden und verhandeln. (Italics mine.)

46. *Ibid.,* p. 41.
47. Compare *Sein und Zeit,* pp. 267–80.
48. For Heidegger's analysis of this poem, see *Hölderlin,* pp. 75–143.
49. *Ibid.,* p. 90:

    Die Geschichtlichkeit der Geschichte hat ihr Wesen in der Rückkehr zum Eigenen, welche Rückkehr erst sein kann als Ausfahrt in das Fremde.

50. *Ibid.,* p. 97:

    Aber das Wirkliche, in das uns der Alltag gewöhnt hat, vermag das Offene nicht offen zu halten. Nur das Ungewöhnliche kann das Offene lichten, sofern das Ungewöhnliche sein verborgenes Mass in der Seltenheit des Einfachen hat, worin sich die Wirklichkeit des gewöhnten Wirklichen verbirgt.

51. See Werner Marx, p. 17.
52. In "Der Ursprung des Kunstwerkes," *Holzwege,* p. 50. For an account of the after-gleanings of Heidegger's early Nazi political activity, see Guido Schneeberger, *Nachlese zu Heidegger* (Bern: Schneeberger, 1962).
53. Second printing (Frankfurt a.M.: Klostermann, 1959), pp. 30–31.

54. Heidegger's general theory of linguistics is a topic going beyond the scope of the intent of this piece. *Unterwegs,* defining "method" merely as an opening up of ways of thinking, moreover, promises no systematic handling of the subject.

55. See *Holzwege,* pp. 248–95.

56. *Ibid.,* pp. 250–51.

57. *Holzwege,* p. 50.

58. See his *Gelassenheit* (Pfullingen: Neske, 1959).

59. In *Vorträge,* pp. 187–204.

60. *Ibid.,* p. 147:

> Bauen, buan, bhu, beo ist nämlich unser Wort 'bin' in den Wendungen: ich bin, du bist, die Imperativform bis, sei. Was heisst dann ich bin? Das alte Wort bauen, zu dem das 'bin' gehört, antwortet: 'ich bin,' 'du bist' besagt: ich wohne, du wohnst.

61. *Ibid.,* p. 189:

> Dichten ist, als Wohnenlassen, ein Bauen.

62. *Ibid.,* p. 190:

> Der Mensch spricht erst und nur, insofern er der Sprache entspricht, indem er auf ihren Zuspruch hört.

63. *Unterwegs,* pp. 9–33.

64. *Vorträge,* p. 192.

V

65. Summarily delineated in *Identität und Differenz;* see pp. 46–47.

66. *Vorträge,* p. 195.

67. *Ibid.:*

> Das Wohnen des Menschen beruht im aufschauenden Vermessen der Dimension, in die der Himmel so gut gehört wie die Erde.

Compare his description of the "world-square," *ibid.,* pp. 153–54.

68. *Ibid.,* p. 196:

> Im Dichten ereignet sich das Nehmen des Masses. Das Dichten ist die im strengen Sinne des Wortes verstandene Mass-nahme, durch die der Mensch erst das Mass für die Weite seines Wesens empfängt.

69. *Ibid.,* p. 197:

> Das Mass besteht in der Weise, wie der unbekannte Gott als dieser durch den Himmel offenbar ist.

70. *Ibid.*

71. *Ibid.:*

> So erscheint der unbekannte Gott als der Unbekannte durch die

Offenbarkeit des Himmels. Dieses Erscheinen ist das Mass, woran der Mensch sich misset.

72. *Ibid.*, p. 145:

Zum Wohnen, so scheint es, gelangen wir erst durch das Bauen.

73. *Ibid.*, p. 200:

Allein der Dichter beschreibt nicht, wenn er Dichter ist, das blosse Erscheinen des Himmels und der Erde. Der Dichter ruft in den Anblicken des Himmels Jenes, was im Sichenthüllen gerade das Sichverbergende erscheinen lässt und zwar: als das Sichverbergende.

74. *Unterwegs*, pp. 176, 181, 184, 200: "Das Wesen der Sprache: die Sprache des Wesens." I interpret: we will have understood the essence of language when we have succeeded in expressing the essences of things in language." Heidegger puts this task on the shoulders of poets and philosophers.

VI

75. *Unterwegs*, pp. 9–33.
76. *Sein und Zeit*, pp. 15–16; 43–44.
77. *Vorträge*, pp. 145–62.
78. *Unterwegs*, p. 205.
79. *Ibid.*, p. 215:

Die Sage versammelt als das Be-wëgende des Weltgeviertes alles in die Nähe des Gegen-einander-über and zwar lautlos, so still wie die Zeit zeitigt, der Raum räumt, so still wie der Zeit-Spiel-Raum spielt.

80. *Ibid.*:

Wir nennen das lautlos rufende Versammeln, als welches die Sage das Welt-Verhältnis be-wëgt, das Geläut der Stille. Es ist: die Sprache des Wesens.

81. See R. P. Blackmur, *Language as Gesture* (New York: Harcourt, Brace and Co., 1952).
82. Pfullingen: Neske, 1957, p. 92.

9

NOTES TOWARD THE CRITICISM OF THE FILM

I

If a work of art is created and experienced as a context of significance, it becomes the business of criticism to elucidate the significance unique to its context. Aesthetic criticism in particular will employ some viable set of aesthetic categories for interpretation of the experience, which may then be shared by those members of an artist's audience who, for any reason, may have missed the significance on a first encounter. The critic's primary function, then, is to ensure aesthetic communication, and not to pass judgment, to assess "values," to place an artist in history as a "major" or "minor" contributor to his culture, or to create a new—verbal—work of art, which merely happens to be inspired by the experience of the work under consideration. In short, criticism is not essentially normative because our perception already is; it is not historiological, even though, taking place in time, it is always historical; and, lastly, it is not itself a work of fine art. Wherever the arts are taken seriously, criticism is dependent upon the discoveries of individual artists and upon the developments—having both individual and social consequences—of the institutions giving form and substance to man's creative activity.

Art itself is perhaps the most free of human institutions, having in general only two determining conditions: the limitation of materials presenting obstacles to man's expression, and those of the human imagination for transforming these obstacles into means of expression.[1] The open society's role is, if not to set up those conditions making artistic expression possible, at least to permit it by making no laws restricting creative individuals from exercising their right of self-discovery in meaningful activity.[2] The gain to society for such permissiveness is the guarantee of its continued openness.

But this is not to deny that society has an interest in *how* an artist is to achieve his personality. All social institutions perform a double function in the lives of individuals: they not only permit the expression of licit human impulses, they also supply the restraints necessary for effective social control.

Where creation and appreciation are pursued without external constraints or restraints, the aesthetic institution is liberative of human impulse; where criticism is performed within the limits of contextual constraints and restraints, the aesthetic institution supplies all the controls necessary or desirable for the demands of social equity. Viewed in this light, the claims of an artist to creativity are counterbalanced by those of his society, that his expression be genuine. The social function of the perceptive critic is to describe this genuineness. That a work of art be found aesthetically significant should constitute sufficient grounds for approving of it; that it be found insignificant, sufficient grounds for disapproving of it. The fact that such judgments are currently made in our own society is attested to in the many court trials of individuals arraigned for publishing "obscene" literature, in which respected critics are asked to plead for the aesthetic validity of the questionable product.

But to be able to make such a plea, any critic must have experienced the work in question, and must be equipped to explain the significance of an artistic product in aesthetic terms. My argument is that contemporary phenomenology has developed a method of artistic interpretation sufficiently powerful to allow anyone possessing it to fulfill this critical function within the aesthetic institution, be he a critic, a judge or juror, or merely the man on the street. For purely illustrative purposes, the medium to be discussed is the film.

II

Aesthetic criticism is phenomenological description of the structures perceivable in works of fine art. It can begin only after the work has been set off in its intentionality, i.e., defined in its perceptual characteristics alone, as distinguished from an object of the natural world that is the effect of some cause and itself the cause of another effect. In this so-called phenomenological attitude, in which our consciousness is "reduced" to its essential character of intending an object, the aesthetic experience is found in its purest form. All our beliefs, prejudices, and preferences are "bracketed out" of relevance, along with our knowledge of formal systems or of the real empirical world. We are, in effect, attending only to how the thing looks, sounds, or feels; in a word, to its sensuous surface as organized by the artist for our perception.

Failure to distinguish the phenomenological from the natural attitude, as Husserl called them,[3] has led more than one aesthetician astray. Witness the account of Seigfried Kracauer, whose "material aesthetics" consists of treating the film as if it were an extension of still photography:

> My book differs from most writings in the field in that it is a *material* aesthetics, not a formal one. It is concerned with content. It rests upon the assumption that film is essentially an extension of photography and therefore shares with this medium a marked affinity for the visible world around us. Films come into their own when they record and reveal physical reality. Now this reality includes many phenomena which would hardly be perceived were it not for the motion picture camera's ability to catch them on the wing.[4]

Catching moving phenomena on the wing, however, can be as hazardous as catching flies the same way.

We understand, of course, that one of the first uses for the newly developed moving picture camera was to win a bet—that all the horses' legs are off the ground simultaneously in a given single moment of its canter. But if this is the case, the man who won the bet had already perceived the phenomenon on the wing, as it were, with his own two unaided eyes. And if his adversary accepted the "proof," he did so because the moving picture camera was able to "stop" the movement of the horse in a single freezing frame at the very instant the horse's four feet were all in mid-air. A still and a moving camera are both technological tools; both may be used to represent nature in a high degree of accuracy; but, in either case, the aesthetic value of the object produced—the photograph—has nothing to do with "recording or revealing physical reality." The question always remains, what is the aesthetic import of this recording?

We do not start our critical analyses by asking, What

does this photograph look like? but, How does it look? And if one is true to his visual experience, with all reference to the external world bracketed out, a still photograph will always appear as a more or less well-organized gestalt with a felt tension of visual counters (lines, forms, spaces) blending into maximal significance. The experience is one of intentional space.

Moving pictures, for the most part, do not look that way at all. Their essence is to move, as we all can see; but as we all likewise know, this motion is an illusion entertained only in the mind of the viewer and caused only by the persistence of vision. The projector's reel plays itself out at a rate of 24 frames per second, and between each of the frames nothing is being projected at all. The apparent movement of the film, then, is a figment of the viewer's imagination—which is not to say that it does not exist. It too is intentional, like any other phenomenologically reduced object, and exhibits properties peculiar to its own ontological structure. Our perception of its intentional motion yields a different kind of tension—temporal, this—which we must perceive kinaesthetically, if at all.

A film that is perceived in "slow motion" must be shot at a speed greater than that at which it is to be projected, or projected at a speed less than that at which it was shot. The differential between the shooting and the projecting speeds creates the illusion of unnaturally slow motion. And for accelerated motion, the reverse is true. What, then, is the "natural motion"? How does one adjust the camera and projector speeds to synchronize with the "natural" tempo of a changing event? It seems we find ourselves in the position of being able to recognize slow and accelerated motions depicted within a film's representational frame of reference without being able to tell exactly what is the rate of the continuous changes of nature, or if, as a matter of fact, they are continuous at all.

Add to this empirical foundation for an understanding of the illusion of natural motion in films the further knowledge that no one film is a continuously moving shot, but a compilation of various shots into scenes, and scenes into sequences—all through the simple act of cutting and splicing, and it is very easily understood that the significance of an entire movie depends as much upon these formal conditions of the art as upon the purely material condition of a single frame's representing a real, moving object. Since a movie is not only shot, but put together in any sequence fitting the director's purpose, a good movie may be as formalistic or as realistic as the context of expression demands. This is something Kracauer would have understood if he had practiced but twice the phenomenological reduction.

The truth is that his method is deficient. He still believes that content and form may be distinguished in a realistic film; because his own intuitions are perhaps something less than trustworthy, he supplants them with a historical survey of the natural "affinities" of photography:

> A phenomenological description based on intuitive insight will hardly get at the core of the matter. Historical movements cannot be grasped with the aid of concepts formed, so to speak, in a vacuum. Rather, analysis must build from the views held of photography in the course of its evolution—views which in some way or other must reflect actually existing trends and practices.[5]

Let us overlook the naïveté of the assumption that official views must somehow be borne out in practice, and put aside the strange notion that analysis builds something. Phenomenological descriptions, in contradistinction, do build the groundwork for an understanding of the working of a particular work of art.

Acceptable phenomenological descriptions are intuitive only in the sense that any meaning must be intuited. If they are not of the significance itself, they must be of the structures of a context of relational elements, each of which contributes to the meaningfulness of the whole construct. Our understanding of the description, however, is not a simple intuitive act. We must have experienced the tensions of the work to be able to judge the accuracy of the description. In this process, as explained in Chapter 4, the sensuous construct is experienced, and forms the basis for all further conceptual interpretation. True, the concepts used in the description are not to be formed in a vacuum; this is a red herring. All concepts applicable to the context are in fact grounded by an interpretation of the context in which they inhere. In any genuine phenomenological description of a representational art-work, then, we have two functional determinants of the artistic context: the surface "spread" of sensuous organization and an emergent order of signification, which I prefer to call "depth." This order of signification may itself control an affective response, and thus becomes relatable to the significance of the surface. This relation too is affectively toned; it is felt in perception as a tension, and may be called the "total expressiveness of the piece."

If one adopts one context, one sort of significance is found; if another, a second. For Kracauer's own personal reasons, which he states as follows: "This study rests upon the assumption that each medium has a specific nature which invites certain kinds of communications while obstructing others,"[6] he has chosen the natural attitude, and uses aesthetic categories of second-order signification. But he fails to realize that neither this attitude nor these second-order concepts will yield valid knowledge of the phenomenological data unless valid descriptions are given for the data themselves. And these are by definition phenomenological, and not natural events at all.

If any concepts occur within the context of expression, they too must be given phenomenological treatment. Kracauer, ignoring these distinctions, commits a common error of traditional aesthetics: he is looking for the essence of cinematic quality, with respect to which all particular cinematic expressions are to be judged adequate or inadequate, cinematic or uncinematic, when he should have been looking for the "essence" of a single filmic experience, i.e., its manner of coming into existence and remaining what it is. Any aesthetic theory that fails to do this fails for precisely the reason stated by Kracauer: it develops its concepts in a vacuum.

I shall try to avoid constructing my concepts in a vacuum by presenting two of my own phenomenological descriptions of cinematic experiences. The fact that they were originally film reviews written for the purpose of a group discussion of the films should be interpreted only as an attestation to the aforementioned necessity for aesthetic theory to grow out of attempts at first-hand criticism. Wherever this first level is lacking, the second can have no foundation in fact.

"Matter" and "form" or "substance" and "manner"

simply will not do as interpretive aesthetic categories. We are presented with organized sensuous surfaces, and some of these—not all filmic surfaces do—deepen as further significance accrues to the organization of sensuous gestalten. Some represent objects or the moving relations between objects we call "events" or "action," and each of these may be illustrative of a still more general idea. The job of the critic is to perceive how this happens and to describe how the deepening work engages his consciousness more fully. The context is always there; unlike a musical performance, which is an unrepeatable, real temporal process, we can always rerun the film, and perceive the same temporal tensional spread. Any hypothesis we may bring to the work must be made to fit the developing scheme. Even the occurrence of symbols, when they work, functions to focus consciousness by establishing an interrelatedness of elements within the context; so much so, that the attentive viewer, following the imaginative content of the references, is led back to a new perception of form; for, the counters (or elements) in their relatedness constitute the structure of the context whose significance we must be led to perceive. Given a knowledge of the film medium, a modicum of cultural development, and a state of mind open enough to let the work happen, one could do no better than adopt the following rule: "Anything in a film which is clumsy or abrupt or meaningless is so because the spectator's mind has been jarred or checked or led astray."[7] It is still the effect on our consciousness of what we perceive that constitutes the value of the film.

How then does the deepening of the surface affect the consciousness of the viewer? If we are to take Kracauer at his word, too much intellect is always anti-cinematic.

But this charge, if anything more than a tautology owing to the identical connotative values of "too much" and "anti-cinematic," covers over an obvious truth: that concepts may be effective within an artistic context only insofar as they function to intensify the consciousness induced by the structure of the context to entertain them.

The best phenomenological account of the function of such "concepts" is to be found in Heidegger's discussion of "a hermeneutical situation."[8] The translators of *Sein und Zeit* begin well,

> In interpreting, we do not, so to speak, throw a "signification" over some naked thing which is present-at-hand, we do not stick a value on it; but when something within-the-world is encountered as such, the thing in question already has an involvement which is disclosed in our understanding of the world, and this involvement is one which gets laid out by the interpretation. . . .[9]

but they continue badly. For the "fore-structure" of understanding (which is never at this stage explicit, but only an item of experience determined by the interaction of the work, in its intentionality, with the consciousness that has called it into being by its act of intending) contains three determinant attitudes, without which no implicit understanding could ever be made explicit through interpretation. Heidegger called them "Vorhabe," "Vorsicht," and "Vorgriff." Macquarrie and Robinson translate them "fore-having," "fore-sight," and "fore-conception."[10] The first and third of these renderings must go by the board. Heidegger's terms were coined from two common German verbs, *vorhaben* (to be occupied with, to intend, to have before one) and *vorgreifen* (to stretch out in front, to anticipate.)

It must be remembered that one has already had an experience of the object to be interpreted, whose meaning must be laid bare through the interpretation. The "Vorhabe" is what one is occupied with, what one intends in a general way, what is already laid out before one, but in a confused fashion: hence, *a developing context.* The "Vorsicht", for which "fore-sight" is at least suggestive, is the specific direction or end-point of the developing context, toward which the elements of the construct are being organized: it is, indeed, *the specific intent of the piece* as viewed by the consciousness seeking further interpretation of the developing scheme. Thus, consciousness must begin at the beginning, with what lies before it—a context of significance; it then projects a future as an optimal point of significant development, and must return to a fuller anticipation of the manner in which the total significance of the piece is stretched out in front of the interpreter. In this return, consciousness comes to its *hermeneutical hypothesis.*

Such is the internal structure of Heidegger's "hermeneutical circle." Explanation begins with knowledge (which is only implicit) and ends with the same knowledge, now stretched out before one in explicit, comprehensible terms. The final step in its application to criticism is to re-apply the hypothesis to the original context, to check, as it were, the validity of the conscious movement.

Heidegger applies this circle in explanation of the structure of the human being's being, and finds three correlative stages for Dasein's existence, or mode of self-transcendence.[11] They are of little import here, except to indicate that consciousness or psychic temporality undergoes structural modification in so far as it is *understanding,* and understanding projects three temporal dimensions as it intends objects within its world. *Dasein* (our human existence) is always already engaged in a world—in criticism, in a context of developing significance; and it projects ahead of itself, through its own fore-sight into a possible future, which gives meaning to the entities composing the context's structure. Call them, ontologically, "facticity," "existentiality," and "fallenness"; or, from the point of view of Dasein's own temporality, "past," "future," and "present"; and you have so many reoccurrences of the eternal return of consciousness to itself.

It is in this manner that a good hypothesis intensifies our experience, at the same time it explains the aesthetic facts of our initial awareness. And except for the value to be placed upon the intensification of consciousness—the aesthetic significance of the piece in question—scientific explanations are no different in structure. In spite of the incurrence of "concepts" within the aesthetic context—or perhaps because of them—our experience can and does become more intense for our having perceived the value structure of an organized set of qualities. Science has merely chosen to exclude the qualitative ordering of aesthetic contexts as irrelevant to its measurable realities. So much the worse for our scientists, and their merely natural attitude.

If this same sort of hermeneutical structure is to be found in each act of conscious interpretation, it is not clear at all that too much intellect is essentially anti-cinematic. All we have to do is to form an interpretive hypothesis, and apply it to the facts of the context of significance it lays out before us. The film reviews presented here are intended to be read as an attempt to show

how a hermeneutical hypothesis is formed to interpret the significance of the developing filmic contexts.

III

Film review of *Variety*: UFA, Germany, 1925. Adapted from the novel and directed by E. A. Dupont; starring Emil Jannings.

Siegfried Kracauer's psychological study of the German film represents *Variety*, an adaption of a novel by Felix Hollander, as a treatment of German middle-class rebellion and submission to societal authority. Since the principal characters all represent the lower classes, this hypothesis is hard to understand; but whether or not Kracauer's account is faithful to the film as originally produced or to the novel as written is a matter of historical interest only. The fact of the matter is, his account accords little with the present copy of the film distributed by the Museum of Modern Art Film Library. The following is taken from his description of the plot:

> The film, made after a popular prewar novel by Felix Hollander, opens with a sequence inside a penitentiary. Emil Jannings as "Boss" Huller has been pardoned before the end of his prison term, and now agrees to tell the prison director the story of his crime. This prefacing sequence is significant in that it emphasizes Huller's ultimate submission. At the outset of the story proper, Huller is running a shabby show in an amusement park, but neither that nor his faded wife can compensate for the sensations he had once experienced as a trapeze artist. One day, a sailor brings Huller a girl from a remote southern country. Huller hires her, and soon her sensuous beauty

> stirs him to rebel against his humdrum existence. He runs away with her. . . .[12]

In the version of the film under discussion, Huller has not yet been pardoned at the time of his interview with the warden; and there is no mention of a previous, faded wife. That the story of the crime should be placed within the frame of the parole interview is significant, but whether this significance may be laid to his submission or to something else depends upon a finer analysis of the film.

As the initial scene opens, Number 28, who has been imprisoned for ten years and who has never spoken of his crime, is called before the warden (sitting in an eerie light under a crucifix). Warden, judge, God, and priest rolled into one, the man asks for an explanation of the prisoner's crime and his subsequent behavior. It begins, we are told, in Berlin at the carnival. The story within the story is a sordid tale of elemental passions. A middle-aged man, the consort of a young, passionate beauty, lives the life of a vagabond performer who becomes the victim of his desire for his mate. We view him cooking her meals, even darning her stockings, all for love.

There appears on the scene a seductive Italian trapezist in need of new partners for his aerial act. The girl persuades her lover to accept the offer of a partnership, and the three aerialists become the Three Artinellis in the new variety show opening at the Wintergarten. The inevitable eventually happens: the young girl succumbs to the seduction of Artinelli, Huller learns of her deception, and Artinelli is murdered. Realizing the enormity of his crime while still under the influence of his own strong feelings of innocence, Huller surrenders to the police.

Following this account of his story, Huller is released from prison and returned to the freedom of nature.

If the story is banal, its telling is not, in spite of the hackneyed device of framing the story within a story. The film is a remarkable technical achievement in that the expressionistic and symbolic filmic representations actually succeed in communicating more about the fable than any synopsis of the plot may suggest. There is never a loss of visual interest. Although the parole interview begins with an expressionistic sequence, including the mystical representation of the warden intimated above, a deep angled shot into the prison courtyard, and the receding planes of door-frames along an enclosed corridor (symbolic of the degree of confinement suffered by the inmates), Dupont has taken pains to avoid the pitfalls of the expressionistic film. He has kept the formal balance of the individual shots, but introduced frenetic activity within the enclosing structure of most of them. The play of the lights and darks, the double exposures on fade-out, the single pyramid of white focusing into the statuesque exposure of the nude dancer is little short of cinematographic genius: and to prove the point, the audience within the film continues to view the dance obliquely, as the dancer's image is reflected off the business end of opera glasses. These same eyes will be magnified a thousandfold when Huller experiences the anguish of his decision to kill or not to kill his rival while swinging on a trapeze.

Further visual interest is maintained by the skill in variation of close-ups with moving camera shots of middle range. The few long shots are used to prolong the tension of an emotional scene, as in those cases when the camera follows the Hullers down the hall past the room of Artinelli. The symbols are used mostly as "plants" to foreshadow the impending crime. The ring Artinelli offers Berta-Marie predicts her adultery; the bracelet, her emotional fulfillment with his love. Although Huller could have been ignorant of the old German proverb—lucky at cards, unlucky in love—he insists that he is lucky in both even while Artinelli is making love to his wife. At the celebration of their first performance, hadn't Boss rather symbolically thrown the tipsy Berta into the arms of his rival?

The final trapeze act comes as a surprise. First of all, Boss imagines what would happen should he fail to catch Artinelli; but this premonition of death is a false lead—as false as that provided by the almost preternatural fall of the death's head from Artinelli's costume. Boss catches Artinelli, and Berta replaces the skull. Neither, at this particular time, could have done otherwise. Boss's tragedy at this point is not entirely a matter of having lost out to a younger, more passionate lover; rather, it is the fact that he is too much of an artist to spoil an act; and Berta is now completely in love with Artinelli. The applause of the audience revives Huller for a moment, as he lives in the glory of an act well performed. But the glory is shortlived, and he meditates an act of murder that could never be passed off as an accident. He traps the lovers into accepting the opportunity of a final tryst, and coldly kills his rival with the kitchen knife, which seems to have materialized from nowhere. The Freudians in the audience will love this scene.

Following the murder, Huller returns to his own room, where he washes the blood off his hands, and we would be obtuse not to draw the inference indicated: he is innocent of the blood of this man. But Huller is too confused to realize the significance of this symbolic act, and delivers himself up to the law. Berta, in some of the best acrobatics in the film, abandons herself to her grief as she has abandoned herself to each of her lovers before, somersaulting down two flights of stairs and coming to rest in a position of Petrine crucifixion, a victim of her own passion.

It might be thought that Huller's tragedy could have been told without the framing story. And apparently this is how Kracauer viewed the film. The appearance of the warden, you will remember, was taken as significant only of Huller's submission to the law. He failed to perceive the full mysticism of the opening sequence, which is buttressed by the symbol of the heart carved into the back of the warden's chair. Religiously understanding and humanly forgiving, the warden returns Huller to his freedom, more sinned against than sinning. The Boss's failing was in having loved too much, and in being too proud an artist to make his crime look like an accident. As the opening tells us, the story is portrayed in an unrelieved atmosphere of sordidness and tension; and therein is laid bare the secret of one suffering heart, having made an oath and expiated a crime.

Film review of *Nicht Mehr Fliehen*: Filmaufbau, Germany, 1955. Script by Herbert Vesely and Hubert Aratym; directed by Herbert Vesely.

Nicht Mehr Fliehen is an experimental film constructed on the principle of the anti-plot. It tells no story, contains no significance beyond itself, and invites each viewer to reconstruct the universe it endeavors to present. The theme of the film derives from existentialist philosophy, as it was understood or misunderstood at the time the film was made. The title itself is a clue to the film's structure.

Existentialists have defined man as a flight unto death, as an ever-ongoing process of becoming what one is called to be, during which one is constantly faced with the fear of answering or of not answering the call in authentic fashion. It matters little that one is both caller and called; having chosen a possibility as one's own, one must live it resolutely to the end. The fear one has in face of this awesome responsibility is *Angst,* and the emotion as felt constitutes a special access to nothingness.

"Nothingness" then, is a subjective concept, fitting nothing in the outside or objective world, be it ever so desolate; it is not to be mistaken for death, since it is with us always, even when we are most alive. It is neither here nor there, but everywhere—which is the same as to say nowhere at all. The sound track tells us that this place does not exist, and designates it as ground-zero, where time is about to run out. So much for the theme.

Since the anti-plot is an unspeakable one, the theme of the anti-fable will have to be portrayed indirectly. The one realistic representation in the film, a scene of vast desolation, sets the mood; and the seemingly chaotic cutting enhances the initial impression of stark emptiness. The music is sometimes melodic, but highly syncopated; more often it is "musique concrète," composed of natural sounds, including the human voice ranging from complete silence to frenetic shouting; and at times it is electronic, synthesized from a sound-making machine. The film is synchronized in vivid counterpoint; at times the images lead the music, and at others the sounds lead the image. Single shots stand out of the sequence like paintings, and single notes out of the 12-tone score like a complete melody.

The film makers have borrowed their techniques from the literary and pictorial arts. From literature they have taken the technique of symbolism and (insofar as it has one) of existentialism; from painting, that of surrealism. The art of symbolism is to understate—to say little and to suggest much; a single object or image is presented, and suggests another that has already been, or will be, presented in its own right at another place in the imaginative construct. The symbol thus serves to produce multi-relatedness in the art-work, introducing an intellectual content into the established mood. The literary surrealists made one of these objects a dream image, not making clear whether the symbol or its referent was to be taken for "reality." In this way they hoped to allow for the appearance of a super- or surreal object to be understood by the mind contemplating the images. Existentialism has added an ontological description of various kinds of objects. The techniques of the literary "existentialists" have generally varied according to the level of reality to be depicted in their representational universe; it can be shown, for example, that Sartre has used three diverse writing techniques in the narrative of *La Nausée. Which* device is to be used *when* is determined by the metaphysical significance of the event to be recounted. The metaphysical event in this film is the end of the flight, at a time when there is no longer any place to go. Pictorially, the camera angle presents forms arranged in the "metaphysical" style created by di Chirico, and Dali's influence is felt in the mingling of the human with mechanical and natural forms.

In summary, then, *Nicht Mehr Fliehen* is an eclectic piece. It has borrowed its theme from contemporary existentialism (principally Martin Heidegger's *Sein zum Tode*), and its techniques from other art genres. As is fitting for an experimental film of this type, the music is of the latest to have been developed. Such is the cultural background, or at least the most relevant parts of it, with which Vesely has tried to construct his anti-plot movie. When we switch attention from the background to the figure appearing thereon, we enter the movie's own context of significance.

To the whirring strain of a heavy motor, the viewer is presented with the last flight of two passengers, the man who drives and the woman being driven. Following a countdown of the space leading into ground-zero, we are introduced to an armed driver whose North African countenance announces the presence of an Ishmael-figure, or outcast. Gerard is obviously at the service of his machines (the pistol, the truck) as well as in the service of his passenger, a semi-automaton, but beautiful and vain European woman. She speaks only French; he speaks French and German.

Death is everywhere around us, seen in the desolation of the place, the death's head configuration made by the front of the truck, the body lying half hidden behind a wall. The driver's pistol promises another death to come, and his partner's mask of a face indicates that she too is only half alive. The child they meet speaks no language at all, and he finally vanishes, having died for no reason at all. Sisyphus-like, Gerard is condemned to bear the lady's baggage from place to place. And in the middle of nowhere she rents a "room" with no roof, no wall (only symbolic curtains), no floor. The bags must be put down nowhere. The money exchanged is a dead symbol, its value having been lost; nonetheless, the game of the bargain is undergone.

There appears another woman, Ines, who is racially akin to the driver. She is attracted to the lady's finery, but comes too close. Gerard pushes her down and carries her away to that place near ground-zero where the railroad tracks lead meaninglessly (directionlessly) to the end of the desert, where they are bent out of shape. A large unused crane, as significant as the bleeding truck, stands facing the sea. But the sun is hot, and only the lady and the police possess sun glasses, so they cannot feel what Gerard has to do. He rapes Ines, and feels grateful for her existence. Under the gaze of the lady, however, he feels shame and the obligation to explain to his passenger, who feels nothing. Gerard then throws stones at Ines, the one person there with whom he might have communicated. Later he fills her body with bullets, his earlier germ warfare having proved itself ineffective. Why? Like Meursault's murder, for no reason whatever.

This appeal to Camus's novel is not fortuitous. The script writers have intercalated a long excursus on the Myth of Sisyphus, in which Gerard is shown bound to his burnt-out truck. Man must redo what he has already done. The camera switches to the lady's "vanity," the child's pebble building, the man's gun-cleaning, the lady's vanity—a sequence of images in strict symbolist fashion. In the child's pebbles there are shells of dead fish and a starfish, likewise dead. Sapphire, the lady, could see her image there, dead, as she had seen it before in the reflection on a bar table; the man wields the instrument of death; the difference between life and death is only the woman's vanity. In love with herself, wearing black narcissus perfume, clad in her most glamorous dress, she idly taps an empty oil drum as Gerard murders Ines.

Following the murder, Sapphire, who is no precious jewel, breaks into the barest hint of a smile, and the music becomes recognizably jazz while she trots off across the desert in search of her own image. When the police arrive, they find only Gerard, a dead body, and three bags. The empty significance of the money exchange is repeated in the empty perusal of Gerard's passport. All sit down to await the final count-down, this one in time. The last shot picks up a precedent death's head image; it is the front of the jeep, which resembles that of the truck but which bears a meaningless license plate. Man and his machine, man the machine (the one policeman walks with the aid of a mechanical leg) has come to the end of time. There can be no more fleeing, as the soundtrack rather obtrusively tells us, for time has run out.

Admittedly experimental, *Nicht Mehr Fliehen* seems more ambitious than successful. It succeeds to a limited extent in creating a powerful mood by sheer weight of surface manipulation: the film montage and music are harmoniously intercut into concurrent patterns of jagged rhythms, and the modulation of the human voices to fit the musical score is an effective device. If the voices are unrecognizable, we are reassured by the thought that we never really hear the other anyway. The ambition of the piece, however, is to present nothingness—an apparent impossibility. Since this existentialist concept is purely subjective, *whose* nothingness, *whose* subjectivity, is being presented? Not Sapphire's; although her life is empty enough, she feels no anguish. Not Gerard's; he feels only the oppression of the sun and his burdens. Nor that of the child, a puppet who vanishes into the dust never betokening any conscious trait; nor of Ines, who is only a woman to be killed; nor of the police, nor of the society they represent. This reviewer's vanity is to suggest that it can only be the nothingness of the viewer. We are told that the place does not exist; it must be a figment of our imagination. We are told that symbols need the imagination of a viewer for their life to take form. We are told that the conditions of ground-zero constitute the fate awaiting all the world.

All of this takes a great deal of telling for a film that might otherwise have succeeded in presenting an audience with its own anguish, each member in his own way. But to do that, the film must draw the viewer into its life. Too much symbolism, the chief device used to procure the desired result, has as its effect an intellectual response, and the intellectual activity prevents our being drawn into the universe of the film until after analysis, when the mood is considerably weakened.

Moreover, it is cheating for the analyst to give the patient clues in the interpretation of his Rorschach blots. Camus's commentary, although pertinent in life, is impertinent in the film, and too many symbols have been directly borrowed from the literature of our times: the sun, desert, and sea, from Camus; the wall, from Sartre; the metamorphosis, from Kafka; and so on. The movie proves if anything, that philosophy may yet be embodied within the textures of a film, but only when its concepts are understood.

The makers of this film have mistaken absurdity, which is a metaphysical concept in Sartre and a moral one in Camus, for mere incongruity. (Sapphire wears heels with slacks and sandals in full dress, which combination itself is absurdly incongruous anywhere, but which seems even more so in view of the desolation of the place.) Before or after the bomb, such a confusion of philosophical ideas will still be a mistake. If the desert is to be read as a symbol for our own nothingness, then everything that occurred in the film was a dream of our own. Such a result would be surreal, but not existentialistic; it might produce fright, but not anguish.

IV

Two films, the one silent and the other very talky indeed, have provided the occasion for initially suspending all judgments on the nature of the universe in which we live in favor of the appearance of two unique contexts of significance intended by our attentive consciousness. Although silent, the first shows the tragic character of a man who suffers for having loved too much. The other, more ambitious, attempts to show the meaninglessness of any human attempt to discover significance on this side of death, that point in a projection toward which all human endeavor must achieve its summation. In aesthetic terms, both films are "depth" dominated. The first recounts a story; the second argues for the uselessness of telling any story at all, and in fact does not, since all stories must end when there is no more time for the telling. We judge the first to be successful, because in telling its story our interpretive hypothesis is carried out in the accrued significance attributed to each of the isolable incidents, including those functioning only symbolically to call attention to others funding to suggest the *signification* of the piece.

But criticism does not stop with the determination of the signification of symbolic reference within the growing context. If the movie is to be judged successful, our judgment must fall on—or we must be led to perceive (which is the same)—the manner in which our understanding of this signification has served to concentrate or to diffuse the intensity of our consciousness. We follow the rhythm of Boss Huller's tragedy up to the moment of his murderous act; the intensity of this act is rendered more intense still by the cineast's skillful manipulation of shot upon shot, which together become scenes freighted with future consequences. The scenes fund into sequences becoming momentous movements: the opening (Boss and Berta in their original state of innocent love); the complication (the introduction of Artinelli and the defection of Berta); the obligatory scene (in which Boss enacts his revenge by murdering the cause of his unhappiness); and the dénouement (in which Boss himself undergoes the revenge of society). But there is more. The film has no end, as Boss's punishment cannot end with parole: he has learned that in killing his antagonist he has also destroyed the most revered object in the life of his beloved, thereby likewise killing a part of her. As long as he is conscious he shall continue to expiate this, his more serious crime.

Thus, in applying our hypothesis, we find that our consciousness is constantly brought back to the expressiveness of the surface counters themselves, which have established the mood in the first place, for the development of sordid human involvements. Each developing strand of the depth signification in turn produces a reinforcement of this original mood, thereby enhancing the significance of the overall context, which intensifies our consciousness. The depth is not pursued for its own sake, and therefore does not carry our attention beyond its function to increase the tension of the expressive surface. But this is only to say that Dupont's film withstands any of our attempts to mock or jeer at its significance.

Vesely is not so felicitous. The signification we place upon his display of symbols, although unifying the details, fails to function at its own level to intensify the significance of the surface counters. Image follows image in shot after shot, but scenes do not fund into meaningful sequences, even with the aid of one of the most sophisticated sound tracks ever devised for a movie. The visual rhythms are intercut by the aural, and they do achieve a measure of significant contrapuntal unity; but all this interesting surface is lost, not being picked up in the depth. There, sterility is piled on sterility, yielding only a sense of reinforced futility. The editor admits as much by including the final recitation of Camus's verbal description of the meaninglessness of life.

Vesely and his cohorts have indeed attempted the impossible: to present a mood possible only by contemplating one's own death. Instead, *Nicht Mehr Fliehen* presents two lines of significance that remain nonfunctionally related in context. Our understanding of the hypothesis yields a signification that adds nothing to the significance of the context, and our entertainment of it merely serves to disperse our conscious energy.

If there is anything to be learned from all this, it is precisely that not all intellection is wasted effort in the contemplation of an aesthetic product. Where it functions, it can indeed be very good; and where it fails to function, it is always destructive of any attempt to perceive embodied significance. And where both of these phenomena—the goodness and the good and the badness of the bad—cannot be perceived, either because one is incapable of making the necessary interpretive hypothesis or because one has in theory excluded the relevance of all intellectual activity in the perception of an aesthetic context, there is still room for criticism as phenomenological description to contribute its function to the ongoing aesthetic institution. This has always been the case; only the phenomenological critics have been lacking.

V

Two ironic conclusions follow from the foregoing discussion. The first is my use of Heidegger's hermeneutical method to show the inadequacy of Vesely's attempt to express in the cinematic medium Heidegger's own ontological description of human existence. But surely this is no fault of the philosopher.

At the same time, it shows the vacuity of Kracauer's judgment concerning the existence of "truly" cinematic content as opposed to "the theatrical story" (which is merely photographed) and "experimental films" having "problematic symbolism." The reason, of course, is to be found in his own attempt to show that the unique cinematic purpose is to "redeem physical reality"[13]—a mighty purpose, indeed, to be perceived by a person in a dream state, who is said to have his consciousness "lowered."[14]

If it is true that "Films . . . tend to weaken the spectator's consciousness,"[15] it would be difficult to explain the "true" cinematic motive in any terms other than those of an unconscious desire to escape. As Freud has shown, and surrealists never tired of reiterating, consciousness is liberated in sleep, becomes more active, and loses itself in the creation of its own symbolic fantasies fulfilling otherwise inexpressible desires.

The second irony stems from this source. For what is lulled to sleep in our awareness of a cinematic creation is precisely *our concern with the true nature of physical reality,* which we gladly exchange for the significance to be found in any successfully organized cinematic experience. And we do this merely by practicing the phenomenological reduction.

Content is important to film, as to any other art, only because without it we could not have an experience of one kind of significant form. If we must apply a hermeneutical hypothesis to the display of formed content, then we shall do so, and without leaving the context in question or having the intensity of our consciousness necessarily weakened. If it does become weakened, our only judgments can be either that the hypothesis is wrong or that the movie is bad. In his own study of the German expressionistic film, Kracauer uses a wrong hypothesis, and is led later on to deny the validity of the content in films of that kind. But as Croce said so long ago, aesthetic judgment has nothing to do with kinds.

There are, after all, good and bad realistic films, just as there are good and bad expressionistic or symbolic films. Only the experience of their goodness or badness will convince us that these judgments are valid.

Phenomenological description is still the best devised method of critical procedure for the arts. And it is not too difficult. The only trick is to accept what appears as true; for in our phenomenologically reduced consciousness the only relevant objects are those which, in one way or another, make their appearance felt.

Further tests of phenomenology as a method of aesthetic inquiry are easy to imagine: sculpture, architecture, costume and jewelry, interior and civic design, religious ritual are all capable of supplying the context in which surface, sensuous counters are manipulable in the control of the qualitatively unique experiences by which human beings have learned by nature, habit, or taste to enrich their own circumstances. Human subjects transcend the limits of their past experience by projecting and establishing a more meaningful future. And in our experiences of the arts, we are given an expression of such meanings with a minimum of distracting, insignificant detail.

When surface counters are arranged in such a way as to suggest objects, ideas, and images, or other practical functions of intercourse between man and other men or between men and things, the goodness of these depth constructions depends upon the way in which they emerge from, only to have their absolute value changed by ultimately remerging with, the qualitative structures of the surface itself. Hence, what a successful art-work expresses is never anything less than a completely fulfilled intention.

One thought remains: There is no royal road to aesthetic expertness, for in aesthetic judgment there is no authority beyond the qualification that having an experience gives to the person capable of reflecting upon, and describing, the conditions of that experience. That these conditions are existential, rather than physical or psychological, can no longer be a surprise, and in the end, Husserl has been found to be right from the beginning: to understand an experience one must go back to the things themselves, which are the objects of our conscious intentions.

In the final chapter of this book, I shall summarize the sources used in the construction of the theory.

NOTES

1. See Chapter 3 above, for the existential-phenomenological account of this process; also compare John Dewey, *Experience and Nature* (Chicago: Norton and Co., 1929), pp. 357–59.

2. For a description of the socio-economic conditions favorable to the development of a particular style of film production, see George A. Huaco, *The Sociology of Film Art* (New York and London: Basic Books, Inc., 1965).

3. Edmund Husserl, *Ideas,* B. Gibson, trans. (New York: Collier Books, 1962), pp. 91–100.

4. See his *Theory of Film* (New York: Oxford University Press, 1965), p. ix.

5. *Ibid.,* p. 3.

6. *Ibid.*

7. Formulated by Ernest Lindgren, *The Art of the Film* (London: Allen and Unwin, 1948), pp. 114–15.

8. *Being and Time,* J. Macquarrie and E. Robinson, trans. (London: SCM Press, Ltd., 1962), pp. 190–91.

9. *Ibid.*

10. See the original *Sein und Zeit* (Tübingen: Niemeyer Verlag, 1957), pp. 148–53, 310–16.

11. The methodological significance of Heidegger's account of "the hermeneutical situation" has been developed by Hans-Georg Gadamer, *Wahreit und Methode* (Tübingen: Niemeyer Verlag, 1960). In shorter compass the same is presented in "Vom Zirkel des Verstehens," in *Martin Heidegger zum siebzigsten Geburtstag* (Pfullingen: Neske, 1959), pp. 24–34.

12. Kracauer, *From Caligari to Hitler* (Princeton, N.J.: Princeton University Press, 1947), pp. 125–26.

13. Kracauer, *Theory of Film,* pp. 300–301.

14. *Ibid.,* p. 303.

15. *Ibid.,* p. 159.

PART III
Conclusion

10

MERLEAU-PONTY: THE NATURE AND SCOPE OF PHENOMENOLOGICAL CRITICISM

I

Although the argument of the foregoing chapters has been culled from many sources, the distinctively phenomenological method it prescribes stems from the philosophy of Edmund Husserl. Sartre and Merleau-Ponty were instrumental in making phenomenology popular in France, even if in doing so the musical Gallic tongue was forced to violate our ears with the harsh, guttural sounds of the imported German. Along with an interest in Husserl (and Hegel), however, Sartre was always concerned with ontologizing phenomenology in the Heideggerian mode: i.e., he was more interested in describing "human being" than aesthetic experiences *per se*. Merleau-Ponty, who likewise began with Husserl but was brought over to ontology in the latter stages of his career, is the central influence on the development of the thesis of this book.

In 1960, when my own account of Merleau-Ponty's then existing philosophical corpus was being prepared for the press,[1] I made the seemingly safe prediction that this subtle Frenchman's major works would not be translated for some time to come. The same year he was himself preparing another important addition to his *oeuvre, Signes.*[2] But, even with this new work, my prediction proved to be somewhat more than rash. I was clearly wrong. Since 1962 all the major works have found their way into English, and in 1964 the Northwestern University Press published translations of *Signes* and a collection of essays by Merleau-Ponty illustrating his principal thesis—the primacy of perception for determining the significance of human existence.

What follows is an attempt to evaluate the central significance of Merleau-Ponty's aesthetic theory within the mainstream of the phenomenological movement. My task is aided by the publication in English of the major portion of the controversial Frenchman's critical works. Besides *Signs* and *The Primacy of Perception,* mentioned above, even his posthumous *Le Visible et l'invisible* has been prepared for readers of English.[3] The greater part of the essays in the first two mentioned volumes is professionally "philosophical," treating of subjects ranging from the arts and linguistics to science and politics. Merleau-Ponty wrote these essays for an audience familiar with the tradition of continental philosophy, or for students seeking an introduction to that tradition.

These volumes contain two essays in aesthetics that are markedly different in tone. "Indirect Language and the Voices of Silence,"[4] one of the last pieces by Merleau-Ponty to appear in *Les Temps Modernes,* of which he was co-editor with Sartre, is an attempt to compare the expressive capabilities of language with those of painting, and was conceived as a part of a larger work left unfinished at the time of his death in 1961. The second aesthetic essay, "Eye and Mind,"[5] first appeared in the inaugural issue of *Art de France* with illustrations, and then without illustrations in the memorial issue of *Les Temps Modernes* dedicated to him; both came out in the original French in 1961. This essay was reedited by Gallimard, with the original illustrations, in 1964.[6]

Since the first of these essays was a study of expressiveness, and the second, an "ontology of painting"—two different tasks, two different subjects, two different styles for two different audiences—we shall have to consider the importance of each for the development of Merleau-Ponty's aesthetics. In the main, his translators have made the task easier than before.

Enough will be said, perhaps, about the complexities of Merleau-Ponty's style for the casual reader to comprehend the translators' difficulties, if we mention that the minimally prepared linguist must also be familiar with the range of Merleau-Ponty's subjective interests—the history of philosophy, phenomenology, literature, painting, aesthetics, politics, psychology, anthropology, and sociology—to do justice to his work. McCleary, who was the sole translator of the entire *Signes*, had the correspondingly more difficult job; *The Primacy of Perception* was prepared by a team of translators.

Richard C. McCleary is one of the few interpreters of Merleau-Ponty who have realized that "conduite" bears a special meaning in phenomenological thought, and that to translate the word as "conduct" is inadequate. "Conduct" in English (as in one of its senses in French), even when written in the singular, is already plural, since it is a generic term. "Une conduite," however, is not a generic term; it thus may have a plural form. It is used to refer to a single, significant, manner of behaving. Thus, when the translator meets "conduites" in the text he opts for "ways of behaving,"[7] which is close, but not technical enough to convey Merleau-Ponty's meaning, which is "patterns of behavior." We are certainly interested in showing the typical ways in which artists and their audiences behave, but we may find the more technical sense of the term a clearer interpretation of our task.

A pattern of behavior is an act of a human subject, having, in Aristotelian terms, a beginning, middle, and end that make it a unity. In Merleau-Ponty's terms, however, the unity of the act is phenomenologically described as an intention, or relatedness outward toward a transcendent object (one other than the intending subject). In short, as explained in Chapter 5, a pattern of behavior is a form or structural unity of the human corporeal schema reacting to its environment—physical, vital, or cultural.

To anyone who has worked his way through *The Structure of Behavior*,[8] the importance of this correction will be apparent. In that book Merleau-Ponty was at pains to show the continuity between the orders of forms —syncretic, mutable, and symbolic—each representing a different kind of patterning of behavior in the life of human subjects, who are presumably the only species of organism to have completed the "dialectic of orders" from the physical to the vital and thence to the cultural; the only living species, that is, to have transformed its lived into recorded history. Our interpretation of the dance medium (Chapter 5) is entirely based on the derivation of significance in each of these orders.

The Structure of Behavior was in effect an essay on the relations of mind and body, in which these terms were found to be strictly correlative: each lower order of the dialectic was "body" for the immediately higher order of conduct, which constituted "mind." In this dialectical development of behavior, man was found to reach an absolute of self-consciousness (philosophy, or reflection on the lower orders implicit in his behavior), primarily through the acquisition of speech, which enabled the reflective individual to represent to himself the relationships between the elements implicit in a primary human intention (transcendence), the most basic pattern (Husserl would have said "essence") of which is perception.

We have been interested, of course, in showing the relevance of these distinctions for a description of the human behavior implicit in artistic, or creative, communication. Merleau-Ponty never did lose his interest in the basic patterns of human behavior, or his faith in the ability of philosophical reflection on the behavioral sciences and other "primary expressions," such as art, to cast new light on Husserl's philosophy. As proof, read "The Philosopher and Sociology" and "From Mauss to Claude Lévi-Strauss" in *Signs,*[9] and "Phenomenology and the Sciences of Man" and "The Child's Relations with Others" in *The Primacy of Perception.*[10]

If, in translating Merleau-Ponty's remarks on the patterning of behavior, McCleary came close (missing only the close tie between the Frenchman's idea of behavioral patterns and Husserl's doctrine of essences), on the nature of philosophical reflection he was further off the mark. But he is not alone on this; John Wild and James M. Edie have made the same misleading error in their translations in *The Primacy of Perception.* I refer to their rendering of "l'irréfléchi" as "the unreflected."[11] What we find in this association of the two terms is a strict one-to-one correlation between the past participles of "réflechir" and "to reflect," indicating, perhaps, that the translators were working with words rather than with ideas.

In French, the article in "l'irréfléchi" causes no difficulty, since it is common in that language to change adjectives into nouns in this way; we do it in English too, as when we speak of the true, the good, and the beautiful. But for us, there always results an aura of oddity, as if the noun so created wore a halo. This otherworldliness of the naturally ambiguous terms "reflected" and "unreflected" is too much to take, especially since the appropriate meaning of "irréfléchi" is "nonreflective." It, too, is a behavioral term referring to a stratum of human experience, to that consciousness before self-consciousness, in which the human being intends an external object. Within the context of an aesthetic theory, the nonreflective component of human experience represents our basic intuitive or prereflective intercourse with aesthetic stimuli. In reflecting upon these, that is, in an attempt to bring these experiences to fully conscious appreciation, we are led to the fullest heights of critical appreciation.

For a statement of Merleau-Ponty's notions of the relation between philosophy and other human disciplines, we read in McCleary's translation:

> . . . this philosophy which searches *beneath* science is not in turn "deeper" than passions, politics and life. There is nothing more profound than experience which passes through the wall of being. . . . Those who go by the way of passion and desire up to this being know all there is to know. Philosophy does not comprehend them better than they are comprehended [sic]; it is in their experience that it learns about being. Philosophy does not hold the world supine at its feet. It is not a "higher point of view" from

> which one embraces all local perspectives. It seeks contact with brute being, and in any case informs itself in the company of those who have never lost that contact.[12]

Why, then, should the translator not distinguish between the reflective and the nonreflective aspects of human experience, rather than between reflection and "the unreflected?" Appreciation of art is just that: either nonreflective and intuitive or reflective and fully self-conscious.

With the publication of *Signes*, however, and again in the composition of "L'oeil et l'esprit," Merleau-Ponty introduced a notion of "brute being" that may or may not be the same as that of "Being," which played an important role in his later discussions on painting.[13] Whatever the relationship between these two concepts, they afford a clue to the inspiration of the later aesthetic works: Merleau-Ponty, the crypto-positivist, was moving toward ontological speculation.

It is to this movement in his thought that the remainder of this chapter is dedicated. In ontology, interpreted as a theoretical explanation of human being, the question arises as to whether one's being takes precedence over one's creativity, or whether creation is only one way a human being has of working out the significance of his personal transcendence. If therefore ontology is thought to be a useful tool for aesthetic analysis, we should be led to question what it adds to Merleau-Ponty's earlier case, which was based entirely upon his "philosophical anthropology."

II

The American editors of Merleau-Ponty's works were

motivated by a noble aim, to produce dialogue between continental and British and American philosophy. But this purpose is poorly served by the attitudes of those historians of philosophy who would trace the ideas of Merleau-Ponty to their origins, then judge them on their fidelity to the original sources. Edie points out that Merleau-Ponty's scholarship would hardly pass American standards, and to anyone who has tried to trace down sources for Merleau-Ponty's citations, this is an understatement. But to say, with Herbert Spiegelberg, ". . . that some of the citations and doctrine Merleau-Ponty professes to find in Husserl's later writings have not been discovered by anyone else, as, for instance, his quotation 'Transcendental subjectivity is an intersubjectivity. . . .' "[14] is to show an excessive interest in the preservation of the sources, and thus to place oneself in a scholarly phone booth to which all lines of communication have been cut; no dialogue of any sort will emanate from such a position. For if Husserl did not say "Transcendental subjectivity is an intersubjectivity," he did say

> In meiner original erfahrenden Monade *spiegeln* sich die anderen Monaden (Liebniz). Die Enthüllung der Konstitution des alter ego ergibt dieses als transzendentales, und so erweitert sich die phänomenologische Reduktion auf die transzendentale Subjectivität als transzendentale Monadengemeinschaft. Diese ist nun der transzendentale Boden für die Konstitution der objektiven Welt als für alle Monaden der Gemeinschaft identisch seiende und für die intersubjektive Geltung der Idealen Gegenständlichkeiten.[15]
> Translation:
> The other monads are *mirrored* in my own original experiencing monad (Leibniz). The uncovering of the consti-

> tution of the alter ego shows it to be transcendental, and so the phenomenological reduction is broadened into a transcendental subjectivity that is a transcendental community of monads. This latter is now the transcendental basis for the constitution of the objective world, as for all the identically existing monads of the community and for the intersubjective validity of the ideal objectivities [revealed in the reduction].

Merleau-Ponty's rendering of the passage is merely briefer, and perhaps more to the point, which was to show that my own being is conditioned by the being of others as each of these existents is related to the external objects of the world. Creative communication, if the hypothesis of this book is correct, is a privileged locus for the observation of interpersonal relations, a subject Merleau-Ponty was never to lose from sight.

When he died at the age of 53, Merleau-Ponty was gradually approaching full possession of his philosophical powers. His inaugural lecture at the Collège de France[16] had promised a philosophy that was to be the "conscience of history," an institution whose special interest and concern was to serve as criticism of other human institutions; it goes without saying that philosophy could perform this function only if it were itself fully self-conscious and in complete control of its own powers. Sensitive to the differences with his friends and their criticisms of his analyses, he returned once again to the sources.

The conclusions of the *Phenomenology of Perception*[17] are fairly restated in *The Primacy of Perception* and in the synopsis of his prior works presented to the judges of his candidacy for the chair in philosophy at the Collège de France.[18] Reading the discussion following the presentation of the first paper to a 1946 meeting of the *Société française de la philosophie,* especially the misunderstandings of those who had just heard it, attests amply to the fact that he had perhaps taken too much for granted in assuming that his hearers were familiar with his first works. He admits this himself in the discussion.[19] It simply was not understood by the convened philosophers how the phenomenological method of Husserl and the *cogito* of Descartes could be interpreted as a phenomenon of corporeal existence. But Merleau-Ponty insisted that

> . . . there is a third meaning of the *cogito,* the only solid one: the act of doubting in which I put into question all possible objects of my experience. This act grasps itself in its own operation . . . and thus cannot doubt itself. The very fact of doubting obdurates doubt. The certitude I have of myself is here a veritable perception: I grasp myself, not as a constituting subject that is transparent to itself, and that constitutes the totality of every possible object of thought and experience, but as a particular thought, as a thought engaged with certain objects, as a thought in act; and it in this sense that I am certain of myself.[20]

Besides defining his own position, this passage points up Merleau-Ponty's specific differences with Descartes and Husserl. But it is clear that he accepted the "bracketing" of the phenomenological reduction, and claimed absolute certitude for the knowledge it gives the practitioner. Thus, if we allow a work of art to display its own essential structure, our reward is self-epiphany; for in the phenomenological attitude we are said to grasp ourselves perceiving the significance of the work.

In further refining his notion of the primacy of perception, Merleau-Ponty attempted to relate *all* rationality to the life conditions of the reasoning organism, since men go on living, even after thinking, with their particular syntheses of the lower orders implicit in their structures. To establish the primacy of perception in the theory of knowledge, however, ". . . is not a question of reducing human knowledge to sensation, but of assisting at the birth of this knowledge . . .";[21] it is, rather, an attempt

> to make it as sensible as the sensible, to recover the consciousness of rationality. This experience of rationality is lost when we take it for granted as self-evident, but is, on the contrary, rediscovered when it is made to appear against the background of non-human nature.[22]

Only one proposition needs to be added: perception is truly a *bodily* phenomenon.

In his fifth Cartesian meditation Husserl had stumbled onto this fact,[23] and, according to Merleau-Ponty, never really faced up to the problem:

> Positing another person as another myself is not as a matter of fact possible if it is *consciousness* that must do it. To be conscious is to constitute, so that I cannot be conscious of another person, since that would involve constituting him as constituting, and as constituting in respect to the very act through which I constitute him.[24]

For a formal schematization of bodily perception Merleau-Ponty referred once again to the reflexive action by which we know our own bodies: "This subject that experiences itself as constituted at the moment it functions as constituting is my body."[25] In this act of corporeal reflexivity the *cogito* is complete.

Yet speech is the bodily phenomenon that gives privileged access to a fully developed intelligence. Hence, needed next was a thoroughgoing, phenomenologically developed, interpretation of language, one that related the corporeal structure of human beings to its expression in speech. It is for this reason that Merleau-Ponty published "On the Phenomenology of Language" following his article "Indirect Language. . . ."[26] The problem, specifically, was not merely one of making Saussure[27] consistent with Husserl, but of bringing their theoretical structures to bear upon the conclusions of the behavioral sciences that study the same phenomenon.

The most apparent evidence that a bridge may yet be built across the English Channel between philosophers of a predominantly positivistic bias and those of a continental or "phenomenological" persuasion is Merleau-Ponty's fine analysis of the relations between "Wesensschau" (essence reading), as he practices it, and inductive reasoning. In brief, we read

> After closer examination, the only difference we find between inductive procedure—so far as it is justifiable and moves toward what is truly essential—and the procedure of eidetic psychology is that the latter applies imaginary variation to its examples, while the former refers to effective variations in considering cases that are *actually realized.*[28]

To the kind of positivism that seeks its evidence in the conclusions of the empirical sciences, then, there can be no question of contradicting the validly established results of phenomenological analysis. Both methods are fallible and corrigible; phenomenology is so by virtue of the language used to describe the "essences" or structures that are revealed to perceptual intuition.

Perhaps the greatest divergence Merleau-Ponty himself saw between "Anglo-Saxon" positivism and his own philosophical interests was the almost exclusive attention the former has paid to the scientific enterprise. But this is true only of its earlier developments. As the followers of Wittgenstein II gradually replaced those of Wittgenstein I, the range of contemporary British and American philosophy was extended, thanks to its exclusive interest in language and its use, which now became extended to include other fields of traditional philosophical activity. Ethics and aesthetics became "meta-ethics" and "meta-aesthetics," and value judgments were readmitted to the realm of philosophical discourse even though the philosopher's interest was restricted to determining, at a second level, what the words used to express value judgments meant in the first-order occurrence of their use.

But why, asks Merleau-Ponty, should we restrict ourselves to examining a fully developed language? Is this not the same as to restrict our discourse on reason to those procedures we associate with the "major rationalists,"[29] i.e., to a self-contained set of principles that define everything that may be consistently thought, and this prior to any experience of a possible fact to the contrary? The study of language must be brought back to encompass the "nonreflective" elements of expression, to a consideration of the uses of language before its irrationality has been removed by arbitrary decision; back, in other words, to language as it is being created in use. If this can be done, we shall see further that the creative use of language bears fruitful comparison with other human expressions, especially, according to Merleau-Ponty, with painting.[30]

The break in Merleau-Ponty's thought from the earlier "primacy of perception" phase to the later interest in ontology is perhaps most apparent in contrasting "The Indirect Language . . ." and "Eye and Mind." In the first he was intent upon describing the ontic conditions for our experience of aesthetic objects, and in the second, upon going beyond these to more speculative claims according to which painters are said to reveal "Being" itself. The two theoretical aims, of course, are not antithetical; only the question of "primacy" has changed. Having made the change, however, Merleau-Ponty ran the risk of losing his chances at dialogue with the majority of British and American philosophers, since they, by and large, rule out the notion of Being as meaningless. It should be interesting, therefore, to consider the steps that brought Merleau-Ponty over to Heidegger's way of doing philosophy.

First of all, it is clear that Merleau-Ponty was not, in his last work, slavishly following the imponderable German, any more than he was formerly an undiscriminating disciple of Heidegger's mentor, Husserl. He was outspoken in condemnation of Heidegger's rejection of the continental tradition:

> The same philosopher who now regrets Parmenides and would like to give us back our relationships to Being such as they are prior to self-consciousness owes his idea of and taste for primordial ontology to just this self-consciousness.[31]

And he continued, "There are some ideas that make it impossible for us to return to a time prior to their existence, even and especially if we have moved beyond them, and subjectivity is one of these."[32]

Heidegger's conclusions, if they were to be accepted by Merleau-Ponty, had to be shown as a continuous development of human consciousness. "Being," too, must be grasped on the foundations of perception, if this concept is to have meaning for the self-consciously perceiving subject.

In his letter on humanism, Heidegger had described human beings as "shepherds of Being."[33] What if the same claim could be made for artists, acting not as men but as creators of the new? In reflecting upon our experiences of paintings, our philosophic criticism would show once more the continuity between the nonreflective and the reflective aspects of experience, but this time at the level of ontology itself. What then is the relation between Heidegger's "Being" and Merleau-Ponty's notion of "brute being," announced as early as *Signes*?[34]

In those passages that mark the first clear break in his thought from the crypto-positivistic to the ontological, Merleau-Ponty showed that he had taken in earnest his own counsel, that philosophy must be the reflective criticism of all primary human expressions, and not merely of the scientific or other forms of the fully developed linguistic behavioral patterns of human beings.[35] If seeing is a typically human expression, what, after all, do we see when we say that we see—anything at all?

In answer, consider the basic fact of perspectival perception:

> No thing, no side of a thing, shows itself except by actively hiding the others, denouncing them in the act of concealing them. To see is a matter of principle to see farther than one

> sees, to reach a latent existence. The invisible is the outline and depth of the visible. The visible does not admit of pure positivity any more than the invisible does.[36]

And Merleau-Ponty attributes this discovery to Husserl, in that

> Husserl rediscovers sensible being as the universal form of brute being. Sensible being is not only things, but also everything sketched out there, even virtually; everything that leaves its trace there, even as divergence and a certain absence.[37]

In a word, brute being is that ontological dimension of human experience earlier described by both Heidegger and Sartre as set up and controlled by, as well as revealed in, human affective responses to the environing situation. It is always there, as if concealed from view.

"Being," it will be remembered, was said to be revealed in boredom (Heidegger) or in nausea (Sartre). And the complementary notion, "nothingness," was equally amenable to phenomenological interpretation, both thinkers relying upon "anguish" as the behavioral pattern whose significance is uniquely determined by the revelation of the ontological nought human beings are. Each interpreted "existence" as a relationship to the world of a being transcending itself toward its own possibilities. The last of these possibilities is death itself, which, as possibility, must be resolutely relived each moment of our lives.

Although Merleau-Ponty rejected the evidence offered by Heidegger and Sartre, he did not reject their ontological intention. "Le néant" and "das Nichts," when interpreted in the light of perception, merely became "l'invisible."[38] And to suggest its hidden relationships to the visible things of our common world, he referred to it as the "in-visible."

The invisible is constituted by "the other side of things," the under side or the far side, the overlapped side or the foreshortened side of visible objects. This move is a step back to Husserl, and his perspectival theory of perception. But if he is to live in the thickness of the world the "philosopher must bear his shadow":[39] men must live with other men, and their thought must find some basis in nonthought, reflection in the nonreflective responses of human organisms. Thus fundamental thought is an understanding of ". . . that jointing and framing of Being, being realized through man"[40]—a bold step forward, here, to join in the Heideggerian transformation of Husserl.

In such passages as the last, Merleau-Ponty's language has obviously become metaphorical. But this he could see as no defect. A functional metaphor expresses what no simple declarative sentence can state. In the metaphors he himself used he was giving examples of the kind of language "that states anew,"[41] by silence and allusion; and so, he asked,

> . . . what if, hidden in empirical language, there is a secondary language in which signs once again lead the vague life of colors, and in which significations never free themselves completely from the intercourse of signs?[42]

If this is the case, the "jointing and framing of Being" is not an inept metaphor; it is perhaps the clearest indication of the phenomenological basis upon which language and painting may be compared, as well as an indication of how language may be used in the criticism of art.

For the earlier works of Merleau-Ponty this comparison has already been elaborated.[43] It remains to be seen, however, what was being jointed and framed in Merleau-Ponty's "ontology of painting," as it appeared in "Eye and Mind."[44] Its central idea is that all painting, figurative and nonfigurative, is spatial, but that the space of painting is not what is represented in literal Renaissance-style projection. So far, so good; this is true. It is likewise true that Descartes in the *Dioptrics* describes a space that has no essential connection with the space we actually see, but one which, like that of the Renaissance painters, can only be thought.

The aim of painting, on the other hand, is to reduce what is to what is visible;[45] to present for our enjoyment the visibility of things seen. And it is for this reason, according to Merleau-Ponty, that any consistent theory of painting is likewise an ontology[46]—so long as that ontology is not Cartesian, and the paintings involved in the theoretical discussion are not of the Renaissance. For the Being that shows through the two-dimensional surface of the painting (the "window" of the Renaissance and the "picture plane" of the moderns) can only be fully positive: "Space is in itself; rather, it is the in-itself *par excellence*."[47] The weakness of this metaphysical view of painting is said to be an elementary ontological error: ". . . like all classical ontologies, this one builds certain properties of beings into a structure of Being itself."[48] And if Merleau-Ponty is right, then it is clear that aestheticians, too, must make the ontical-ontological distinction that forms the crux of Heideggerian philosophy.[49]

But what is the ontological difference as Merleau-Ponty sees it? This is hard to determine, even from a fifth reading of the essay. His answers are flooded with metaphorical expressions which, this time, do not communicate in their silence. I name only a few: Being is "polymorphous";[50] and in our experiences of painting we find "a system of equivalences, a *logos* of lines, of lighting, of colors, of reliefs, of masses—a conceptless presentation of universal Being . . .";[51] in short, "Vision encounters, as at a crossroads, all the aspects of Being."[52] Painters themselves are called "artisans of Being,"[53] and their works are said to contain "an ontological formula,"[54] i.e., they make possible an aesthetic experience in which we find "an access to Being."[55] Our gaze, it is said, "wanders [in a painting] as in the halos of Being."[56] And, finally, it is there that we can find the "texture of Being itself."[57]

All this is a lot of Being, but if it does not suffice, there is more. According to Merleau-Ponty, in painting "there is inspiration and expiration of Being, action and passion so slightly discernible that it becomes impossible to distinguish between what sees and what is seen, what paints and what is painted."[58] Now, while we may be led to accept the identity of the artist and his work if the medium is dance, it is harder to conceive of a painter's vision as presenting "the metamorphosis of Being,"[59] and we ordinary humans will never know this until some finer analysis of the concept of Being is forthcoming. But Merleau-Ponty is no more; his analyses of the visible and the invisible were left unfinished.

There are, however, some clues as to how this analysis would have gone:

> In principle all my changes of place figure in a corner of my landscape; they are recorded on the map of the visible. Everything I see is in principle within my reach, at least within reach of my sight, and is marked upon the map of

> the "I can." Each of the two maps is complete. The visible world and the world of my motor projects are each total parts of the same Being.[60]

Here we glimpse in a new context how perception is conceived as bodily reaction to the things of our world, of an intentional arc between "brute being" and a bodily schema expanding itself outward. And in aesthetics the idea is repeated: "Quality, light, color, depth, which are there before us, are there only because they awaken an echo in our body and because our body welcomes them."[61] But this he had said much earlier in his career, and we have interpreted our experiences of the expressiveness of dance (Chapter 5) entirely in the same terms. The question remains whether the same explanation may be made for the expressiveness of the novel, music, or films.

Thus, the problem Merleau-Ponty left aestheticians is the same after the publication of "Eye and Mind" as it had been before. What is needed, if we are to succeed in making sense of the sensible, is a phenomenological analysis of *paintings*, and not an eidetic-ontological description of *painting*. (See Chapter 6.) Although Merleau-Ponty had included illustrations for his "ontology" of painting, he ominously avoided analyzing a single one of them. In my own treatment of this subject, I have attempted to furnish this missing dimension of phenomenological analysis. I cannot agree, therefore, with the judgments of Sartre and de Waehlens quoted by the editor of *The Primacy of Perception*, that "Eye and Mind" is ". . . one of Merleau-Ponty's most important works, standing apart as one of the richest, most synthetic (and most difficult) presentations of his thought we have."[62] Difficult, however, it is.

Nor can I agree with the editor that comparison with Heidegger's *Daseinsanalytik* is bootless. Heidegger had forged the concepts necessary to elucidate his notion of Being and he has presented at least two pieces on the derivation of an art-work, of which the most important, "Der Ursprung des Kunstwerkes," contains an analysis of a painting by Van Gogh.[63]

The truth is that Heidegger's work in phenomenological aesthetics is little known, even by those American philosophers who consider themselves most "phenomenological." All one has to do to question the relevancy of Heideggerian ontology for Merleau-Ponty's analysis of perception is to read *The Visible and the Invisible*. And I have offered a further test by examining the function of hermeneutics in my critical appreciation of aesthetic contexts enriched by a "depth" dimension. Poetry and the film, in the analyses given above, illustrate how the relation between the "eye" and the "mind" is no simple disjunction: poetry makes us hear what only the mind can fully comprehend; and the film, as a simple felt tension of sight and sound, image and idea, brings into focus the full potentiality of our being. But for this mystery to occur, space and time must undergo transformation into corporeal transcendence, i.e., man's being must be stretched into a temporal schema, the understanding of which is the experience itself.

The postulates given in Chapter 4 represent nothing more, nor less, than a set of second-level (or reflective) categories for interpreting the significance of such first-order (nonreflective) experiences. Most of us love the arts, and some of us are reflective enough to seek an understanding of our own loving natures—gratifying thereby those Greeks who gave to the philosophical discipline the name of "love of wisdom," according to which the highest virtue is to know oneself.

III

The argument of the preceding chapters is simple, in spite of its complex appearance. Earlier claims made concerning the value of aesthetic experiences are declared meaningless in that the dichotomy between "cognitive" and "emotive" theories is found to be baseless. All works of art have some affective component, and "ideas" may very well serve to control the affect of a literary, pictorial, or cinematic work. Likewise, the structure of an aesthetic surface itself may be interpreted as an "ideal" affective expression. We have argued that the question to be answered is not *what* is expressed in a work of art, but *how* an aesthetic expression is achieved by means of the process of creative communication, in which one human transcendence proposes a meaningful change in the environment and another acquiesces in the change by intending the same (aesthetic) object.

The task to be accomplished is the derivation of the categories necessary to explain how these two transcendences actually intend the same object. I referred to these categories as "sensuous surface," "experiential depth," and "total expressiveness." The theory of Sartre was rejected as being depth dominant, i.e., as minimizing the value of the medium or surface counters, while extolling the virtues of imaginative responses to objects only represented by aesthetic surfaces. Merleau-Ponty, on the other hand, tended to emphasize the value of the surface over the imaginative content of representative works. He, too, knew that the medium is the message.

Our experience tells us that some works are entirely surface expressions, and others both surface and depth; and that in the latter case, the value of the expression must be a function of the *manner* in which the depth content is presented on the surface, defined by the medium an artist has chosen to express his "idea."

Two theoretical (or methodological) problems are therefore required to supplement Merleau-Ponty's interest in an ontological interpretation of visual expression. We must show how a medium becomes a means of expression (see Chapters 5 and 7), and at the same time how this medium becomes a further means of representing ideas (Chapters 6, 8, and 9). Music, whose phenomenological description is best illustrated in the work of Ingarden, remains a paradigm of surface expressiveness; the techniques of Heideggerian hermeneutics applied to depth-dominant expressions indicate what one must do to bring human cognition back to the foundations of human experience considered as ultimate, or primordial, transcendence. Merleau-Ponty was obviously moving in this direction at the time of his death, and only his fatal coronary prevented him from unifying in theory what the value-laden experiences of works of art always accomplish in fact: the unity of the senses and the mind intending a single, significant object.

But what is presented in fact is experienced nonreflectively; mine has been the task of making the nonreflective bases of experience the foundation of our fully self-conscious reflection.

Starting with Husserl, therefore, we moved to Sartre and Merleau-Ponty, only to return to Ingarden and Heidegger (and thus to Husserl once again by one remove). No matter where we start in theory, and however we end, the purpose of phenomenological criticism must be the elucidation of the things themselves—in aesthetics, of works of art, whose very existence demands the complicity of our most characteristically human qualities. For this reason art is a privileged means of enriching human existence.

If the *what* of artistic expression remains problematic, to be displayed only on its own conditions in individual contexts, and determinable only by a defensible reading of those contexts, phenomenology affords a method for showing *how* the expressiveness is controlled, and thereby affords a means of determining how each of us experiences personal significance while surface and depth counters fund within our conscious attention. As with any other method, its validity is to be determined only by its success in operation.

Thus we need only try the method to see whether our aesthetic experiences become clearer and more intense. If they do, we need look no further; the experience is its own reward. And if they do not, no amount of theory will convince us of the claim that we "ought" to find enjoyable what quite obviously leaves us cold.

No wonder, then, that the simple expression "to see" englobes all the problems of aesthetic theory: we sense, we understand, and we feel what we sense we understand, all in an act of responding to the creative gestures of a human transcendence. All the problems of epistemology must, in some sense, derive from this intercourse between openness in the creator to the unorganized stimuli of his environment, and the openness of an appreciative audience to the specific qualities of the new stimulus organized by the artist's creative responses.

Given more time to reflect, Merleau-Ponty might have

discovered this fact in Heidegger's account of human disclosedness (*Erschlossenheit*): wherever we find ourselves, we do so in feeling; and we bring that feeling to the level of understanding (*Verstehen*) by an act of expression (*Rede*). Effective speech takes place only in act, whether creative or critical.

But unlike Valéry and Alain, we should no longer state that the creative act is purely physical; nor, like Croce, that it is primarily mental. Implicating not just the space and time of nature, whose effects we bracket out of an aesthetic experience by practicing the phenomenological *epoché*, but our very existence as spatializing and temporalizing beings (transcendence), creation is existential through and through.

Art and existence was our theme, because without art our existence is impoverished, and without existence there can be no art.

NOTES

1. See my *An Existentialist Aesthetic* (Madison, Wis.: The University of Wisconsin Press, 1962).
2. In the Bibliothèque des Idées, Paris: Gallimard, 1960.
3. In the Bibliothèque des Idées, Paris: Gallimard, 1964; text prepared by Claude Lefort. English translation: *The Visible and the Invisible,* translated by A. Lingis (Evanston, Ill.: The Northwestern University Press, 1968). See also *Signs*, translated by R. C. McCleary (Evanston, Ill.: The Northwestern University Press, 1964), and *The Primacy of Perception*, translated by J. M. Edie, *et al.* (Evanston, Ill.: The Northwestern University Press, 1964).
4. *Signs*, pp. 39–83.
5. *The Primacy of Perception*, pp. 159–90.
6. The illustrations, however, are not discussed as examples of aesthetic structures.
7. *Signs*, p. 94.
8. Merleau-Ponty, *La Structure du comportement* (Paris: Les Presses Universitaires de France, 1942).

9. Pp. 98–113 and 114–25.
10. Pp. 39–95 and 96–155.
11. See *Primacy of Perception*, p. 6.
12. *Signs*, p. 22.
13. *Primacy of Perception*, pp. 159–90, *passim.*
14. *Ibid.*, pp. xvii–xviii.
15. This section of Husserl's "Inhaltsübersicht" to the *Cartesian Meditations* was available in the first printing of the *Husserliana*, Band I (*Cartesianische Meditationen*) (The Hague: Martinus Nijhoff, 1950). I quote from the second printing, 1963, p. 192. No pun intended on Husserl's "spiegeln"; the emphasis is his.
16. Published as *Eloge de la philosophie* (Paris: Gallimard, 1953).
17. Paris: Gallimard, 1945.
18. *Primacy of Perception*, pp. 3–11.
19. *Ibid.*, p. 42.
20. *Ibid.*, p. 22.
21. *Ibid.*, p. 25.
22. *Ibid.*
23. See his *Cartesianische Meditationen, Husserliana*, Band I, 2nd ed. (The Hague: Nijhoff, 1963), pp. 121ff.
24. *Signs*, pp. 93–94.
25. *Ibid.*, p. 94.
26. *Ibid.*, pp. 84–97, following pp. 39–83.
27. See Ferdinand de Saussure, *Cours de linguistique générale*, Charles Bally, Albert Sechehaye, Albert Riedlinger, eds. (Paris: Payot, 1949); and my *An Existentialistic Aesthetic*, pp. 279, 324–26.
28. *Primacy of Perception*, p. 70; emphasis his.
29. *Signs*, pp. 147–53.
30. "Indirect Language and the Voices of Silence," *Signs*, pp. 39–83.
31. *Signs*, p. 154.
32. *Ibid.*
33. *Über den Humanismus* (Frankfurt am Main: V. Klostermann, 1946), pp. 19, 29.
34. *Signs*, pp. 22, 170–72, 179–80, 185.
35. See his *In Praise of Philosophy*, translated by J. Wild and J. M. Edie (Evanston: Northwestern University Press, 1963).
36. *Signs*, p. 21.
37. *Ibid.*, p. 172.
38. See *Le Visible et l'invisible, passim.*
39. *Signs*, pp. 159–81.
40. *Ibid.*, p. 181.
41. *Ibid.*, pp. 17–19, 44–45.

42. *Ibid.*, p. 45.
43. See my *An Existentialist Aesthetic*, pp. 258–90.
44. The *Primacy of Perception*, pp. 159–90.
45. *Ibid.*, p. 166.
46. *Ibid.*, p. 171.
47. *Ibid.*, p. 173; emphasis his.
48. *Ibid.*, p. 174.
49. See M. Heidegger, *Being and Time*, translated by J. Macquarrie and E. Robinson (London: SCM Press, 1962), pp. 21–35.
50. *Primacy of Perception*, p. 174.
51. *Ibid.*, p. 182.
52. *Ibid.*, p. 188.
53. *Ibid.*, p. 180.
54. *Ibid.*, p. 188.
55. *Ibid.*, p. 171.
56. *Ibid.*, p. 164.
57. *Ibid.*, p. 166.
58. *Ibid.*, p. 167.
59. *Ibid.*, p. 166.
60. *Ibid.*, p. 162.
61. *Ibid.*, p. 164.
62. *Ibid.*, p. xiv.
63. *In Holzwege* (Frankfurt am Main: Klostermann, 1950), pp. 7–68.

BIBLIOGRAPHY

BOOKS

Alain (pseud., Chartier, Emile). *Système des beaux arts.* Twenty-eighth edition; Paris: Gallimard, 1953.

———. *Vingt leçons sur les beaux-arts.* Sixth edition; Paris: Gallimard, 1931.

———. *Eléments de philosophie.* Twentieth edition; Paris: Gallimard, 1953.

Austin, John. *Sense and Sensibilia.* Oxford: The University Press, 1962.

Ballard, E. G. *Art and Analysis.* The Hague: Nyhoff, 1957.

Beardsley, Monroe C. *Aesthetics: Problems in the Philosophy of Criticism.* New York: Harcourt, Brace and Co., 1958.

———. and Schueller, H., eds. *Aesthetic Inquiry.* Belmont, Calif.: Dickenson Pub. Co., 1967.

Benjamin, A. C. *An Introduction to the Philosophy of Science.* New York: Macmillan, 1937.

Blackmur, R. G. *Language as Gesture.* New York: Harcourt, Brace and Co., 1952.

Collingwood, R. G. *The Principles of Art,* paperback reprint. New York: Oxford University Press, 1958.

Croce, Benedetto. *Aesthetic.* Translated by D. Ainslie. London: Macmillan and Co., Ltd., 1922.

Dewey, John. *Experience and Nature.* Chicago: Norton and Co., 1929.

———. *Art as Experience.* New York: Minton, Balch, and Co., 1934.

Dufrenne, Mikel. *Phénoménologie de l'expérience esthétique.* Paris: Presses Universitaires de France, 1953.

Fallico, A. B. *Art and Existentialism.* Englewood Cliffs, N.J.: Prentice-Hall, 1962.

Focillon, Henri. *La vie des formes.* Paris: Presses Universitaires de France, 1947.

Gadamer, Hans-Georg. *Wahrheit und Methode.* Tübingen: Niemeyer, 1960.

Ghiselin, Brewster, ed. *The Creative Process.* Paperback edition; New York: Mentor Books, 1955.

Hanslick, E. *The Beautiful in Music.* Translated by G. Cohen. New York: The Liberal Arts Press, 1957.

Heidegger, Martin. *Über den Humanismus.* Frankfurt a.M.: Klostermann, 1946.

———. *Existence and Being.* Translated by W. Brock. Chicago: Regnery Gateway Editions, 1949.

———. *Holzwege.* Frankfurt a.M.: Klostermann, 1950.

———. *Erläuterungen zur Hölderlins Dichtung.* Frankfurt a.M.: Klostermann, 1951.

———. *Vorträge und Aufsätze.* Pfullingen: Neske, 1954.

———. *Vom Wesen des Grundes.* Frankfurt a.M.: Klostermann, 1955.

———. *Was ist das, die Philosophie?* Pfullingen: Neske, 1956.

———. *Identität und Differenz.* Pfullingen: Neske, 1957.

———. *Der Satz vom Grund.* Pfullingen: Neske, 1957.

———. *Sein und Zeit.* 8th ed. Tübingen: Niemeyer Verlag, 1957.

———. *Being and Time.* Translated by J. Macquarrie and E. Robinson. London: SCM Press, Ltd., 1962.

———. *Einführung in die Metaphysik.* Tübingen: Niemeyer, 1958.

———. *Zur Seinsfrage.* 2d printing. Frankfurt a.M.: Klostermann, 1959.

———. *Gelassenheit.* Pfullingen: Neske, 1959.

———. *Unterwegs zur Sprache.* Pfullingen: Neske, 1959.

———. *Was ist Metaphysik?* 8th printing. Frankfurt a.M.: Klostermann, 1960.

———. *Nietzsche.* 2 vols. Pfullingen: Neske, 1961.

———. *Was Heisst Denken?* Tübingen: Niemeyer, 1961.

Hogben, Lancelot. *From Cave Painting to Comic Strip.* New York: Chanticleer Press, 1949.

Huaco, George A. *The Sociology of Film Art.* New York and London: Basic Books, 1965.

Husserl, Edmund. *Cartesianische Meditationen. Husserliana,* Band I. The Hague: Nyhoff, 1950.

——. *Ideas,* Boyce Gibson trans. New York: Collier Books, 1962.

Ingarden, R. *Das literarische Kunstwerk.* Halle: Max Niemeyer Verlag, 1931.

——. *Untersuchungen zur Ontologie der Kunst.* Tübingen: Niemeyer Verlag, 1962.

James, Henry. *The Art of Fiction and Other Essays.* New York: Oxford University Press, 1948.

Jarrett, James L. *The Quest for Beauty.* Englewood Cliffs, N. J.: Prentice-Hall, Inc., 1957.

Kaelin, E. F. *An Existentialist Aesthetic.* Madison, Wis.: The University of Wisconsin Press, 1962.

Kant, Immanuel. *Critique of Judgment.* Translated by J. H. Bernard. New York: Hafner Publishing Co., 1951.

Kepes, Gyorgy. *Language of Vision.* Chicago: Paul Theobald, 1944.

Kracauer, Siegfried. *From Caligari to Hitler.* Princeton, N. J.: Princeton University Press, 1947.

———. *Theory of Film.* New York: Oxford University Press, 1965.

Langer, S.K. *Philosophy in a New Key.* Paperback edition; New York: Penguin Books, 1948.

———. *Feeling and Form.* New York: Scribner's Sons, 1953.

Lewis, C. I. *Analysis of Language and Valuation.* LaSalle, Ill.: Open Court, 1946.

Lindgren, Ernest. *The Art of the Film.* London: Allen and Unwin, 1948.

Malraux, André. *Les voix du silence.* In *La Gallérie de la Pléiade*; Paris: Nouvelle Revue Française, 1951.

Marx, Werner. *Heidegger und die Tradition.* Stuttgart: Kohlhammer, 1961.

May, Rollo, ed. *Existence: A New Dimension in Psychiatry and Psychology.* New York: Basic Books, 1958.

Mead, G. H. *Mind, Self and Society.* Chicago: The University of Chicago Press, 1934.

Merleau-Ponty, Maurice. *La Structure du comportement.* Paris: Presses Universitaires de France, 1942.

———. *La Phénoménologie de la perception.* Paris: Gallimard, 1945.

———. *Sens et non-sens.* Paris: Editions Nagel, 1948.

———. *Les Aventures de la dialectique.* Paris: Gallimard, 1955.

———, ed. *Les Philosophes célèbres.* Geneva: Mazenod, 1956.

———. *Signes.* Paris: Gallimard, 1960.

———. *Signs.* Translated by R. C. McCleary. Evanston, Ill.: The Northwestern University Press, 1964.

———. *Le visible et l'invisible.* Paris: Gallimard, 1964.

———. *The Visible and the Invisible.* Translated by A. Lingis. Evanston, Ill.: The Northwestern University Press, 1968.

———. *Eloge de la philosophie.* Paris: Gallimard, 1953.

———. *In Praise of Philosophy.* Translated by J. Wild and J. Edie. Evanston, Ill.: Northwestern University Press, 1963.

———. *The Primacy of Perception and Other Essays.* Edited by J. Edie. Evanston, Ill.: The Northwestern University Press, 1964.

Meyer, Leonard B. *Emotion and Meaning in Music.* Chicago: The University of Chicago Press, 1956.

Morris, Charles. *Foundations of a Theory of Signs.* In *Inter-*

national Encyclopedia of Unified Science. Vol. 1, no. 2. Chicago: The University of Chicago Press, 1938.

Morris, Van C. *Existentialism in Education.* New York: Harper and Row, 1966.

Müller, Max. *Existenz-philosophie im geistigen Leben der Gegenwart.* Heidelberg: Kerl, 1949.

Nahm, M. C. *The Artist as Creator.* Baltimore: The Johns Hopkins University Press, 1956.

Naumburg, Margaret. *Psychoneurotic Art: Its Function in Psychotherapy.* New York: Grune and Stratton, Inc., 1953.

Newman, William S. *Understanding Music.* New York: Harper and Bros., 1952.

Prall, D. W. *Aesthetic Judgment.* New York: Crowell, 1929.

Pratt, Carrol C. *The Meaning of Music.* New York and London: McGraw-Hill, 1931.

Richards, I. A. *Science and Poetry.* 2nd rev. ed. London: Kegan Paul, Trench, Trubner and Co., Ltd., 1935.

———. *Principles of Literary Criticism.* New York: Harcourt Brace and Co., 1947.

Ruesch, J. and Kees, W. *Non-verbal Communication.* Berkeley and Los Angeles: University of California Press, 1956.

Ryle, Gilbert. *The Concept of Mind.* New York: Barnes and Noble, 1950.

Santayana, George. *The Sense of Beauty.* New York: The Modern Library, 1955.

Sartre, J.-P. *L'Imagination.* Paris: Presses Universitaires de France, 1936.

———. *L'Etre et le néant.* Paris: Gallimard, 1943.

———. *Being and Nothingness.* Translated by H. Barnes. New York: Philosophical Library, 1956.

———. *L'Existentialisme est un humanisme.* Paris: Nagel, 1946.

———. *L'Imaginaire.* 18th ed. Paris: Gallimard, 1948.

Saussure, Ferdinand de. *Cours de linguistique générale.*

Edited by C. Bally, A. Sechehay, and A. Riedlinger. Paris: Payot, 1949.

Schneeberger, Guido. *Nachlese zu Heidegger.* Bern: Schneeberger, 1962.

Taine, Hippolyte. *Philosophie de l'art.* Paris: Hachette, 1906.

Tillich, Paul. *Systematic Theology.* Vol. 1. Chicago: The University of Chicago Press, 1951.

Valéry, Paul. *Charmes.* Commentary by Alain. Paris: Gallimard, 1929.

———. *Introduction à la poétique.* Paris: Gallimard, 1938.

Vivas, E. and Krueger, M. *The Problem of Aesthetics.* New York and Toronto: Rinehart and Co., 1953.

Weitz, Morris. *Philosophy of the Arts.* Cambridge, Mass.: Harvard University Press, 1950.

Woolf, Virginia. *To the Lighthouse.* New York: Harcourt, Brace and Co., 1927.

ARTICLES

Beauvoir, S. "Merleau-Ponty et le pseudo-Sartrisme." *Les Temps Modernes* 10 (1955):2072–122.

Ecker, D. W. "The Artistic Process as Qualitative Problem Solving." *Journal of Aesthetics and Art Criticism* 21 (1963):283–90.

Ehrenzweig, Anton. "Unconscious Porm-creation in Art." *British Journal of Medical Psychology* 21 (1948):185–214; 22 (1949):88–109.

Feldman, E. B. "Man Transcends Himself through Art." *Arts in Society* 2 (1962):90–98.

Gadamer, Hans-Georg. "Vom Zirkel des Verstehens." In *Martin Heidegger zum siebzigsten Geburtstag,* pp. 24–34. Pfullingen: Neske, 1959.

Goldstein, K. "Über Zeigen und Greifen." *Der Nervenarzt* 4 (1931):453–66.

Hospers, John. "The Croce-Collingwood Theory of Art." *Philosophy* 31 (1956):291–308.

Kaelin, E. F. "The Arts and Communication." *Arts in Society* 1 (1959):71–85.

———. "Aesthetics and the Teaching of Art." *Studies in Art Education* 5 (1964):42–56.

———. "The Existential Ground for Aesthetic Education." *Studies in Art Education* 8 (1966):3–12.

———. "Notes toward an Understanding of Heidegger's Aesthetics." In *Phenomenology and Existentialism,* edited by E. N. Lee and M. Mandelbaum, pp. 59–92. Baltimore: The Johns Hopkins University Press, 1967.

Merleau-Ponty, Maurice. "Le Langage indirect et les voix du silence." *Les Temps Modernes* 7 (1952):2113–44; 8 (1952):70–94.

———. "L'Oeil et l'esprit." *Les Temps Modernes* 17 (1961): 193–227.

Morgan, Douglas, "Psychology and Art Today: A Summary and Critique." *Journal of Aesthetics and Art Criticism* 10 (1950):81–96.

Morris, Charles. "Esthetics and the Theory of Signs." *Journal of Unified Science* 8 (June, 1938):131–50.

———. "Science, Art and Technology." *The Kenyon Review* 1 (1939):409–23.

Nagel, Ernest. "In review of S. K. Langer's *Philosophy in a New Key." Journal of Philosophy* 11 (1943):323.

Price, Kingsley. "Is a Work of Art a Symbol?" *Journal of Philosophy* 50 (1953):485–503.

Read, Herbert. "Psychoanalysis and the Problem of Esthetic Value." *International Journal of Psychoanalysis* 32 (1951): 73–82.

Sartre, J.-P. "Merleau-Ponty vivant." *Les Temps Modernes* 17 (1961):304–76.

Taylor, J. F. A. "The Art of Encounter." *Arts in Society* 3 (1965):249–55.

Vivas, Eliseo. "What is a Poem?" *Sewanee Review* 62 (1954): 578–97.

Wellisch, E. "The Use of Projective Paintings in the Rorschach Method." *British Journal of Medical Psychology* 22 (1959):66–71.

Wilson, Robert N. "The Poet and the Projective Test." *Journal of Aesthetics and Art Criticism* 16 (1958):319–27.

Ziff, Paul. "Art and 'the Object of Art,'" In *Essays in Aesthetics and Language,* edited by Wm. Elton, pp. 170–86. Oxford: Blackwell, 1954.

Zink, Sidney. "The Cognitive Element in Art." *Ethics* 64 (April, 1954):186–204.

INDEX